PLATO'S PSYCHOLOGY

PHOENIX

JOURNAL OF THE CLASSICAL ASSOCIATION

OF CANADA

REVUE DE LA SOCIETE CANADIENNE

DES ETUDES CLASSIQUES

SUPPLEMENTARY VOLUME VIII

TOME SUPPLEMENTAIRE VIII

PLATO'S PSYCHOLOGY

T. M. ROBINSON

UNIVERSITY OF TORONTO PRESS

©University of Toronto Press 1970
Printed in Canada by
University of Toronto Press, Toronto and Buffalo
SBN 8020-5220-7

FOR RONALD FOX

Foreword

The following pages are an attempt to fill what seems to be an important gap in current literature on the philosophy of Plato. Since the war a large amount of work has been done on his Theory of Knowledge, and this has thrown light on a number of hitherto dark corners in the dialogues. That other "pillar of Platonism," however, the doctrine of *psyche* (soul, mind), has only received sporadic attention, and this is surprising, since a Theory of Mind and a Theory of Knowledge would appear to be very closely linked. In a century not a single comprehensive work on Plato's notion of *psyche* has appeared in English. In 1862 A.-Ed. Chaignet produced a work entitled *De la Psychologie de Platon*, but the work is so instinct with his own brand of (philosophical) idealism that the Plato of the dialogues is seldom given an impartial hearing. A better book, J. Simson's *Der Begriff der Seele bei Platon*, appeared in 1889. This has the great merit of treating Plato's own words dispassionately, and references to the text of the dialogues are used to corroborate practically every general statement. The only trouble is that the book is too slight to be comprehensive. What it says, as far as it goes, is admirable, but it does not go far enough. Nearer our own times, H. Barth's *Die Seele in der Philosophie Platons* was published in 1921, and this can only be considered retrogressive. As in the case of Chaignet's monograph, Barth's book is so riddled with his own philosophical prejudices (this time in the direction of *Lebensphilosophie*) as to be rendered almost valueless.

The present study attempts to give as lucid and comprehensive an account as possible of all that Plato has to say on the nature of *psyche*, personal and cosmic, in each of the dialogues. This inevitably involves a good deal of interpretation, but I have tried, as much as possible, to let the texts speak for themselves. As far as the doctrine of "personal" *psyche* is concerned, the dialogues, I argue, suggest no particular "development" on Plato's part. On the contrary, he appears to use particular "models" of *psyche* (uniform, bipartite, tripartite, etc.) to suit particular contexts, and seems to be peculiarly unbound by dogmatism in this regard till the end of his life. As for the notion of "cosmic" *psyche*, it is suggested that there is some development here, though many obscurities still remain.

The relative order of the dialogues is a problem every student of Plato must face, and I have followed generally accepted opinions except in the case of the *Timaeus* and the *Phaedrus*, which I tentatively place (in that order) soon after the *Republic*. To defend this would demand another book; suffice it for the moment to say that the move seems to me to make Plato's cosmic psychology and cosmo-theology follow a more comprehensible pattern of development than has been suggested hitherto. Though this is my own opinion on the matter, I hope that it has not so influenced my analysis of the "later" dialogues that the reader will be precluded from forming his own judgment on the basis of what Plato says on any particular occasion. For that, ultimately, is the aim of the book – to put the reader into a position where he can make up his own mind concerning particular problems on the basis of precise and, one hopes, unbiassed exposition of the relevant texts. In this sense I should like to see myself as performing that "under-labourer's" task of which Locke speaks in the *Essay*.

The translation of the term *psyche* is always difficult. Is it "soul," or "mind," or "person"? Translators are in constant disagreement. After much thought I finally opted for the uniform translation "soul," on the grounds that this would be the least misleading. For the term "soul," to most people (including those who reject it as nonsense), suggests an "inner person" or "ghost in the machine" (to use Ryle's phrase) that is, in my opinion, very close to Plato's usual view on the matter. The translation "mind," though occasionally useful in those few contexts (like the *Phaedo*) in which *psyche* is seen as an almost totally intellective principle, is misleading in those many more contexts where intellect is seen as only one of a number of subdivisions of *psyche*. It would be less misleading, of course, if it could be assumed that every reader of this book adhered to a Rylean view of mind; but this is hardly likely to be the case.

I have used standard translations throughout, reducing them to uniformity in one respect only – that of translating ψυχή in every instance as "soul." Apart from the *Timaeus* and parts of the *Republic*, where I employ Cornford's translations, a few passages of the *Phaedo*, where I have used Hackforth's translation, and a few passages of the *Gorgias*, where I have used the Jowett translation, all translations are drawn from *The Collected Dialogues of Plato*, edited by Hamilton and Cairns (Bollingen Series LXXI). Unless otherwise indicated, the Greek text that I have followed is that of

Burnet (Oxford University Press 1900-7). I must also thank the editors of the following journals for permission to use material which originally appeared in them: *The American Journal of Philology* (LXXXVIII (1967) 57–66), *Phronesis* (XII (1967) 147–51), and *Apeiron* ((1968) 12–18).

To keep abreast of all Platonic scholarship (even within a specialized area) is a formidable, if not impossible, task. If I have come anywhere near success in this regard, it is largely the result of constant reference to the outstanding Bibliography of Platonic Scholarship published in *Lustrum* (1959–60) by Professor H. Cherniss. For works appearing in more recent years I have relied for my bibliographical information upon *L'Année philologique* and the *Bulletin signalétique*. Even so, a number of items were (inevitably) overlooked, and I should like to draw attention to them now, since they came to my notice too late for me to use: D. J. Schulz *Das Problem der Materie in Platons Timaios* Bonn 1966; H. J. Easterling "Causation in the *Timaeus* and *Laws* x" *Eranos* LXV (1967) 25–38; M. Corvez "Le Dieu de Platon" *Revue philosophique de Louvain* LXV (1967) 5–35; J. B. Skemp *The Theory of Motion in Plato's Later Dialogues*[2] Amsterdam 1967.

No doubt there are more such items; but I have every confidence that, Platonic scholarship being the maze that it is, their authors will be understanding, and will attribute the omission to my ignorance of the existence of their contributions, rather than to any unwillingness on my part to consider them.

Finally, it is my pleasant task to thank the many scholars who have offered advice on particular topics. In particular I should like to mention Dr. D. A. Rees, of Jesus College, Oxford, and Professors G. M. A. Grube and D. Gallop of the University of Toronto. Of course, this in no way commits them to the contents of the book; I myself take full responsibility for that. But their advice made me re-consider large tracts of the argument, and almost invariably, I think, for the better. If occasionally I stuck stubbornly to my original opinion, I cheerfully accept what blame and retribution may come my way.

This book has been published with the help of grants from the Humanities Research Council, using funds provided by the Canada Council, and from the Publications Fund of the University of Toronto Press. I should like to thank Miss Prudence Tracy, of the same press, for her careful and good-humoured supervision of the manuscript from its earliest stages through to publication.

T.M.R.

Toronto, June 1969

Contents

PLATO'S PSYCHOLOGY

I

The "Socratic" Dialogues

In a well-known lecture John Burnet has argued that the core of Socrates' teaching is to be found at *Apology* 29D4 ff. and 30A7 ff., where stress is laid on the care of the soul, and how to make it as good as possible.[1] Few would dispute this as a correct account of an important element in Socrates' philosophical activity, but as such it throws little light on the nature of the soul in question. Any hope of elucidating this will depend upon a close examination of the usage of the term in dialogues largely admitted to be Socratic. Even here our findings can carry no particular conviction that the view of soul envisaged is that of the "historical" Socrates, but for our present purposes this is not really important. What matters initially is to see what picture of soul emerges from the earlier dialogues which Plato wrote; such an examination of its beginnings may help to explain the structure and raison d'être of the more complex psychology to come.

Perhaps the first thing to notice is the rather tentative nature of some of Socrates' remarks. At *Crito* 47E–48A, for example, he says:

> What about the part of us which is mutilated by wrong actions and benefited by right ones? Is life worth living with this part ruined? Or do we believe that this part of us, whatever it may be, in which right and wrong operate, is of less importance than the body?

Burnet, in keeping with his thesis that Socrates' view of soul introduced something new into Greek thought, takes this hesitant comment (in which the word soul is not mentioned as such) as indicating in some way that Socrates was aware of the newness of his doctrine.[2] One might compare a comment at *Crito* 47D3–4, where Socrates exclaims: "Shall we not corrupt and outrage that principle in us which may be assumed to be improved by justice and deteriorated by injustice?"

1 J. Burnet (1) 235 ff. See also W. Jaeger (3) 38–44.
2 J. Burnet (3) n. *ad Cri.* 47D4.

Again this looks like a clear reference to soul.[3] That the word is in neither case explicitly mentioned does call for an explanation, and Burnet's suggestion may well be right. More important for us, however, is the fact that soul is here seen to be the principle in terms of which a man is characterized as good or bad. What is more, it can apparently be itself said to possess moral qualities, of varieties both desirable and undesirable. This is of some consequence, for in the case of the unjust man badness of soul apparently means its deterioration or even destruction (ἀπώλλυτο). Finally, in words at least, a distinction seems to be drawn between the *man* who is "just" and his *soul* which is correlatively "better." Whatever this may turn out to mean, one can at any rate offer the minimal observation that soul is seen here as a principle of man's moral activities, and that it is described in a way which suggests substantial, rather than qualitative existence.

But this is far from the whole story. At *Euthydemus* 295E4–5 we read the following: "Answer then," he said, "again, whether you know what you know with something or with nothing." "Yes," I said, "I know with my soul." Here the soul is clearly taken to be some sort of cognitive principle, and the indefinite plural ἅ is sufficiently vague to cover knowledge that, knowledge how, and knowledge by acquaintance. Be this as it may, soul and knowledge are intimately linked, and "mind" looks a fair and natural translation of the term in the context.

At *Charmides* 156D ff. we have a discussion about health, where Socrates propounds the views which he claims to have learned from a doctor who had served the Thracian king, Zalmoxis. The passage is worth quoting in full:

> This Thracian told me that in these notions of theirs, which I was just now mentioning, the Greek physicians are quite right as far as they go, but Zalmoxis, he added, our king, who is also a god, says further, "that as you ought not to attempt to cure the eyes without the head, or the head without the body, so neither ought you to attempt to cure the body without the soul. And this," he said, "is the reason why the cure of many diseases is unknown to the physicians of Hellas, because they disregard the whole, which ought to be studied also, for the part can never be well unless the whole is well." For all good and evil, whether in the body or in the whole man, originates, as he declared, in the soul, and overflows from thence, as if from the head into the eyes. And

3 J. Adam (1) n. *ad loc.*, where the principle is called νοῦς.

therefore if the head and body are to be well, you must begin by curing the soul – that is the first and essential thing.

What is one to make of the concept of soul as it seems to emerge from this passage? If the Thracian doctor's language is meant to be anything like exact, the relationship of soul and body is clearly not one of simple numerical addition, the combination equalling the "self" or "whole man." The key to the relationship (and to the concept of soul itself) seems to be in the phrase "because they disregard the whole." This "whole" could conceivably refer to two things: (a) the whole *body*; (b) the whole *man*, that is, body and soul combined.

If (a) is the case, Greek doctors are being castigated for despising courses in general physiology; they fail to realize that ailments of particular organs can only be adequately diagnosed in the light of a more general appreciation of the operations of the human body as a whole. However, this hardly squares with the sentences immediately preceding and immediately following, in which clear reference to "soul" occurs. So the reference is presumably to (b), and the doctors are being taken to task for failing to appreciate that many ailments are in fact (to use modern jargon) psychosomatic; no amount of potions and poultices will cure the stomach-cramp that stems from overpowering guilt-feelings or anxiety, and the physiotherapist should know when to give way gracefully to the psychiatrist. This, if true, is a piece of medical insight antedating a great deal of supposedly modern findings in the field of psychology, but the notion of soul which it seems to entail appears even more remarkable in its acuteness. For, in this context, "soul" and "the whole man" appear to be interchangeable terms. If the Thracian doctor's language means anything at all, soul is to body as head is to eye or body is to head. The analogy, if seriously meant, is a startling one, and would compel us to see soul as the "whole" being, of which body is a "part" (in some sense of the word "part"). The reasoning behind this conclusion seems to be as follows: the eye and the head can no doubt be viewed as two substances, but the former only has meaning when seen in terms of the latter; and the same can be said of the two substances head and body. In either case, the former is seen to depend on the latter for being and intelligibility. Similarly with the relationship of body and soul: body is *part* of soul, and to deny it the "broader context" of soul is as absurd as to treat the head as a subsistent whole without reference to the living body of which it forms an inalienable part. On this analysis, to say that the "person" is the sum total of body plus soul is as absurd as to say that head equals eye plus head or that body equals head plus body. To attempt to "add up" head and body or eye and head is to fall into a category-mistake, like attempting to "add up" an existentialist and his existentialism. Similarly with attempts to "add up" body and soul. They may both be substances, in some sense of the word "substance," but the first is dependent on the second in a way that other substances are not. If this is true, we seem to be precluded from taking the soul as some sort of ghost or duplicate enjoying substantial existence in addition to the body; one cannot cut away the body, it seems, and find oneself left with a complete psychic substance qualifying for the name of the person or the "real self." The two are so intimately bound together that the destruction of either is the destruction of both, in much the same way as living head and living body become lifeless head and lifeless trunk when the executioner has done his work. Head and body entail each other as concave does convex, and the same can be said of body and soul. In a word, soul seems to be understood here as the total person or "whole man" of which the living body ($\sigma\hat{\omega}\mu\alpha$) is an integral part. (I say "living body" to distinguish it from the νεκρός, or corpse.) On this point the parallelism of Socrates' examples is not perfect, but is adequate. A head deprived of its eyes is still, no doubt, a candidate for the qualification "head," but the point to be stressed is that the eye, deprived of its context in the head, no longer functions as an eye. Even if it is preserved forever under laboratory conditions, it is still only a museum-piece – a small organic camera, the admiration of teleologists, but no longer functioning as part of an integrated whole as it once did when it formed part of a living being. The same might be said of a hand or foot or any other organ. However, even if Socrates' first example makes little immediate impression, the second one, drawn from head and body, is much more convincing. A headless body is only a trunk, and the idea of a head exercising its normal functions without reference to a body is unintelligible, in spite of the odd visions of Empedocles.[4]

That "soul" is here taken as the total self seems to be corroborated by the sentence in which Socrates says: "For all good and evil, whether in the body or in the whole man, originates, as he declared, in the soul, and overflows from thence, as if from the head into the eyes." At first sight this looks like the assertion that the "whole man" is the arithmetical total of body and

4 DK[12] B 57 (Empedocles).

soul, but the parallelism drawn in the final words makes it clear that Socrates' original point still stands. The influence of soul on body is like that of head on eyes, and in searching for the source of trouble one must look in one case to the head, in the other to the soul. This being the case, the phrase "the entire man" (πᾶς ὁ ἄνθρωπος) can only mean "the person" or "the whole man" in the sense that we have already seen – that is, "the soul."

Curing the soul, we are told, is an indispensable preliminary to any curing of the body (157A1 ff.), and this is to be brought about by certain "charms" or "incantations." (157A7) These, we learn, are "noble discourses" (καλοὶ λόγοι),[5] and the sentence continues: "... by them temperance is implanted in the soul, and where temperance comes and stays, there health is more easily imparted, not only to the head, but to the whole body." (157A5–B1)

What are these "noble discourses"? The ambiguities of the word λόγος are notorious, and Croiset's "discours philosophiques" is perhaps as good an interpretation as any.[6] It could be argued, however, that in this context the noun "discourses," particularly when qualified by the epithet "noble," is a phrase whose meaning is as much homiletic as informative, and so perhaps best translated by some such phrase as "good counsel," "sound advice," or the like. That is to say, while good counsel must be *expressed* in λόγοι spoken or written, the emphasis may be upon the value of the advice rather than the expression. It may possibly be that both meanings are intended: the soul is to be charmed by sound advice nobly expressed. Be this as it may, the affirmation of the λόγοι by a charmer and their acceptance by the soul which is charmed is clearly a process of learning, and thus an activity that can be qualified as "intellectual," even though it undoubtedly involves other processes besides. It can also be qualified as "moral," since the soul, or person, as distinct from a cat or a cabbage, can not only see the meaning and implication of "noble discourses," but can also be changed for the better by them. This is in line with comments already noticed in the *Crito* and *Euthydemus*, where it was made equally clear that soul is in some way classifiable as an intellectual and moral principle. But the *Charmides* makes the further affirmation that it is the total person who is the soul, and that only to the person can intellectual and moral activities be meaningfully ascribed. If this analysis is correct, the Thracian doctor is saying something as yet unvoiced

---

5 157A4–5; cf. *Phdr.* 270B7, *Lg.* 689B5–6.
6 Budé translation (Paris 1949).

by the Greeks. So far most comments on body and soul had been frankly dualistic. Souls had been seen as breath,[7] as air,[8] as incarcerated angels,[9] as ectoplasmic wraiths that squeak away like bats to Hades;[10] bodies had been seen by some as tombs[11] and prisons,[12] by others as the true self;[13] cognition had been seen as blood round the heart.[14] Nowhere had it been affirmed that the soul is both the principle of cognition and the "total" self, a being entailed in any affirmation that such-and-such is a living body, in the way that a head functioning as a head entails a living body or an eye functioning as an eye entails a head. This is clear from the fact that no-one had ever said that the body was an integral part of the self. For the Homeric warrior on the one hand the body *was* the self; for the Orphic the self was the incarcerated soul. For the Socrates of the *Charmides*, by contrast, the self is apparently *the whole man* (156E7–8), of which body is an integral and inalienable part. The progress seems to be twofold: Socrates has apparently seen, first, that any talk of the self or person involves talk about *both* body and soul, and, second, that the relationship between the two is not the crude one of numerical addition and subtraction, but the philosophically more respectable one of entailment.

But if the *Charmides* suggests a fruitful and sophisticated approach to the problem of soul and body, it seems that Socrates (or Plato) either failed to see its implications or, seeing them, rejected them for an alternative view, or perhaps a number of alternative views. The best known of these is the notion that the soul alone (without reference to the body) is the self or person, expounded in the (probably apocryphal) dialogue known as *Alcibiades* I. The self of the *Alcibiades*, however, as will be seen, bears little comparison with the self of the *Charmides*. At 130A1–3 we read that the soul "uses" the body and "rules" it, and at 130C5–6 we are informed categorically that the soul *is* the man. The conclusion sounds identical to the one reached in the *Charmides*, but the process by which it is reached shows that a very different image of soul is intended. For at 130A9 three possible candidates for the title "the man" are envisaged: "soul or body or the composite of the

---

7 Homer *passim*. For discussion see E. Bickel, *Homerischer Seelenglaube* (Berlin 1925) 258–9.
8 DK[12] B 2, 17–19 (Anaximenes).
9 DK[12] B 112, 4–5; B 115 (Empedocles).
10 *Od.* 24.9 *et alib.*
11 See *Grg.* 493A1–5, with the comment of E. R. Dodds (3) *ad loc.*
12 *Phd.* 82E3.
13 A useful examination of the evidence can be found in R. Hirzel.
14 DK[12] B 105, 15 (Empedocles).

two." That the self is the body is immediately rejected on the grounds that it does not "rule" itself. (130B2–7) More significantly, it is then denied that the *composite* is the self on the grounds that "if one of the members is subject, the two united cannot possibly rule." (130B11–12) And so by a process of residues Socrates concludes that the man is the soul, for only the latter, he claims, can be said to "use" and "rule" the body. In other words, the body is in no sense seen as part of the true self; it serves simply as an instrument of the soul. The oracular injunction "Know thyself" turns out to be an injunction to know one's soul. (130E8–9) As for knowing the body, this is knowledge about one's possessions but not about oneself. (131A2–3) Possessions, however, are apparently of two sorts. At 131B13–C1 a distinction is made between a man's body and his possessions: if, it is said, the body can be characterized as "one's belongings" (τὰ αὑτοῦ), then a man's "possessions" (χρήματα) will be "at a stage yet further removed from himself." The point is unfortunately not developed further, but the change of epithet does seem to indicate that when Socrates calls the body one of man's "belongings" he wants us to envisage something less crude than the objects we can, say, stow away in a wardrobe or cram into a suitcase. A possible hint of what he means can be found in the passage immediately preceding the discussion on soul, where he talks of the harpist and the tanner as "using" both bodily organs (like eyes and hands) and tools or instruments. (129C7 ff.) The different degrees of engagement involved in the possession of a body and the possession of χρήματα are perhaps meant to be the same as those involved in the use of one's hands and the use of a tool or lyre. If so, the example from use is more telling than that from belonging and possession, for the latter suggest simply a state, while use suggests activity. To talk of body and χρήματα as "belongings" and "possessions" respectively does little in itself to suggest a major difference in kind between the two, whereas the way one "uses" a plectrum and the way one "uses" a hand appear to be significantly different. For the plectrum has a purely passive role to play, while the hand, although in a sense a passive instrument from the point of view of the soul, operates with a purposiveness of activity different in kind from the operation of the plectrum. We are still a long way from the view of the body as an integral part of the person, as integral as living head to living body, but at least the body does not seem to be written off as just a useless burden which the soul is compelled to carry around for a lifetime.[15] Even if the hand is not the

---

15 For the idea see Arist. *Protrept.* 10B (in *Aristotelis Fragmenta Selecta* ed. W. D. Ross (Oxford (1955)) and Epictetus, quoted in *M. Ant.* 4.41.

harpist, the hand is indispensable if the harpist is to do his job, and the hint is perhaps that the body-soul relationship is a similar one. In the *Charmides* the indispensability of the body had involved its being subsumed under the soul as head was subsumed under body; in *Alcibiades* I any such subsuming seems to be rejected, but, if the above reading is correct, the activities attributed to the harpist and the tanner are a suasion that body is indispensable to soul in a way that other possessions are not.

However, while most scholars would admit that the style of *Alcibiades* I is largely Platonic, few feel confident that it is from Plato's own hand. Among the many reasons given as an argument for its apocryphal nature, two touch on the notion of soul. Bidez argues that the formula "soul = the man" is an idea which "certainly has something Platonic about it; but its manner of expression is odd, and belongs to the Academy rather than to Plato himself."[16] He also feels that it is only in the *Phaedo* that we reach the idea of "the distinction between body and soul and the different degree of moral worth which each possesses." (*Ibid.*) As far as the latter point is concerned, one need only refer to *Apology* 29D4 ff., *Crito* 47D3-4, and *Protagoras* 313AC (see below, 11-12) to see that such a statement is somewhat sweeping. As for the former contention, we have seen how in the *Charmides* soul is meant to be the self, even though soul is apparently being envisaged in a sense not usually attributed to Plato. In the *Protagoras*, too, as will be seen, there are hints that soul and self are one and the same, and it will be clearly affirmed in the *Phaedo* (115C) and *Republic* (469D6-9). So I take it, with Allan and others, that "the conception of the soul as the true self is doubtless Socratic,"[17] or, less strongly, that it is not out of keeping with what other evidence tells us about the views of soul held by Socrates and/or the younger Plato. However, the Jowett editors go on to argue that "the view of Reason as an innermost self *within* the human soul is characteristic of the last phase of Plato's thought (*Philebus* and *Timaeus*)." They are referring to a famous passage at 133AE, where the soul is said to glimpse itself in the soul of another, and to possess a compartment "wherein resides her virtue, which is wisdom." In similar vein is the passage 133C1-6:

> *Socrates*: And do we know any part of our souls more divine than that with which wisdom and knowledge have to do?
> *Alcibiades*: There is none.

16 J. Bidez 118 (my translation).
17 B. Jowett, introd. note to *Alc.* I.

Socrates: Then this is that part of the soul which resembles God; and he who looks at this and at the whole class of things divine, at God and at wisdom, will be most likely to know himself.

That this, as it stands, is a succinct outline of a view of soul adopted in the *Timaeus* few would dispute. It could be argued, however, that the *Timaeus* doctrine on the individual soul is no advance on doctrine outlined at *Republic* x, and that the latter in turn, at any rate as far as Reason is concerned, can be squared with the *Phaedo*. Since the *Phaedo* is probably the first or among the first of the new-style dialogues, after the "aporetic" or Socratic ones, one could then perhaps argue that in *Alcibiades* 1 Plato is toying with ideas which will come to fruition within the very near future. However this may be, at least the doctrine "soul = the man" is in line with what we know of soul from other early dialogues which are admitted to be genuine, and so perhaps has value as corroborative evidence.

Turning to the *Protagoras*, we find, in a passage in which Socrates is advising a would-be pupil of a sophist teacher, that stress is laid on the greater *importance* of soul than of body:

Well then, I continued, do you realize the sort of danger to which you are going to expose your soul? If it were a case of putting your body [σῶμα] into the hands of someone and risking the treatment's turning out beneficial or the reverse, you would ponder deeply whether to entrust it to him or not, and would spend many days over the question, calling on the counsel of your friends and relations. But when it comes to something which you value more highly than your body, namely your soul [ψυχήν] – something on whose beneficial or harmful treatment your whole welfare depends – you have not consulted either your father or your brother or any of us who are your friends on the question whether or not to entrust your soul [ψυχήν] to this stranger who has arrived among us. On the contrary, having heard the news in the evening, so you tell me, here you come at dawn, not to discuss or consult me on this question of whether or not to entrust yourself [σαυτόν] to Protagoras, but ready to spend both your own money and that of your friends as if you had already made up your mind that you must at all costs associate with this man – whom you say you do not know and have never spoken to, but call a Sophist, and then turn out not to know what a Sophist is, though you intend to put yourself into his hands. (313A1–C3)

Perhaps the most remarkable thing about this passage is the (apparently) unconscious way in which Socrates slips over from talk about "soul" to talk about "self." At 313A2, for example, Hippocrates is said to be going to expose his *soul* (ψυχήν) to danger. At 313B2 he has not asked advice about whether to entrust his *soul* (ψυχήν) to a stranger. And then immediately following (in fact, in the very same sentence) he has apparently not discussed the question whether to entrust *himself* (σαυτόν) to Protagoras! Since Plato offers no hint to the contrary, "soul" and "self" are presumably meant to be one and the same. If this is not the case, and σαυτόν is meant to refer to the *composite* of soul and body, this misleadingly blurs the careful distinction already drawn between the soul and body in the same paragraph. As the doctor or gymnastic trainer is said to treat the body, the itinerant sophist in turn treats the soul; so that if, after this precise distinction, Plato goes on to talk about giving *oneself* to the sophist, one can only assume that he means self and soul to be taken as one and the same. In a word, I do not *possess* a soul; I *am* my soul.

Adopting a metaphor from the processes of nutrition, Socrates then argues that as the wholesale and retail merchants supply food for the body, the sophist supplies food for the soul, and such food is "pieces of knowledge" (μαθήματα 313C7). However, just as food can do the body good or ill, so can knowledge the soul, with the result that the purchase of either demands circumspection. With physical food there is the least danger; one can take it away in a basket and ask the advice of experienced friends before consuming it. As for the other, "you cannot buy the wares of knowledge and carry them away in another vessel; when you have paid for them you must receive them into the soul and go your way, either harmed or benefited ..." (314B1–4) Only the "physician of the soul" can know beforehand which will harm and which will help. (313E2)

Such a picture of soul might be described as paramechanical. Like the body it needs sustenance and can enjoy a state of health; like a material basket it is described as a type of container, and the process of learning is seen as the storing of pieces of knowledge in itself. It is clearly seen as exhausting the totality of self or person, as in the *Charmides* and *Alcibiades* I; it is an intellectual principle in that it can learn; it is a moral principle in that it can be classified as "righteous" (χρηστόν 313A3) or "depraved" (πονηρόν 313A4); and apparently its moral state is a direct result of what it learns. While the "harm" or "help" which is done to the soul by different "pieces of knowledge" is not explicitly stated, it seems fair to infer from 313A3–4 that the degree to which a soul is said to be "harmed" is the degree to which it can be described (or further described) as "depraved." If, too, from the term "physician" we are to infer that it is meaningful to talk about the "health" of the soul, such health will presumably consist in the state describable as "righteous." But when all this is said, it remains true that important questions are left untouched. If the soul is the totality of the self, in what way is it related to the body? In what do its two states, "righteous" and "depraved," consist? And how seriously is one to take the paramechanical status which is (by implication at least) attributed to it?

In the hope of further enlightenment one might perhaps turn to the *Gorgias*. At 464A ff. a distinction between body and soul is drawn. We are told that each has its appropriate state of well-being and that for each there is a specific art to maintain or, if necessary, to restore such a state. In the case of the body the art is not named, but its two branches are given as gymnastic training and medicine. In the case of the soul, the appropriate art is politics, whose two branches are legislation and justice. As for the body-soul relationship, we are told that it is soul which guides body and "has it under its charge." This notion appears, by implication at least, in the possibly spurious *Alcibiades* I, as we have seen, and Dodds sees it as perhaps the first clear appearance of that "sharp Platonic antithesis between mind as the dominant and body as the subject part of man" which will become more and more evident from the *Meno* and *Phaedo* onwards.[18] But does such a soul exhaust the totality of the self, or is the body meant to be part of it, as in the *Charmides*? No clear indication is given, except perhaps in the use of the very "personal" verb "to be in charge" (ἐπιστατεῖν 465D1) to describe soul's activities. This no doubt proves little, but it is worth noticing that in the *Phaedo*, to which Dodds refers (*ibid.*), and where soul is once more seen as the dominant partner,[19] soul is equally clearly meant to be taken as the true self, without reference to body.[20]

As far as the *Gorgias* is concerned, the distinction between body and soul seems to be a numerical one. At 464B3, for example, one reads the striking sentence: "To the pair, body and soul, there correspond two arts – that concerned with the soul I call the political art; to the single art that relates to the body I cannot give a name offhand." The use of the term "pair" (δυοῖν πραγμάτοιν) to describe body and soul suggests that Plato wants to

---

18 E. R. Dodds (3) n. *ad loc.*
19 E.g., *Phd.* 79E ff. and *passim.*
20 E.g., *Phd.* 115C.

treat the two as though they possess similar ontological status – that is, substantial status – and the close parallelism of the arts treating them seems to corroborate the point. If this is true, there seems to be, as in the *Protagoras*, a shift of emphasis from the viewpoint expressed in the *Charmides*. By contrast with the mitigated monism of the latter we seem to be confronted with straight numerical dualism, with all its attendant problems. Though the soul, for example, is unequivocally said to have "charge" over the body, the details of this are not explained, so that the new information adds little to the notion, hazy enough, that we already have. Indeed, throughout the dialogue we are told much about the moral qualities of soul, and the vices to which it is subject, without having any very clear notion of what a soul is meant to be: its existence and (substantial) ontological status are simply assumed.

While this is somewhat frustrating, a lot of what is said is still very memorable. For example, the three different evils of possessions, body, and soul (for the distinction see above, 9), are listed as poverty, disease, and injustice respectively. (477B8–C2) Of these quite the worst is seen to be "injustice, and in general the evil of the soul." (477C3–4) From the context this is clearly meant to be the equivalent of disease in the body, and hints at a view of soul which will prevail in the *Republic* (444D3–E3) and *Sophist* (227D–228E). The same point is developed at 506E4–5, where the good soul is described as that "in which there is harmony and order." The parallel harmony and order in the body is described as "health," and the position is summed up as follows:

> "Healthy," as I conceive, is the name which is given to the regular order of the body, whence comes health and every other bodily excellence ... And "lawful" and "law" are the names which are given to the regular order and action of the soul, and these make men lawful and orderly; and so we have temperance and justice. (504C7–D3)

This is something new. Soul, it seems, is not a homogeneous entity, but a complex of elements, the balance or imbalance of which will characterize·it as morally good or bad. The number and nature of these are not stated, but from 493A4–5 it seems that Plato is following the popular bipartition of soul into reason and impulse. He mentions how the sick body is – in its own interest – forbidden to indulge all its yearnings, and the same rule, he says, obtains for the sick (i.e., depraved) soul: "While she is in a bad state and is senseless and intemperate and unjust and unholy, the desires ought to be controlled, and she ought to be prevented from doing anything which does not tend to her own improvement." (505B2–4)

What are we to understand by these desires? An examination of what he has said immediately before, concerning bodily desires, may help us: "When a man is in health the physicians will generally allow him to eat when he is hungry and drink when he is thirsty, and to satisfy his desires when he likes, but when he is sick they hardly suffer him to satisfy his desires at all." (505A6–9) If this is true, the bodily desires seem to be what he will later class as "necessary" desires, which in the balanced person are usually neutral.[21] But what, if any, can be the psychic equivalent of such desires? That they should be desires for different virtues, or for freedom from a state of ignorance, is hardly possible, for presumably no soul-doctor would wish to curb the very desires which would lead to a direct cure of the ailment. Plato himself at this stage offers no solution to the problem, but in later dialogues its unravelling will figure prominently in his descriptions of soul and its activities.

One cannot leave the dialogue without at least mentioning the so-called Myth of the Watercarriers. (493A ff.) It is a vexed problem how seriously we are to take the passage. Is it Socrates talking, or Plato himself, or is it simply a story from which Plato wishes to dissociate both Socrates and himself? If, as Dodds has argued,[22] the evidence of the text favours the third view, this does not mean that the passage is valueless. On the contrary, it is a useful hint that Socrates, and/or the younger Plato, is ready to listen, at least, to Pythagorean-style stories about the fallen estate of man, and the evidence of the *Meno*, *Phaedo*, and *Phaedrus* seems to show that there came a time when he did more than listen.[23] For our purposes the important passage is at 493A1 ff., where, after quoting Euripides' famous lines: "Who knows? Perhaps what we call life/Is really death, and death is really life ..."[24] he continues: "... and perhaps we are really dead; I have heard a philosopher say that at this moment we are really dead and that the body is our tomb and that the part of the soul which is the seat of the desires is liable to be tossed about by words and blown up and down." (493A1–5)

21 *R.* 558EI ff., 571B5, 586E4–587AI.
22 E. R. Dodds (3) 296 ff.
23 Cf. *Men.* 81A, *Phd.* 70C, *Phdr.* 248C ff.
24 For discussion see E. R. Dodds (3) n. *ad loc.*

According to this view the soul is undoubtedly meant to be the real self, with the body serving only as a shell. As a doctrine it is fairly consistent, for "desires" are attributed to the soul alone; the body is treated as (literally) "dead weight" (τέθναμεν), and apparently plays no part in the operations of the person as such. As for the soul, "the part in which the desires are" is liable to persuasion and disturbance, and some unnamed "clever fellow," says Socrates, playing on the adjectives πιθανόν and πειστικόν, once called it a vessel (πίθον). (493A3–7) The quotation continues: "... the ignorant he called the uninitiated or leaky, and the place in the souls of the ignorant in which the desires are seated, being the intemperate and incontinent part, he compared to a vessel full of holes, because it can never be satisfied." (493A7–B3)

This is a considerable qualification. For now apparently it is only the "uninitiated" or ignorant who are under discussion, and the argument has narrowed appreciably. The exposition of the term "uninitiated" in terms of ignorance is certainly in keeping with Socratic intellectualism, and, if the quotation does stem from some "clever fellow" other than Plato himself, one can see why Socrates is shown as being prepared to listen. Whatever the provenance of the image, however, the point to note is that only in the case of the uninitiated or ignorant is that part of the soul which houses the desires called a sieve or leaky vessel. In the earlier brief quotation from the Pythagorean-style "philosopher" no such distinction between knowledgeable and ignorant souls is drawn, but we are simply told that the seat of desire in (any) soul is "liable to be tossed about by words and blown up and down." The second doctrine, however, seems to go beyond this more popular statement in assuming some difference in kind between the "desiderative part" of the soul of the knowledgeable man (see 493B1) and that of the soul of the ignorant man. What this is in the case of the ignorant man is explained (493A7–B3), but we are left in the dark about the position of the wise man. The only hint seems to be in the phrase "*liable to be* persuaded" (οἷον ἀναπείθεσθαι 493A4), where perhaps he means to suggest that the ignorant man is *in fact* persuaded and disturbed, while the wise man is not necessarily so. Whether such intelligence denotes the exercise of effort as well as the possession of knowledge – in other words, whether it has the moral overtones of nouns like "intelligence" (φρόνησις) or "wisdom" (σοφία) – is a question which is not investigated.[25] As for the nature of the desires in ques-

25 See E. R. Dodds (3) n. *ad loc.*

tion, the strong language used by both the "philosopher" and the "clever fellow" (493A2–B3) suggests that it is what will later be called the "unnecessary" desires which are involved, or at any rate "necessary" and "unnecessary" desires lumped together indiscriminately.

The final views of the "clever fellow" confuse the picture considerably. It now turns out that in the case of the uninitiated in Hades the *whole* soul – not just a part of it – is perforated, "being incontinent, owing to a bad memory and want of faith" (493C2–3), and Socrates is compelled to admit that he finds the whole thing "a bit odd." (493C3–4) However, the moral lessons of the myth are not to be missed. It bids us "choose, instead of the intemperate and insatiate life, that which is orderly and contents itself with what it has for its daily needs." (493C5–7) This again suggests that for Socrates the desires under discussion have been what will later be called "unnecessary" desires, by contrast with those "necessary" desires whose satisfaction is a legitimate part of the life of simple sufficiency.

One must be careful not to lay too much stress on this myth, but one minimal observation can be made. If it does not express the views of Socrates or Plato, it does seem to contain in general views which later on will be categorically theirs. Dodds talks of Plato's continual efforts "to transpose his religious beliefs from the mythical to the philosophical level, thus transforming them into truths of reason. This has the curious result that his conclusions often emerge earlier than the philosophical arguments by which they are established: thus his doctrine of the soul appears in mythical guise in the *Gorgias* before it is presented as a truth of reason in the *Phaedo*."[26] This is undoubtedly true of the body-tomb doctrine (493A1 ff.), but his attribution of desires to both body and soul will undergo a number of modifications first. For the moment Socrates is content to juxtapose two views of soul, the one of which he clearly holds with conviction, as the *Phaedo* will show, the other of which he is perhaps still busy appraising. How they are integrated into Plato's more mature psychology will appear in the *Republic* and *Philebus*.

The *Gorgias* myth had hinted at a doctrine which underlay the notion of body as a tomb, namely that of pre-existence. A show of argument in support of this belief is offered in the *Meno*, where Socrates tries to show that a slave's "knowledge" of geometrical truths can only mean that he already knew these before he was born. (82B–86C) This is remarkable enough, but Socrates sees it as sufficient evidence in itself for one to conclude to the soul's immortality:

26 E. R. Dodds (1) 24.

Socrates: ... may we say that his soul has been forever in a state of knowledge? Clearly he always either is or is not a man.
Meno: Clearly.
Socrates: And if the truth about reality is always in our soul, the soul must be immortal. (86A8–B2)

No formal proof is offered; the step is simply taken. One can hardly doubt that friendly criticism of such strange-looking assertions led Plato to more serious attempts at proof in the *Phaedo*. It is also worth noticing that the religious beliefs sketched in the *Gorgias* and characterized there as "a bit odd" (493C4) seem to be starting to gain a stronger hold:

Socrates: I have heard from men and women who understand the truths of religion ...
Meno: What did they say?
Socrates: Something true, I thought, and fine. (81A5–8)

This truth is in fact the assertion of the immortality and palingenesis of soul, with the injunction to live "as righteously as possible." (81B3–6) It is followed by a long quotation from Pindar or someone very like him, and how cogent Socrates sees it to be can be gathered from his comment, "Thus the soul, since [ἅτε] it is immortal and has been born many times ... has learned everything that is." (81C5–7) Proof, it seems, is not needed; if a divine poet says the soul is immortal, it *is* immortal, and can therefore be said to have seen and learnt all things. What is important for present purposes is not so much the conclusion as Socrates' apparent willingness to accept as a *point de départ* the outpourings of an Orphic poet. The warmth and conviction with which they are uttered (and indeed treated as quasi-biblical, self-evident truth) leave us in no doubt of the importance to him of such religious belief.

What is the nature of this migrating and immortal soul? Its status as the true self or person, as distinct from the body, is a necessary corollary of what has been said above, and some of its qualities are discussed at 88A6 ff. Among these are mentioned "temperance, justice, courage, quickness of mind, memory, nobility of character and all other such qualities." (88A6–8) None of the qualities, it is argued, can qualify for the name of "knowledge," for knowledge is invariably beneficial, whereas they are sometimes beneficial, sometimes the opposite, depending on the presence or absence of intelligence (88B1–7). Socrates continues:

In short, everything that the [soul] undertakes or suffers will lead to happiness when it is guided by wisdom, but to the opposite, when guided by folly.

Meno: A reasonable conclusion.

Socrates: If then virtue is an attribute of the [soul], and one which cannot fail to be beneficial, it must be wisdom ... (88c1-5)

Socrates then goes on to suggest that there is an analogy between the goodness or harmfulness of qualities of soul, and the goodness or harmfulness of things like wealth. In either instance, he says, we are dealing with that which is in itself neutral, and which only takes on an ethical colour when wisdom (φρόνησις) or folly (ἀφροσύνη) is in control of a man's soul. The passage – an important one, since it makes a clear distinction between "wisdom" (φρόνησις) and "the rest of the soul" (τῇ ἄλλῃ ψυχῇ 88c6), which in turn is said to have certain characteristics or properties (τὰ τῆς ψυχῆς 88D7) – runs:

Just as wisdom when it governs our other psychological impulses turns them to advantage [or rather: Just as wisdom, when it controls the rest of the soul, turns the impulses (or properties) of that part of soul to advantage, TMR], and folly turns them to harm, so the [soul] by its right use and control of these material assets makes them profitable, and by wrong use renders them harmful.

Meno: Certainly.

Socrates: And the right user is the [soul] of the wise man, the wrong user the [soul] of the foolish.

Meno: That is so. (88D4-E4)

Here, as at *Gorgias* 493A3-5, there seems to be the popular distinction of the soul into a rational and a non-rational part or aspect, without reference to the later, more elaborate doctrine of tripartition. What is of particular interest about it, however, is the way in which the non-rational part or aspect is seen as possessing a useful, worthwhile role in the functioning of the soul, provided intelligence or wisdom (φρόνησις) holds the reins. This seems definitely to prefigure the psychology of the *Republic*. The same could be said of the balanced statement at 88c6-D1, in which Socrates maintains that "all qualities of soul [πάντα τὰ κατὰ τὴν ψυχήν] in and by themselves are *neither* advantageous *nor* harmful, but *become* advantageous or harmful by the presence with them of wisdom [φρόνησις] or folly." Sober comments like this should be borne in mind when one is reading some of the more extreme statements on desire and pleasure to be found in, say, the *Phaedo*.

The passage concludes as follows:

> *Socrates*: ... in general the goodness of [material] assets depends on [the character of our soul], and the goodness of that on wisdom. This argument shows that the advantageous element must be wisdom, and virtue, we agree, is advantageous; so that amounts to saying that virtue, either in whole or in part, is wisdom.
> *Meno*: The argument seems to me fair enough. (88E4–89A5)

This conclusion had already figured hypothetically in an earlier sentence (88C4–D3). But what, in that case, is the status of the original qualities of soul which started off the discussion? Are they to be classed as genuine virtues (or vices), or are they morally neutral, only taking on colour as virtues (or vices) when, under the guidance of wisdom or folly, they are useful or deleterious? (88B7) According to this argument, at least, they can only be morally neutral; the title of virtue is reserved for wisdom and for wisdom only, which alone is *invariably* useful to the soul. (88C4–D1) If this is true, what are commonly called justice, prudence, bravery, etc., are merely potentially virtues; only when combined with wisdom do they become virtues in the truest sense, and then presumably they qualify for the title of genuine virtue in the way that wisdom itself does. We seem to have here the first move in the direction of a distinction between "ordinary" and "philosophic" virtue which will prove particularly important in the *Phaedo* and *Republic*.[27]

What has emerged therefore from the earlier dialogues are two groups of problems: (a) soul seems to be used in several distinguishable senses; (b) as a result, the body-soul relationship is expressed in rather different ways. In particular soul is seen as the true "self" or person, with sometimes its cognitive and sometimes its moral characteristics being stressed. But the nature of this "self" is ambiguous. In the *Charmides* it is such that it seems to include body as an integral part of itself; in the *Protagoras* it completely excludes it; in the *Gorgias* and *Alcibiades* I it excludes it, but at least body is seen to have a "special relationship" with soul not shared by other possessions.

Over and against this general view of soul is the Orphic-style picture of soul as a counter-person, imprisoned in the body as in a tomb. This soul, rational and substantial like the other, pre-exists and is immortal, and is composed of a number of elements, notably reason and impulse.

27 For the passages in question see R. D. Archer-Hind (2) app. A.

2

The Phaedo

The *Phaedo* has been from the beginning one of the most widely read of Plato's dialogues, and the reason is not hard to find. For it contains, in a setting where literary brilliance and perception match the pathos of the situation described, a lengthy exposition and defence of what have been called "the twin pillars of Platonism,"[1] the Theory of Ideas and the immortality of the human soul. In this account of soul as it appears in the *Phaedo* we shall be less directly concerned with the so-called proofs of its immortality than with the nature of soul itself, and the problem of the coherence or incoherence of the images of it which emerge from a reading of the text. For our present purpose the proofs of immortality will prove useful more for the concept or concepts of soul which they severally presuppose than for any intrinsic worth as proofs which they happen to possess.

At first sight the Socrates of the *Phaedo* is still the Socrates of the *Apology*, *Protagoras*, and *Crito*, intent upon announcing the importance of soul and its care. But the several concepts of soul itself which emerge are far from clear. Early on in the dialogue Socrates discusses the question of suicide, and death is defined as the separation of soul and body.[2] The language, whatever else it suggests, makes it apparent that body and soul are to be viewed as independent substances, able to exist "alone and by themselves" (αὐτὰ καθ' αὐτά) when in a state of separation from each other.[3] At this stage we have been told nothing of the nature of soul, but it would be fair to infer that such a definition of death is based upon an assumption already seen in the *Gorgias* (464B3), namely that body and soul make two. But what exactly does one mean by soul? Socrates' initial comments are somewhat confusing. At 64E4–6 we are told that the activity of the genuine philosopher is to

1 F. M. Cornford (4) xxv.
2 64C4–9; cf. *Grg.* 524B2–4.
3 See 64E6, 65C7, 65A1–2. This is corroborated later at 93A11–94B3, where it is denied that the soul is an "attunement" (ἁρμονία) of the body's constituent parts. For recent discussion of the latter passage see W. F. Hicken 16–22 and W. J. Verdenius (2) 227–8.

"stand off" (ἀφεστάναι) from the body as far as he can, and "direct his attention to the soul." At 64E8–65A2 he is described as one who "manifests his effort to release his soul from association with his body to a degree that surpasses that of the rest of mankind." An outsider might be forgiven for assuming that we must be dealing here with three substances, body, soul, and the philosopher who possesses body and soul and manipulates them for his purposes. Our first hint of what the soul itself could be comes at 65B9–C2 when we are told, in answer to the question how the soul "reaches truth," that it does so "when it reasons."[4] The soul, then, in addition to its being an independent substance, appears to have some sort of cognition as at least one of its faculties. In order to exercise this faculty to the best advantage, however, it must be untroubled by "either hearing or sight or pain or pleasure." (65C5–7) If we overlook the category-mistake involved in (apparently) treating vision, pleasure, and pain as logical bedfellows, we could sum up the position as roughly describing "bodily sensation." Whatever such bodily sensation turns out to connote in detail, it is considered able to "trouble" the soul, and in view of this the soul must, as far as possible, "bid farewell to the body" and "become alone and by itself." (65C6–8) It is to "reach out after reality," and this will involve "the least possible communion and contact with the body." (65C8–9) The reference to "reality" is a hint of what is to come, when Socrates will explain his views on being and intelligibility; for the moment it is worth noticing the very "personal" language he is using to describe the soul's activities. Even if, for argument's sake, it were granted that all of it is being used metaphorically, it remains minimally true that, for the moment at least, Socrates finds it convenient to at any rate *describe* the soul as some sort of "inner person." This is corroborated by the following sentence, where the philosopher's soul is said to "despise" the body and "avoid" it and seek to be "alone and by itself." (65D1–2)

These introductory comments by Socrates have shown that for him soul is an independent substance, with powers of cognition, and liable to be hindered in the exercise of such powers by "bodily sensation." A preliminary sketch of the means to be taken to avoid any such hindrance as far as possible has involved a description of the soul little removed, if at all, from the normal description of a person. And since there is no compelling evidence so far to suggest that the language is to be taken metaphorically, one could provisionally say that up to this point soul is seen as a "counter-person," or

---

4 For this view of soul as a principle of reason in antecedent and contemporary thought see T. W. Webster 149–54. See also *Prt.* 313C7, 314B, *Euthd.* 295E4–5, *Grg.* 505B2.

"duplicate person," or "inner person," possessed of cognitive faculties. Certainly, soul can hardly be taken to mean *simply* a cognitive principle, as fresh evidence quickly shows. At 65A7, for example, we read of "the pleasures that come by way of the body"; in other words, by implication there exist pleasures other than bodily. This seems to be confirmed by a comment at 64D3–4, where he talks of "the *so-called* pleasures of ... food and drink." Again, the use of the phrase "reach out," already seen at 65C9, can only be taken to mean that the soul is not deprived of desire, either. It is no doubt true that in this early section of the dialogue it is the soul's cognitive faculties which are stressed, but, if language means anything at all, it is seen as much more than a cognitive principle. The coloured and highly emotional language in which it is often described is not, it will be suggested later, to be written off merely as decorative metaphor; on the contrary, it is frequently the clue to varying concepts, in Plato's mind, of the soul whose immortality he is ostensibly trying to prove. To outline what these concepts or tensions are, and to consider whether they are reconcilable, will be the purpose of the rest of this chapter.

We have seen how Plato's initial comments on the soul stress its cognitive activities. This is emphasized even further during a discussion about "popular" and "philosophic" virtue, where it is contended that serious or "philosophic" virtue – a virtue of profound consequence for that element of a man which survives – entails the practice of intelligence.[5] In similar vein Cebes, one of Socrates' young interlocutors, makes it clear that proof of soul's survival is inadequate; one must also show that it "still has some powers and intelligence left." (70B2–4) The idea of personal survival without that of elementary cognition is unthinkable. Socrates recognises this, and concludes his argument from Recollection with the comment, "Our souls, then, Simmias, existed earlier on, before inhabiting human form; they existed apart from bodies, and they had intelligence." (76C11–13) Prominent among the evils of the body which the soul is expected to shun are its "folly" and its "stupidity" (81A6, 67A7), and at one point, where Socrates wishes to equate "preparedness" and "purification," he goes so far as to use the word "intelligence" (διάνοια) in a context which clearly demands the term "soul."[6]

5 See R. 619C, where the choice of life for those to be freshly reincarnated depends on the quality of their "virtue" (ἀρετή) in their previous incarnated existence, and *Phd.* 82A10–E1. For a useful collection of similar texts see R. D. Archer-Hind (2) app. A.
6 67C2–3. For a similar substitution see *Prt.* 326B2, B7, *Sph.* 227C4.

If in this quotation the word "intelligence" sums up one prominent aspect of soul, the adjective "purified" introduces us to another. For in his discussion of the soul Socrates is portrayed as being heavily influenced by Orphic-style religious beliefs. Body is at best a nuisance (66A5–6, 66B7 ff.) and at worst a positive evil (66B6), and it is the body and all that it entails that is said to hinder the soul from possessing "truth and intelligence." (66A6) So the philosopher must spend his lifetime purifying his soul from the body and the bodily as far as possible. Only in this way can he hope to attain the highest possible degree of true knowledge in this life and eternal happiness in the next.[7] The whole dialogue abounds in language like "purification," "religious initiation," "purity of soul," "contamination of the body," and the like. It is the language of the religious believer, and the creed is summed up for us by Socrates himself: "... no soul which has not practised philosophy, and is not absolutely pure when it leaves the body, may attain to the divine nature; that is for the lover of wisdom." (82B10–C1)

But if he has incorporated the religious notion of purification into his thinking, it is no ritual cleansing, no superstitious placation of the powers that be with meticulous ceremony. True purification is the life of philosophy (= "love of wisdom," $\phi\iota\lambda o\sigma o\phi\acute{\iota}\alpha$), or love of learning, or "philosophic virtue": all amount to the same thing.[8] Whatever esoteric creeds may have taught, the notion is transformed into something new by Socratic intellectualism. There is no true virtue without intelligence (69B2), and the utilitarian balancing of pains and pleasures which masquerades under the name of virtue has no claim to the title (69A6 ff.); on the contrary, true virtue is really a process of purification, and intelligence functions as the purge. (69C1–3) Intelligence, to vary the metaphor, is the only valid currency, and all else must be traded in to receive this in exchange. (69A9–10)

But if Socrates has succeeded in transforming the Orphic ethic, the Orphic view of soul is still very much with him. He apparently accepts the ideas of a previous existence,[9] metensomatosis,[10] and the possibility of another life or series of lives after this one (81E ff.), and the view of soul

---

7 66A1–6, 66A6–B1, 66E2–4, 67B8–C3.

8 60E1, 61A8, 69C2–3, 80E2. See also 66E5, 67A5, 67A7, 67B2, 67C3, 67C5, 68B4, 82C1.

9 76C11–13. See *Men.* 81B3–C4. An idea cognate to this which has found eloquent and frightening expression in modern times is to be found in Kafka's novel *The Trial.* Here life is seen as a trial on an unknown charge, by an unseen jury, with an inevitable verdict – guilty, and an inevitable punishment – death.

10 62B. See also Bhagavad Gita II 12.

which these are bound to entail can be clearly discerned in much of the dialogue. This view is essentially that of what I have previously called a "counter-person" or "duplicate person."[11] It is seen at its clearest in the myth of life after death near the end of the dialogue, but, if we leave this aside for later discussion, traces of the view can still be seen in the dialogue proper in much of the language used to describe man in his present state. Some of this we have already seen; in addition, the soul is said to be "bound and cemented"[12] in the body, which he calls its "prison, after a manner of speaking."[13] It "uses" (79c3) the body, and in so doing operates "through sense" (79c5), with the result that "it is dragged by the body towards objects that are never constant, and itself wanders in a sort of dizzy drunken confusion, inasmuch as it is apprehending confused objects." (79c6–8) Such a "personal" view of soul seems to me well illustrated by a number of other passages:

> Another soul departs polluted, uncleansed of the body's taint, inasmuch as it has always associated with the body and tended it, filled with its lusts and so bewitched by its passions and pleasures as to think nothing real save what is bodily. (81b1 ff.)
>
> It seems to me an inevitable result of sharing the body's beliefs and joys that it [i.e. the soul] should adopt its habits and upbringing. (83d6–7) ... this soul secures immunity from its desire by following reason and abiding always in her company, and by contemplating the true and divine and unconjecturable, and drawing inspiration from it... (84a8–b1)

Outstanding is the language used at 94b7 ff., where Plato, aided by a selective quotation from Homer (94d8–e1), is trying to show how soul can *oppose* the feelings and inclinations of the body:

> ... dominating all these alleged sources of its existence, opposing them almost incessantly for a whole lifetime, mastering them in this way and that, sometimes inflicting severe and painful punishment in the course of physical training or medical treatment, sometimes proceeding more gently; threatening here and admonishing there ...

11 For similar contemporary views see T. W. Webster 150–2.
12 82E2; cf. 92A1.
13 82E3. For the *double entendre* involved in the phrase ἔν τινι φρουρᾷ (62B3–4) see J. Burnet (4) *ad loc.* To this should be added the interesting interpretation of P. Frutiger 58 n1. See also *Ax.* 366A1, and P. Courcelle (1) 101–22.

That much of this language would be classed by Plato himself as metaphorical is hardly in doubt; frequently he tones down similar remarks with
a cautionary "as if" or "as though" (ὥσπερ).[14] But if all the language is
metaphorical, it is remarkable how internally coherent it all is, how methodi-
cally it conspires to lead the reader to imagine the soul under one and only
one guise – that of a person.

But these two views of soul, the one cognitive, the other personal, are
far from being the only ones which the dialogue presents to us. The first
Heraclitus-style proof of soul's immortality, that based upon Opposition
(69E–72D),[15] and the final proof, based upon entailment (102A ff.), both
involve the popular view of soul as "life-principle" or "life-carrier" or
something similar.[16] Cognition is not discussed, and Plato's apparent assumption that this "life-soul" and the cognitive soul are one and the same is
nowhere subjected to critical examination. To the modern mind it is odd,
to say the least, to claim that an invisible noetic substance should be the
direct and sufficient cause of a man's physical existence, without offering
some semblance of argument to support the claim. Yet Socrates first introduces us to the soul as a cognitive principle and then founds his very first
proof of immortality on the fact that it is a *life*-principle![17] That he assumes
the identity of the two seems clear from his concluding comment, "*our* souls,
then, exist in Hades." (71E2, my italics) This can only mean individual
survival, which will in turn entail the survival of at least one cognitive faculty,
memory. The statement is reiterated in a more prolix manner at 72A6–8,
though this time without the same stress on individual survival, and the next
move seems to suggest that Socrates is less sure of his argument than he
appeared at first. For he introduces another one, this time from Recollection.
This, he thinks, proves half of what is desired, namely that "our souls existed
before we were born" (77C2–3), while the preceding argument from Opposition comes into its own by ostensibly proving the other half. (77C6 ff.)
This would have some cogency if it could be shown that life-principle (the
"soul" of the Opposition argument) and cognitive-principle (the "soul" of
the Recollection argument) were one and the same; but that is precisely the
point which Socrates assumes rather than establishes. It could be, of course,

14 E.g. 67D1–2, 83D4.
15 For an excellent short critique of this argument see J. Wolfe 237–8.
16 For this view in Homer and the tragedians see T. W. Webster 150.
17 For a remarkable equation of life-soul and cognitive soul see Antiphon (5,93; 4A7),
where A. appeals to the jury "to deprive the accused of the ψυχή which planned the
crime." (T. W. Webster 151)

that in claiming "our souls ... exist in Hades" Socrates is already assuming the findings of the argument which follows, namely that of Recollection. The dilemma is this – either he *is* assuming the findings of the Recollection argument, in which case he assumes what is to be proved, namely that life-principle and cognitive-principle are one and the same, or he thinks that the Opposition argument by itself does prove *individual* pre-existence and survival, in which case he will be logically compelled to accept a number of curious consequences. For if the Opposition argument is enough to prove our own *individual* pre-existence and survival it will prove it equally for all living beings, human or not. The only difference between us and them will be that we are aware of the continuity of self in the three sets of existence (past, present, and future) by the unifying thread of memory, while other living things, being non-rational, will presumably not. There is indeed some evidence that he would have been willing to accept this latter position, since at 70D9 he applies the argument from Opposition to "everything that admits of generation" (ὅσαπερ ἔχει γένεσιν), and at 72C6 to "everything that has some share of life" (πάντα ὅσα τοῦ ζῆν μεταλάβοι). However, the fact that the argument from Recollection, introduced immediately afterwards, is taken as "proof of one half of what we wanted – that the soul existed before birth" (77C1–3), while the argument from Opposition is adduced as evidence for the other half, on the grounds that in the cycle of births a thing's "pre-existent" state and its "dead" state can be seen as synonymous (77C6–D5), seems to suggest that Socrates may have had some misgivings about his earlier assumption that *individual* pre-existence could be demonstrated by means of the argument from Opposition alone.

The final argument for immortality provides an interesting, if somewhat confused, postscript to all this. For the argument from Opposition had relied upon the life-bestowing powers of soul without offering us any details about their operation, and now we have what at first sight seems a clarification. The soul, we are told, "always brings life along with it to anything that it occupies." The notion of "bringing along" (ἐπιφορά), however, as the context soon shows, is really a logical one, with the same connotation as our own word "entailment." This is clearly shown by the examples which introduce it (105C1–6): heat is the more generic notion entailed by fire, disease by fever, oddness by unity. It is noteworthy that in all the examples what is entailed is not necessarily of substantial status; it is simply a genus of which the first is a specific exemplification. This is clear enough in the case of fever and disease, unity and oddness, where in all cases we seem to be dealing with properties, not substances, and the analogy would lead us to assume that Plato sees both life and soul as *properties* of the living person, soul being but a particular exemplification of the more generic property-concept, life.[18] This is remarkable, for Socrates, in answering Simmias' earlier contention that the soul is only an "attunement" of one's bodily constituents, makes it abundantly clear that the human soul is for him a substance, not merely a property of body (91E5 ff.) How important he sees his refutation to be can be seen from his outline of the danger to his own doctrine of Recollection and pre-existence if the view is accepted. (*Ibid.*) This being the case, it would be rash to assume that Plato is overtly making soul a quality, in the Aristotelian sense. The notion of a quality ($\pi o i \acute{o} \tau \eta s$) is introduced by Plato for the first time in the *Theaetetus* (182A), and one can be reasonably sure that in the *Phaedo* properties are still seen by him as quasi-substantial. Important for present purposes, however, is the fact that their ontological status as "intermediates" between Ideas and sense-objects is frequently suggested by the language Plato uses. The (transcendental) Idea, Coldness-as-Such ($a \dot{v} \tau \grave{o} \ \tau \grave{o} \ \psi v \chi \rho \acute{o} v$), for example, is clearly at one end of the ontological spectrum, while the individual "cold object" ($\psi v \chi \rho \acute{o} v \ \tau \iota$) is at the other. In between appear to be what he calls "the cold" ($\tau \grave{o} \ \psi v \chi \rho \acute{o} v$, $\dot{\eta} \ \psi v \chi \rho \acute{o} \tau \eta s$ 103D7–E1), "the hot" ($\tau \grave{o} \ \theta \epsilon \rho \mu \acute{o} v$, $\dot{\eta} \ \theta \epsilon \rho \mu \acute{o} \tau \eta s$ 103D8, 105C2), etc., and it is these that in this argument serve as analogues of soul for some, if not all, of the time. If this is true, it suggests that Plato is on the verge of the doctrine of soul as "intermediary" between the worlds of quasi-existence and "authentic" existence which will figure prominently in later dialogues like the *Timaeus*. However, it cannot be said with assurance that Plato here unequivocally adopts that position. For, while on the one hand he talks of "the tallness in us" retreating before the approach of "smallness" ($\tau \grave{o} \ \sigma \mu \iota \kappa \rho \acute{o} v$, $\dot{\eta} \ \sigma \mu \iota \kappa \rho \acute{o} \tau \eta s$ 102D8–E2) – a passage which clearly views such properties as "immanent" Ideas – on the other hand he talks later of the apparent *particulars* "snow" and "fire" retreating before "the hot" ($\tau \grave{o} \ \theta \epsilon \rho \mu \acute{o} v$) and "the cold" ($\tau \grave{o} \ \psi v \chi \rho \acute{o} v$, $\dot{\eta} \ \psi v \chi \rho \acute{o} \tau \eta s$ 103D7–E1). This certainly looks anomalous, and a solution that has been suggested is to equate "snow" and "fire" with "immanent" Ideas like "the tallness in us." The clear conclusion will be that soul, too, being the direct analogue of "snow" and "fire," is an "immanent" Idea. However, this need not be so, as a glance at 105E10–106A10 will show. In this passage "three" or "[any] three objects" ($\tau \grave{a} \ \tau \rho \acute{\iota} a$) is substituted for

18 R. Hackforth (6) 162 ff.

"the non-even" (τὸ ἀνάρτιον), "snow" for "the non-hot" (τὸ ἄθερμον) and "fire" for "the non-cold" (τὸ ἄψυκτον). The importance of this is quickly seen when "the deathless" (τὸ ἀθάνατον) – the clear analogue of "the non-even," "the non-hot," and "the non-cold" – is replaced by "soul" at 106B2. As has been pointed out recently, in this latter instance we are undoubtedly dealing with what *is* deathless (i.e. soul), rather than with "deathlessness" *in* the soul. This would seem to suggest that, far from equating "fire" and "snow" with "immanent" Ideas, one ought perhaps instead to have equated "immanent" Ideas with particulars! The truth of the matter is that either move seems to introduce as many anomalies as it is meant to solve, and the more cautious policy would appear to be to reserve judgment concerning the exact ontological status of the different analogues of soul in the argument. Suffice it to say that sometimes they seem to be particulars (fire, snow, etc.), sometimes "immanent" Ideas. If one lays particular stress upon the fact that "immanent" Ideas (like "the tallness in us") are intermediates between the (transcendental) Ideas and sense-objects, one could then just perhaps argue that Plato's view of soul here verges on the view of soul as an "intermediary" championed in later dialogues. But to go further than this would be hazardous.

The ambiguous status of soul in this final argument is paralleled in an earlier passage of the dialogue, where the soul's likeness to the eternal Ideas is stressed. In Socrates' words, "on the one hand we have that which is divine, immortal, indestructible, of a single form, accessible to thought, ever constant and abiding true to itself; and the soul is very like it: on the other hand we have that which is human, mortal, destructible, of many forms, inaccessible to thought, never constant nor abiding true to itself; and the body is very like that." (80B1–5) This, too, makes it look as though soul plays an intermediary role, like that of "the cold" (τὸ ψυχρόν, ἡ ψυχρότης 103D7–E1) between Coldness-as-Such (αὐτὸ τὸ ψυχρόν) and the cold object (ψυχρόν τι 106A9). It is not itself an Idea, but is clearly more proximate to the Ideas than to sense-objects. There is no hint that it is not a substance, though presumably it is of a nature somewhat inferior to the Ideas. But what *sort* of substance can it be? If it is only *like* what is immortal, there is presumably the possibility (however remote) that it is itself mortal; if it is only *like* the indestructible, it could be itself destructible. Only if the soul is unequivocally said to *be* immortal and indestructible – that is, itself an Idea – could this particular statement of Socrates have any cogency. And this is just what he refuses to say with clarity, though some scholars have argued the contrary.[19] Whatever the perfection of soul, it is of a lesser degree than that of the paradigmatic Ideas. All this still tells us little about what soul itself is meant to be, but it is worth noticing that for Socrates the superiority of soul to body lies precisely in its approximation to a reality which is static and unchanging. To anyone who sees soul as a principle of life and activity – that is, change – this reads very curiously, and contrasts sharply with what will be said in later dialogues. The truth seems to be that Socrates is once more emphasizing soul as a cognitive principle. If the known object is static and eternal, the knowing subject will have similar characteristics, on the Empedoclean principle that like knows like.[20] But if this cognitive soul is to be equated with life-soul a serious difficulty presents itself. For the Ideas are in no sense alive; their static permanence suggests just the opposite. In that case, what becomes of Empedocles' principle, since, in one of the most crucial respects of all, soul and the Ideas are completely *un*like? Here, as in the case of the Recollection and Opposition arguments, Socrates tacitly assumes that cognitive-soul and life-soul are one and the same, but emphasizes that cognitive aspect which suits his purpose in the particular context. Quite apart from the fact that this considerably weakens the argument for immortality, little light can be said to have been thrown on the problem of the essential characteristics of soul.

So far we have seen that in this dialogue Socrates looks on the human soul sometimes as a counter-person, sometimes as an intellectual principle, sometimes as a life-bringer or life-principle, and perhaps in one passage even as a formal *property* (with "intermediate" status?) entailing life. But a fifth view remains to be distinguished. This has much in common with the view of soul as a counter-person, but is couched in more materialistic terms. On this view soul is something like what spiritualists call "ectoplasm" and ordinary people a ghost,[21] which can influence and be influenced by the body and the bodily, and is the body's exact non-material replica. Three texts in particular are worth examining:

19 W. Theiler (2) 64 and A.-J. Festugière (1) II 103 have argued that in the final argument of the *Phd.* ψυχή has become, not *like* an Idea, but actually an Idea. Theiler takes it that the soul is an Idea bound up with the Idea of Life, Festugière that the soul is itself the Idea of Life. (*Phd.* 106c) For a criticism of this view see H. Cherniss (3) 208. More recent proponents of the notion that "soul" in the final argument is an Idea are G. Vlastos (3) 93 n14 and (rather more tentatively) D. O'Brien 228.

20 DK[12] B 109 (Empedocles). See W. Theiler (2) 63.

21 See M. P. Nilsson 3.

Purification consists in separating the soul as much as possible from the body, and accustoming it to withdraw from all contact with the body and concentrate itself by itself, and to have its dwelling, so far as it can, both now and in the future, alone by itself, freed from the shackles of the body. (67C7–8)

[The impure and tainted soul] will, I imagine, be permeated by the corporeal, which fellowship and intercourse with the body will have ingrained in its very nature through constant association and long practice. (81C4 ff.)

If at its release the soul is pure and carries with it no contamination of the body, because it has never willingly associated with it in life, but has shunned it and kept itself separate as its regular practice – in other words, if it has pursued philosophy in the right way and really practiced how to face death easily – this is what "practicing death" means, isn't it? (80E2 ff.)

It has been argued that this "spatialist" language can again be written off as metaphorical.[22] Perhaps. But once more, as in the case of soul viewed as some sort of counter-person, all the metaphorical language is remarkable for its internal consistency and coherence, and I suggest that a particular view of soul, if only an unconscious one, underlies it. For the sake of a word, we may call it the "ectoplasm theory." The idea is that the soul is some sort of vital fluid which pervades the entire body and, on separation from the body, retains the latter's shape, at any rate if it has been "tainted" (ἀναπίμπλεσθαι 67A5) by it during the period of their conjunction. The soul on this view is certainly seen in a very "physical" way; it can apparently be "interpenetrated" by the body, and it is the element of the corporeal that it "drags away" which makes it visible as a ghost. And in some way it can be "infected" by the body, as one rotten apple can infect the whole basketful.[23]

22 R. Hackforth (6) 52 n3.
23 *Ibid.* On the materialist tendencies of this view of ψυχή see R. K. Gaye 92 ff., 101. See also A. E. Taylor (3) *ad* 86E3–87A7. The view is not confined to Plato. It seems that the younger Aristotle, in his *Protrepticus*, had something similar to say. He tells how Etruscan pirates had the habit of tying their prisoners to dead bodies, face to face, limb to limb. While he stresses here the body-soul relationship as that of a dead thing to a living thing, there seems also involved the notion that the rotting corpse will *infect* the living body attached to it. Not to mention the fact that once more the one is pictured as a replica of the other. (*Protrept.* 10B, in *Aristotelis Fragmenta Selecta,* ed. W. D. Ross (Oxford 1955)).

As Dodds has written, "the Classical Age inherited a whole series of inconsistent pictures of the 'soul' or 'self,' "[24] and this is nowhere more evident than in the *Phaedo*, where their global assimilation cannot help but weaken the arguments for immortality. The remarkable thing is that the same Socrates who is so adamant about correctness of definition in ethical discourse in the so-called "Socratic" dialogues makes so little attempt to give a coherent and internally consistent definition of the soul in the *Phaedo*. The upshot is that we are presented with conflicting views about the notion of the self, and even stranger views about the body and its desires. Usually (e.g., at *Alcibiades* I, 130E5), self and soul are taken as synonymous. As Socrates puts it:

> I will not stay where I am after I have died, but will take my departure; that will make it easier for Crito: when he sees my body being burnt or put under ground he won't have to distress himself on my behalf, as though *I* were being outraged, and won't have to say at the funeral that it is Socrates whom he is laying out or carrying to the grave or burying. (115D8–E4)

Negative evidence for the same viewpoint is the way in which Socrates frequently uses the first person where he could equally well have talked about the soul. At 67A5–6, for example, he talks about "keeping our*selves* pure and free from bodily infection," when it is in fact the *soul* which is infected and in need of purification. But here, as elsewhere, his views are very fluid. At 66B5–7, for example, he writes, "so long as our *souls* are befouled by this evil admixture, *we* shall assuredly never fully possess that which we desire ..." Here "soul" seems to be viewed as a possession, with the "self" as the possessor. A similar view emerges at 67E6–8, where he writes, "if their continual quarrel with the body, their desire to *have the soul by itself,* were to result in fear and complaint when that is achieved, how unreasonable it would be!" Once more soul and its possessor seem to be distinguished, as also apparently at 64E8–65A2. How seriously this is to be taken is hard to say. If it is taken at its face value, the true self will be some sort of super-Ego beyond soul and body, and this will stand in direct conflict with the view of the self as the soul.[25] Be this as it may, what is quite certain is that Socrates wants to flout the greater part of tradition by maintaining

24 E. R. Dodds (2) 179.
25 Cf. also *R.* 572A5–6. A simple answer to this problem is to suggest that Socrates is using language loosely. This is perhaps true – but it makes for considerable confusion.

that the self or person is definitely *not* the body.[26] The latter is merely the prison in which the soul is incarcerated for a while (82E3); it is nothing but an obstacle and an evil, and its desires a thorough nuisance. (66B6 ff.) The most interesting point here is the assumption that desires are to be deprecated *en bloc*, and that they have the body for their place of origin. (66BD) Conflict, in other words, is between soul and body; the idea of conflict within the soul itself does not appear. But hints of a fresh and more sober approach to this problem can be seen here and there, as I have indicated elsewhere, and their fulfilment we shall find in the *Republic* and *Philebus*. As things stand, however, there is a marked contrast between this view of soul as an incarcerated intelligence, for which desires are bodily nuisances and not part of the true self, and the view of soul which obtains in the myths, in this dialogue and elsewhere. For in the myths the soul is a complete counterpart of the person we know on earth, and desires are as much part and parcel of it as is intelligence. The myths will be treated as a whole elsewhere;[27] for the moment it is sufficient to notice that the one which concludes the *Phaedo* does nothing to allay the confusion about the nature of the soul which the rest of the dialogue has succeeded in engendering. The immortality of "soul" may have been "proved," but we are still left asking the question, "Which soul?"

To sum up. The *Phaedo* presents us with a number of senses of soul, many of them already seen in earlier dialogues. A new one is that of soul as a "life-carrier" or "life-principle," and the assumption that this and the cognitive soul are one and the same weakens much of the argumentation for immortality. It is also noticeable how materialistic the language used to describe the soul can sometimes be. Some pleasures and desires are no doubt attributed to the soul by implication, but, by and large, pleasure and desires are looked upon with distaste and distrust and taken to stem from the body and the bodily. The true person is the soul: the body is a necessary evil *ici bas*. Particularly at the beginning of the dialogue the soul is looked upon as more or less pure intelligence, and desires other than those involved in the search for knowledge are not considered part of this true self. How far such a view can be reconciled with the paramechanical one of the soul in another world, complete with all the attributes, desires, and emotions which we associate with the living person in this world, is not immediately clear. Socrates, however, seems content for the moment to accept both. Refinements can be expected later.

26 For a survey of the tradition that body and self are synonymous see R. Hirzel 1–27.
27 See below, 128ff.

3

The Republic

If the *Phaedo* was as much a manifesto as a dialogue proper, the *Republic* is once more a discussion, taking place in an atmosphere of relative calm. The ostensible theme is justice, its nature and its implications in public and private life. (331C2 ff.) The first book is very much a Socratic dialogue, confining itself in the well-known manner to a search for an adequate definition of the virtue under discussion, and ending in the usual state of inconclusiveness. In the process, however, we have a short discussion on soul which introduces us to some technical terminology of no small interest for the later development of philosophy. I refer to the coupled notions of function and virtue (or "efficiency" ἀρετή). The "end" or "function" of a thing is defined (353A10–11) as "that which it alone can perform or can best perform," and all that has a function is credited with a particular ἀρετή – excellence, or operational efficiency – without which the performance of its particular function is impossible. (353B2–4) In the case of the eye, it is claimed, the function is seeing, and this is out of the question if the eye has a defect and is sightless. It is stressed that Socrates is talking only of a thing's *own and proper* efficient state (οἰκεία ἀρετή) whereby it will perform its task well and efficiently and its own and proper deficient state (κακία) whereby it will perform its task badly, etc. (353C6–7) This terminology is then applied to the soul. The latter is said to have a function in the "stronger" sense – that is, it has a function which is confined to itself alone. (353A10) This function is defined as "management, rule, deliberation and the like," although immediately afterwards we are told that "living" is a function of soul. (353D4–10) It also has its own and proper "virtuous" or "efficient" state (ἀρετή) which is justice, the correspondingly "deficient" state being injustice. (353E7–8) In other words, the soul which is operating at peak efficiency is a "just" one and, it seems, a "good" one. As Socrates puts it, "a bad soul will govern and manage things badly while the good soul will in all these things do well." (353E4–5) It is worth noticing, however, that there is a slight discrepancy in the accounts of the "efficient" and the "good" soul. At 353E1 ff. the question is asked, "Is the soul able to fulfil her own ends [τὰ αὐτῆς ἔργα – plural], Thrasymachus, when deprived of her proper efficient state?" and Thrasymachus replies that she is unable to do so. In other words, the presence of a *single* specific ἀρετή seems to guarantee the proper working of *two* groups of functions, the one neatly summed up as "living," the other rather more loosely as "management, rule, deliberation and the like." (353D4–10) In the next sentence, however, when Socrates is talking of the "good" soul, any reference to "living" is omitted, and it is of such a "good" soul that the efficient operation is defined as "justice" in the sentence immediately following. (353E4–8)

So far the process is intelligible enough. The direct equation of goodness and efficiency is well in keeping with the analogy which Socrates was continually detecting between moral and artistic activity, and there was nothing to stop him from making the further step of defining the particular goodness of the soul as justice. But this conclusion he seems to reach only at the expense of underplaying one of the soul's two groups of functions. If the soul is to be "just" in the same way that it was said to be "good" this can only be because it *plans*, *rules*, etc., well. (See 353E4–5 and D4–6.) Such a definition of justice may be a new one to Greek ears, but it is hardly incoherent. However, Plato had earlier made it clear that the soul's single specific ἀρετή had also covered the function defined as "living" (353D9–10), and he shows in his concluding sentence that the notion plays a crucial part in his reasoning: "The just soul and the just man ... will live well [εὖ βιώσεται] and the unjust ill." (353E10–11) But the man who "lives well," he affirms, is "blessed and happy." (354A1) So the just man, too, will be happy. The conclusion is then drawn: "Injustice can never be more profitable than justice." (354A8–9)

Quite apart from the ambiguities involved in adjectives like "blessed," "happy," and "profitable," the whole argument seems to be vitiated by ambiguities within the notions of "living" and "living well." When it was first introduced at 353D, there was nothing in the notion of "living" to make us think that it was being used in any other than its normal biological sense. To the Greek mind the soul was intimately involved with the notion of biological existence, however hazy their opinions about the relationship of this soul to the living being we see.[1] Socrates himself had taken this for granted in two important arguments in the *Phaedo*.[2] In the absence of evidence to the contrary, therefore, one can hardly be blamed for assuming that such is the meaning of "living" in this context. In such a case, to talk of a person as "just" with reference to his function of "living" can only mean that he is in some way "good at" or "efficient at" living (in a biological sense). The idea that one can be "good at being alive" is so odd, and yet so necessary a conclusion from the notion of "living" as a function of soul, that one feels Socrates ought either to have abandoned the notion of "living" altogether, or perhaps started to question the worth of the analogy between moral and artistic activity. What he in fact does is to retain the formula "living" while tacitly abandoning its *biological* sense. This he does by introducing the composite verb "live *well*" (εὖ ζῆν). Even here, however, he cannot demonstrate his case without (wittingly or unwittingly) exploiting a further ambiguity between the "transitive" and "intransitive" senses of εὖ ζῆν (i.e., "performing morally good actions" and "living prosperously or successfully"). That such senses exist for the verb εὖ πράττειν is a commonplace.[3] What is, to my knowledge, new in the present passage is Socrates' apparent supposition that the same distinctions operate within the verb εὖ ζῆν.

It is perhaps worth noting that the Greeks wanted to make a distinction similar to the one familiar to us in the sentence, "I really live; you just exist." Sophocles (*Ant.* 1165–67) distinguishes between the man who "lives" (ζῆν) and the man who is just a "breathing corpse" (ἔμψυχος νεκρός). A similar contrast is ascribed to his fellow-men by Cephalus at *Republic* 329A8, though this time the antithesis is said to be between ζῆν and εὖ ζῆν. Perhaps Plato means to raise this contrast to a higher plane when he contends later in the dialogue that only the philosopher who has reached communion with the Ideas "truly lives" (ἀληθῶς ζώη 490B6). (Cf. D. J. Allan on *Republic* 329A8.) Be this as it may, it seems not impossible that the popular use of ζῆν and εὖ ζῆν at *Republic* 329A8, which clearly envisages something more than *just* biological existence, is the sort of bridge that Socrates would unconsciously use to pass from the purely biological to the ethical sense of τὸ ζῆν.

1 See J. L. Stocks 217–18.

2 I.e., the argument from Opposition and the final argument based on entailment; see *Phd.* 69E–72D, 102A ff.

3 James Adam (2) n. *ad* 354A2, with references to *Chrm. ad loc.* See also P. Shorey (2) 482, with his references to *Grg.* 507C and Arist. *Pol.* 132B31.

The whole argument can be summed up in syllogistic form as follows:

All men who "live well" ($\epsilon\hat{v}$ $\zeta\hat{\eta}\nu$) are happy.
But all just men are men who "live well" ($\epsilon\hat{v}$ $\zeta\hat{\eta}\nu$).
Ergo all just men are happy.

Put schematically it runs:

M a π
S a μ
Therefore S a π

Here we have what looks like Aristotle's perfect syllogism – First Figure Barbara. So the fallacy, if there is one, could only be in the ambiguity of the middle term. This, I have suggested, is the case. In the major premise "live well" clearly means "act well," and in the minor it means "be prosperous (i.e., *fare* well)," thus exploiting the transitive and intransitive usages of the verb $\epsilon\hat{v}$ $\zeta\hat{\eta}\nu$ and rendering the conclusion vacuous. Socrates, it seems, is caught (wittingly or unwittingly) in the Fallacy of Equivocation.

In the *Phaedo* we have already seen how Socrates takes soul to be both a cognitive principle and a principle of life; now it seems to be a principle of cognition ($\beta ov\lambda\epsilon\acute{v}\epsilon\sigma\theta a\iota$), life (in the purely biological sense) ($\tau\grave{o}$ $\zeta\hat{\eta}\nu$), and morally good or bad conduct ($\tau\grave{o}$ $\epsilon\hat{v}$ or $\kappa a\kappa\hat{\omega}s$ $\zeta\hat{\eta}\nu$), while words like "care for" and "rule over" seem to involve a view of the soul as the "true person" for which we saw evidence in the *Phaedo* and elsewhere.[4] To apply the notion of "justice" to all these aspects of soul in the univocal sense of an excellence or efficiency ($\dot{a}\rho\epsilon\tau\acute{\eta}$) similar to those of the arts and handicrafts leads to incoherence, and we have seen how in fact Socrates vacillates. The dilemma is this: if justice *is* exactly analogous to the $\dot{a}\rho\epsilon\tau a\iota$ of the arts and handicrafts then "living" in its purely biological sense is hardly a function of soul, and if "living" in its biological sense *is* a function of soul then the virtue of "justice" can hardly qualify for the title of soul's unique and specific $\dot{a}\rho\epsilon\tau\acute{\eta}$. Faced with this difficulty Socrates equivocates, and in doing so implicitly admits that the notion of (purely biological) living is either being understressed or, perhaps, dropped altogether. The result is that the definition of justice which survives does not account for all the aspects of soul which have been brought into the discussion, and is plainly out of keeping with one of them (i.e., that of "living" in the purely biological sense). Socrates himself can hardly have failed to see this, for the book concludes with a

4 353D5, 353D9–10, 353E10.

profession of his ignorance of the nature of justice, of whether its possessor is happy or not – in fact, in true Socratic fashion, of everything! (354C1–3) Interesting for our purposes are:

1. The process from the notion of soul as a purely biological principle to that of soul as an ethical principle which is very similar to a process from biological to cognitive principle already noted in the *Phaedo*.

2. The series of senses of soul which emerges during the discussion. That the latter are hard to reconcile is evident from the equivocation in which Socrates is compelled to indulge to make sense of his definition of justice, and the measure of his failure to do this seems to be the measure of his more general failure to come to grips with the unresolved tensions inherent in the notion of soul itself.

Note. I cannot agree with Mr. R. W. Hall that "the phrase τὸ ἐπιμελεῖσθαι καὶ ἄρχειν καὶ βουλεύεσθαι though given earlier would tend to qualify and imbue it with the connotation of morality insofar as that concept entails the rule of reason and self-mastery. In other words the context of the passage allows a moral connotation to τὸ ζῆν."[5] The incontestable meaning of τὸ ζῆν is surely "animal life" (the principal meaning given by Liddell and Scott). For Mr. Hall, however, its "extended meaning" is "to be in full vigour, fresh, strong, efficient." (*Ibid.*) The last adjective here is somewhat unfortunate, since we know that ἀρετή tends to mean "efficiency" anyway,[6] and the use of the word "efficiency" would involve us in precisely the same difficulties as Plato faced by his introduction of the notion of ἀρετή. Nor does it follow that the words "care for," "plan," etc., will always and necessarily refer to the soul of *man*, and hence that "living" will refer to the same, and can be treated as possessing a "moral" sense for that reason. For in the *Timaeus* World Soul is credited with precisely these "personal" characteristics,[7] while in the *Phaedrus* "caring for" what is without soul seems to be a characteristic attributed to (rational) soul-as-such, without reference to any kind of (rational) soul in particular.[8]

In the *Phaedo*, too, Plato seems to make the same mistake as he does here, by attempting to combine arguments based upon two different views of soul: (a) Soul as life-principle (a notion clearly applicable to *all* types of

5 R. W. Hall 70 n1.

6 See Arist. *Ph.* 247A2.

7 See below, 69, 80.

8 *Phdr.* 246B6. See J. B. Skemp (1) 3 n1; A.-J. Festugière (5) 496–7; O. Regenbogen 198–219.

soul); (b) Soul as a principle of rational cognition (applicable to the human or super-human soul only).[9] Whatever can be posited of (a) can be posited of (b) but not – as the *Phaedo* seems to hold – *vice versa*.

In the same way in *Republic* I we seem to have: (a) Soul as life-principle (a notion clearly applicable to *all* souls, rational or otherwise) (353D9–10); (b) Soul as principle of cognition, care, and guidance (in the context almost certainly referring to human souls). (353D4–6) Again, all that can be posited of (a) can be posited of (b) – but not *vice versa*. It is my contention that Plato realised, at least unconsciously, the absurdity of doing the latter, and laid stress on the "moral" sense of "living" (in the ambiguous phrase τὸ εὖ ζῆν) to meet the situation.

II "PARTS" IN THE SOUL

One notable contribution of the *Republic* to the notion of soul is the well-known assertion that it is in some way tripartite. (435B9 ff.) The significance of this has long been the subject of controversy. Some have found its origin and inspiration in a doctrine of Three Lives,[1] which in turn is claimed to be of Pythagorean provenance.[2] Burnet[3] and Taylor[4] went on to make the further assertion that the theory is a piece of popular ethics which Plato never seriously holds as his own; for him soul is essentially a "source of movement." Others have held that the tripartite soul is a view sincerely held by Plato, whatever its source, and defend it as a meaningful piece of psychological analysis in its own right.[5] Others have felt that the doctrine is an uncomfortable one, for it seems to stem immediately from the tri-partition of the State in *Republic* IV; the "soldier-class" in a state may make sense, but the equivalent "spirited element" in a soul is seen as an oddity.[6] Apart from these broader divisions of opinion, further internal questions present themselves. Is there any evidence for the genesis and growth of a doctrine of tripartition in dialogues which precede the *Republic*? Is there any

9 *Phd.* 65B9 ff. The same view underlies the argument from Recollection and the discussion of philosophic virtue.
1 J. L. Stocks 209–10; A. E. Taylor (2) 281.
2 J. L. Stocks *ibid.*; J. Burnet (5) 177; A. E. Taylor (2) 120 n1.
3 J. Burnet (2) 296 and n2.
4 A. E. Taylor (3) 516.
5 J. L. Stocks 214–21; H. W. B. Joseph 67–80.
6 See below, 44–6.

evidence for its reassertion on later occasions? Can Plato's statements on the subject be said to be uniform on all occasions, or show development of thought, or manifest internal contradictions, or reveal the mind of a man more puzzled than dogmatic?

As far as the supposed "antecedents" are concerned, the evidence is very flimsy. At *Gorgias* 493A3–4 we read of "that part of the soul which houses the desires." But, as Dodds has pointed out, "no tripartition is involved here. All that need be assumed is the popular distinction between reason and impulse already present, e.g., at Theognis 631 or Aesch. *Pers.* 767, and is referred to by Aristotle, E.N. 1102ª 26, *de An.* 432ª 26."[7] Again, at *Phaedo* 68C2 we have a reference to the "lover of possessions" and the "lover of honour," and Burnet takes this as implying the tripartite division of soul, and refers to the "Pythagorean" doctrine of Three Lives.[8] While this may indeed be a reference to the problem of the different "types of life" and which of them has a claim to be called "best" – a problem which, no doubt, exercised the Academy as it did the minds of others[9] – it scarcely follows that three parts or types of soul are envisaged. The whole tenor of the *Phaedo* is to the contrary. If in the latter dialogue soul is anything at all it is a unity; any troubles it has to face are *ab extra*; no evidence for internal discord is offered, but all passions and desires other than the purely intellectual are firmly relegated to the body's domain.[10] Friction is between soul on the one hand and body and the bodily on the other; the soul is the self, and the self is an incarcerated intellect. All desires (apart from the specific desire for intelligence) are stated to stem from the body and its exigencies (66E2–3), and how this in particular can be reconciled with the notion of a desiderative element *within* the soul (*Republic* 435B) is hard to see. Again, at 83B we read how the true philosopher tries to free himself from "pleasures, desires, pains and fears" (if "fears" is a genuine part of the text: Burnet doubts it).[11] For Taylor this is once more a hint, like that of *Gorgias* 493A, that we are dealing with a tripartite soul, a doctrine which, he suggests, is "already familiar to educated circles ... [for] φόβος, like its opposite θάρρος, is specifically a state of θυμός."[12] But this view is open to the same objection as that outlined above for 68C2: it runs clean counter to the whole burden of the *Phaedo*

7 E. R. Dodds (3) n. *ad loc.*; cf. *Phdr.* 237D ff, and R. Hackforth (7) 42.
8 J. Burnet (2) 108, 109 n1, 319 n3.
9 E. Zeller 846 n1; A.-J. Festugière (4) 131 ff.; E. R. Dodds (2) 228 n30.
10 See especially 66BD.
11 *Platonis Opera*, ed. J. Burnet (Oxford 1900–7) *ad loc.*
12 A. E. Taylor (3) 497; cf. A. E. Taylor (2) 120 n1; J. Burnet (2) 296 n2.

itself. As for the long list of pains, pleasures, desires, etc., the careless way in which they are strung together suggests that at this stage Plato is little interested in docketing them into their correct logical pigeon-holes; for him the important thing is that they are all of *bodily* provenance. One might compare 65c6–9, where we read that the soul must be untroubled by "hearing" or "sight" or "pain" or "pleasure" of any kind, ignore the body, and become as far as possible independent. The important word is "body": by reference to *this* are words of such different logical status as "hearing" and "pain" seen to have something important in common.

At *Gorgias* 503E ff. Guthrie finds hints of "elements" of the soul, where "justice and temperance" are seen as the "order and regularity" of the soul in the way that the order and regularity of the body are called "health and strength."[13] That this is the embryonic stirring of the theory of "inner conflict" as a sort of disease in the soul, health being a balance or harmony (see *Sophist* 227D–228E), can hardly be doubted; on the same topic Dodds quotes *Gorgias* 482BC, 483A.[14] But again there is no need to assume that the soul's constituents are three; as at 493A1–5, the popular bipartition of soul into reason and impulse fits the case adequately.

The first clear and direct reference to tripartition is in the *Republic* itself, and it certainly seems to be a doctrine invented for a special occasion. For in the early books a *bi*partition of character into what is called the "gentle disposition" and the "great-spirited disposition" suits Plato's purpose (see 375C6–7), and, at 400C ff., when he is discussing Primary Education, the popular dualism of body and soul is taken for granted. The language is fluid and untechnical; the two dispositions are called "opposite natures" (375C7–8), and are later called "the philosophic element" and "the spirited element" respectively, the specific excellence of the former being called "temperance" and that of the latter "bravery." (411E6, 410E10–411A1) Hints of what is to come can perhaps be seen at 404DE, where temperance of the soul is seen as equivalent to health in the body (see *Gorgias* 503E ff.), and 410A–412B, where a sound education is seen to involve the "attunement" (ἡρμόσθαι) of the "philosophic" and "spirited" elements. But to the reader unaware of what is to come both passages make perfect sense when explained in terms of the popular bipartition. It is true that Plato has stressed an aspect of "impulse" which suits his purpose and baptized it as "the spirited element," but his acceptance of bipartition is still clear enough from an evaluative statement

13 W. K. C. Guthrie (1) 5; cf. *Grg.* 525A5.
14 E. R. Dodds (1) 228 n30.

like: "in a man's soul one element is better, one worse." (431A4–5) As has been pointed out, such language is somewhat unfortunate since, if it be allowed to stand, it is a little hard to reconcile with the developed psychology of *Republic* IX, where all three "parts" of soul are recognized to have a worthwhile status.[15] Be this as it may, what we see here is clearly *bi*partition, with not only an evaluative difference between the two parts but apparently even a difference in size. For at 431A7–B1 we read of a situation in which "the better part, which is the smaller, is dominated by the multitude of the worse," and the same idea is repeated on a number of occasions.[16] Such "physical" language is not exceptional. We saw it in the *Phaedo* and it will reappear in much greater detail in the *Timaeus*, where each part of the soul will be described as though it is situated in a particular region of the body.[17]

But if a bipartite psychology has served Plato so far, it is now radically revised. We are informed that, just as a state is called "just" when each of its parts "does its own work," the same will be true in the case of the soul. (435BC) This serves as a basis for subsequently analyzing the soul in terms of tripartition, and many have suspected that the case is prejudged.[18] For, as Cornford argued, the conclusions are "arrived at by the analysis merely of one complex state of mind, the conflict of motives, which is compared to the strife between two factions in a state."[19] In other words, the division of soul into ratiocinative, spirited, and desiderative elements is based upon one narrow aspect of psychic activity – and that the one most readily amenable to political analogy. That Plato himself was aware of the non-conclusive nature of his arguments seems clear enough from 443D3–7, where he talks of "three principles ... and all others there may be between them." And earlier on he had said: "And let me tell you, Glaucon, that in my opinion we shall never apprehend this matter accurately from such methods as we

15 N. R. Murphy 26, 28; *R.* 586E4–587A1.

16 For the references see J. Adam (2) n. *ad* 379C.

17 See *Ti.* 69D ff. and L. Robin (3) 284, who lays much stress on the fact that for Plato soul is a μέγεθος. His evidence for this is *Ti.* 34B, 36E (cf. 33B 1ff), Arist. *de An.* 1 3, 406B27 ff., 407A2 ff., and Speusippus' view of the soul as the ἰδέα τοῦ πάντῃ διαστάτου. For the view that soul is not a μέγεθος at all, and that Aristotle misunderstands the psychology of the *Ti.* when he takes soul's κινήσεις to be ἐν τόπῳ, see H. Cherniss (5) 395, 405, and J. B. Skemp (1) 86. A.-Ed. Chaignet 87 takes it that the so-called κινήσεις of soul in the *Ti.* are simply "thought" ("la pensée"). For another statement of the immaterial nature of soul see F. Solmsen (3) 458.

18 M. Pohlenz 229, 231 ff.; F. M. Cornford (3) 259 ff.; L. Robin (4) cxviii; E. Pfeiderer (1) 24; E. Pfeiderer (2) 233; E. Hoffmann (1) 165 f.; E. Topitsch (3) 125; F. A. Wilford 54; N. R. Murphy 29 f.; E. R. Dodds (3) n. *ad* 493A3–4.

19 F. M. Cornford (3) 262.

are now employing in discussion. For there is another longer and harder way that conducts to this." (435D1–3)

The phrase "this matter" here seems to refer grammatically to the question whether the soul has three parts or not, and Adam admits this.[20] However, at *Republic* 504B ff., where this passage is clearly referred to, the question is not raised at all. So Adam concludes that the phrase must really refer to "the ethical question to which the psychological enquiry is introductory." In this way he preserves the "artistic unity" of the dialogue. (*Ibid.*) If this is true, Plato can be said to preserve artistic unity only at the expense of grammatical coherence. One ought, perhaps, to take into consideration a passage in book ten, where the whole question of the soul's true nature is discussed. Here Plato seems to suggest that the soul in its true, purified state is in fact single rather than manifold (612A4), and (by implication) that the man who will see the truth of this is the man who has undergone the intellectual and moral disciplines outlined in books five to seven. So that, indirectly at any rate, the "longer and harder way" *has* led to certain conclusions about the soul's true nature. But since we are there left in some doubt about whether the soul can ever fully realize its true nature in this earthly life,[21] the problem of its simplicity or tripartition *hic et nunc* can hardly be said to have been solved.

Whatever reservations Plato may have about his new doctrine, elements of it are an undoubted advance on the psychology of the *Phaedo*. Conflict of motives – a conflict within the soul itself – is now fully recognized, and a psychology is outlined which to a large degree caters for it. No longer is the conflict between body and soul, as in the *Phaedo*;[22] the conflict lies rather within the soul itself, as in the *Gorgias*. (493A1–5) Even in the bipartite soul of the early *Republic* the conflict was seen to be internal; the two "natures" were "opposite," and needed to be "attuned." (375C7–8, 410E8) This is no less true when the "philosophic element" is seen to be really the "ratiocinative element," and when the "spirited element," far from being something desiderative, is seen to be quite distinct from what is genuinely desiderative.[23] Justice, in the individual as in the state, turns out to be the "doing of its work"

20 J. Adam (2) n. *ad loc.*
21 See below, 52–4.
22 See R. Hackforth (7) 12. For an antithetical point of view see J. Moreau (1) 249–57.
23 441E4, 439E6 ff., 440E3–4. The word "desiderative part" (ἐπιθυμητικόν 440E3–4) is a little confusing, since in book nine Plato is prepared to admit that all three parts of the soul possess their own proper "desires" (ἐπιθυμίαι), which serve a useful purpose when sensibly canalized.

by each of the constituent elements in either, and injustice the opposite. (443CE) In the same way, "sobriety" or "balance" is defined in terms closely fitting the analogy with a departmentalized city or state: a man is "sober" "by reason of the friendship and concord of these same parts, when, namely, the ruling principle and its two subjects are at one in the belief that the reason ought to rule, and do not raise faction against it." (442C11–D1)

True to the analogy, vice is seen as a state of civil conflict, and it is also called a lack of attunement, a state of ill-health or disease, and a state of ugliness.[24] These epithets tell us nothing that we do not already know from the *Gorgias*, and all of them, including that of civil strife, could equally well be applied to a soul of "two or more" parts; tripartition fits the picture, but could hardly be said to be a necessary constituent of it.

Even without reference to the political analogy the position of ratiocinative and desiderative elements would be understandable enough. It is a more technical expression of the popular distinction of reason and impulse, and the balanced man will be the one who sees to it that reason reigns supreme. The "spirited element" is more ambiguous, however. But for the political analogy, one's first reaction would be to place it among the "desires," or "crude impulses," which go to form the "desiderative" element. Plato, however, arguing from the conflict of motives, concludes to its intermediate position: its function in the soul is the analogue of that of soldiers in the state. (440D4–E5) But soldiers themselves are frequently torn by a conflict of motives; although their role is to defend law and order (i.e., effect the rules and regulations laid down by authority) they can and do on occasion unite with the ruled and mutiny. Is the same true of the "spirited element"? A passage at 440AB has suggested the contrary to some scholars, and taken by itself it would certainly give the impression that the "spirited element" is always on the side of reason.[25] At 441E6 it is called the "subject-ally" of reason, and at 441A2–3 its "natural ally." But at this stage the important proviso is inserted, "unless it be corrupted by evil nurture." (441A3) Such a proviso, taken in conjunction with evidence of the subversion of the "spirited element" in book eight,[26] implies that Plato did after all think of

---

24 442D1, 444B1, 440E5, 443D5, 443E2, 444D3–E3.

25 440A8–B8. See J. Adam (2) app. IV; F. M. Cornford (3) 263; E. Topitsch (3) 127.

26 553C ff. Of a number of passages 572A is important, showing as it does that the θυμοειδές is *impulsive* (εἰς ὀργάς A4), and needs *allaying* (πραΰνας A4) by the λογιστικόν. 586CD is valuable, too, since it shows in short compass the gamut of meanings which the term θυμοειδές enjoys. For E. *Supp.* 1102, where ψυχή is seen as the organ of courage and endurance, see T. W. Webster 150.

it as liable to mutiny against reason, and this is not surprising when one considers its political analogue. Adam, relying on the evidence of 440AB, is prepared to underplay conflicting evidence,[27] but this perhaps underestimates the force of that political analogy which seems to account for the birth of the notion of the "spirited element" anyway. Cornford, too, taking 440AB at its face value, finds Plato saying things which imply the opposite; like the passage (441C) in which the "spirited element" is described as "that which feels unreasoning anger."[28] On the face of it Plato stands open to the charge of a mild self-contradiction here, and one probably does him most justice by letting it stand as such. If, however, we are determined (like Adam) to reduce him to coherence, we should probably do better to accept the numerous indications that he *does* accept an occasional alliance between the "spirited" and "desiderative" elements rather than the single, isolated statement to the contrary. In this way the political analogy is also saved. But the ambiguous, amphibian status of the "spirited element" still remains obscure. Some have seen in it a profound piece of psychological analysis,[29] but Cornford is probably nearer the mark when he taxes Plato with failing "to distinguish mere anger from a quite different psychological factor, best described as a *sentiment* – the *sentiment* of honour, or of self-respect."[30] The word "spirited element" (θυμοειδές) certainly does cover a whole gamut of emotional states, from pure anger on the one hand to a feeling of noble courage, self-respect, and self-defence on the other.[31] It is Plato's exploitation of these different meanings which gives to his discussion of the term any plausibility that it has. In his account of Leontius, for example, it is "spirit" as equivalent to "anger" which is stressed (439E6 ff.), but in other cases "spirit" as legitimate self-assertion and self-defence is underlined, in keeping with the political analogy.[32] In this Plato is doing nothing new. I have argued that the proofs of immortality in the *Phaedo* fail to convince precisely because they stem from exploitation of ambiguities within the notion of soul itself; the same can be said for the ambiguities within the notions of "living"

27 J. Adam (2) app. IV 271. His case is bolstered by an implicit use of *Phdr.* 253D-256E. It is far from clear, however, that the supposed 'tripartite soul' of the *Phdr.* is precisely the same as the one outlined in *R.* IV. See below, 116ff.

28 F. M. Cornford (3) 264.

29 See above, 39n5.

30 F. M. Cornford (3) 264.

31 H. W. B. Joseph 65 ff., and F. M. Cornford (4) tr. *ad loc.*

32 For the view that θυμός has basically two senses, the one indistinguishable from ἐπιθυμητικόν, the other from λογιστικόν, see W. F. R. Hardie 141-3.

and "living well" in *Republic* I.[33] In the same way the ambiguous status of the "spirited element" allows it to be fitted with some show of plausibility into a scheme of tripartition invented as an imposing analogue to the tripartite state. It serves a purpose in a context, and should not be pressed. In the same context Plato outlines four "virtues" of soul and state (435B1 ff.), based upon the tripartition of both,[34] and then (445D1 ff.) five "types" of soul and state (later examined in detail in books eight to nine). One might reasonably ask whether he would have reached the same conclusions without the initial political analogue.

III SENSES OF SOUL

If we pass over a single reference to soul in its popular sense of "life" (590A2), a common meaning given to the word is that of the true or genuine self, as was the case in *Alcibiades* I (130A1 ff.) and the *Phaedo*. (115D8 ff.)[1] According to this view a man *is* his soul, with the body functioning merely as an instrument. The most striking example is at 469D6–9, where we read: "And is there not illiberality and avarice in robbing a corpse, and also a degree of meanness and womanishness in making an enemy of the dead body when the real enemy has flown away and left only his fighting gear behind him?"

This view seems to underlie passages like 526AB and 535BD, where Plato uses the plural noun "souls" in contexts where we should normally say "people" or "persons." It is an image closely bound up with another, again to be found in the *Phaedo*, of soul as a sort of inner person, a duplicate self with all the characteristics which we normally attribute to standard human beings. The most notable example of this is in a passage where Plato is discussing the relation between soul and sense-objects. The object of perception and the soul are brought into contact by the good offices of an intermediary "sensation" or "perception," and soul is seen as the recipient of the latter's pronouncements.[2] These can reduce it to a state of stress and be-

33 See above, 35–9.

34 This is not to suggest, of course, that the doctrine of four virtues is Plato's own invention. For its existence in earlier Greek thought see H. North 304–8. What is in doubt is whether Plato would have explained the nature and operation of the four virtues in man (and the relation of each of them to the other three) in quite the way he does had he not been influenced by the doctrine of tripartition in the human soul and, *a fortiori*, by the doctrine of the tripartition of the state which is the latter's analogue.

1 For a similar idea see Bhagavad Gita II 19, where it is said that a soul can neither slay nor be slain. The parallelism with Socrates' comment at *R.* 469D6–9 is striking.

2 524A1 ff. For a similar view see *Tht.* 184–6.

wilderment, which it resolves by supplicating the aid of mind and intelligence. (λογισμός τε καὶ νόησις 524B4–5) No doubt verbs like "to be at a loss" (ἀπορεῖν), "to supplicate the aid of" (παρακαλεῖν) and "to hand down word" (παραγγέλλειν) are to be taken metaphorically, as in parallel passages of the *Phaedo*, but it is noticeable how they all tend to be of a particular pattern, stemming from a notion of soul as an inner person, or, to use a now famous phrase, "ghost in a machine."[3]

An apparent contradiction of this view is to be found at 462CD, where the self or person seems to be the compound of soul and body, not simply soul by itself. In an important note *ad loc.* Adam agrees that the passage means that the "whole man" is to be seen as a composite, but goes on to say that in this partnership "it is ὁ ἄνθρωπος who rules ... although he is himself a partner only in the sense in which the whole is partner with its parts." The passage is an obscure one, and his guess may be correct. Certainly from the evidence of the *Charmides* it seems clear that Plato at least *knew* of the notion of a "biological part," for there the self is the biological, rather than the arithmetical combination of soul and body.[4] If the present passage is to be taken as saying something similar it will be the most philosophically sophisticated statement about soul in the dialogue. For now the body, far from being merely an instrument or tool, will have a vital part to play in the concept of a person, being as necessary to it as a biological part to its whole.

This view of soul has something in common with one at 572A, where the self or person seems to be seen as a super-Ego transcending the body-soul complex. The operative phrase is found at 572A5–6: "But if he has thus quieted the two elements in his soul and quickened the third, in which reason resides, and so goes to his rest, you are aware that in such case he is most likely to apprehend truth, and the visions of his dreams are least likely to be lawless."

The question is, *what* pacifies and moves the three parts of the soul? Hardly the body. Perhaps the whole soul, in the sense seen above, where a whole might be partner with its parts. If this is true, the doctrine will now be somewhat different, for there the "whole" was the entire man, body and soul combined, whereas here the "whole" will be soul taken by itself. However, even in this dialogue we have seen evidence for believing that Plato sometimes treats soul as exhausting the totality of self,[5] and if he means soul

3 G. Ryle chap. 1 *passim*.
4 See above, 5–8.
5 See above, 46.

to be taken in the same sense here the two passages under discussion may have more in common than at first sight appeared. But even if this is the case, the former passage apparently finds a meaningful place for the *body* in the concept of a person while the latter does nothing of the sort, and this alone would serve to distinguish the two theories as different in kind.

A third view of the passage is to see it as evidence for a fourth "part" of soul, which has powers to arouse or calm the others.[6] In view of Plato's evident hesitation about the tripartition of soul this cannot be ruled out a priori, but it seems odd that so interesting a thing as a fourth part of soul should be introduced in so abrupt a manner, without explanation, and then never be mentioned again.

A fourth view sees the passage as implicitly admitting the self as a separate entity, over and above and distinct from the body-soul complex.[7] And it could be argued that such a notion would not be new. In the *Phaedo*, as we saw, the philosopher is described as "[freeing] his soul from association with the body, so far as possible, to a greater extent than other men." (64E8–65A2) To the outsider this looks very like a distinction of three substances: body, soul, and the philosopher who possesses and uses them. If this interpretation is correct, Plato is saying that *neither* body *nor* soul has anything to do with the genuine self! No doubt, if pressed, he would have argued that self and soul are really one, so that any talk about the control of one's soul is to be interpreted as *self*-control. But such interpretation is surely necessary.

Another view of soul, similar to one outlined in the *Phaedo*, is that of a substance in some way "akin" to the Ideas. In the *Phaedo* (70A) Cebes expresses the fear that the soul may leave the body at death and be dispersed – and so be eternally destroyed – particularly if one is unlucky enough to die in a gale. Socrates replies that only what is composite can decompose; hence the body's decomposition. But what is constant and invariable is likely to be incomposite; it is things subject to *change* which tend to be composite. He then goes on to suggest in what ways the soul is more akin to the (incomposite and unchanging) Ideas. (80B ff.) This is really a suasion, rather than an argument, and leaves us with no clear idea about the status of soul. It cannot be set among the objects of the world of motion, for it is precisely these which, like body, are subject to change and decomposition. Yet it is apparently not an Idea; it is only "very like" the Ideas. But if the argument is to succeed it must *be* an Idea. For only the reality of Ideas is absolute, and any

6 J. Adam (2) *ad loc.*, quoting Schleiermacher.
7 *Ibid.*, quoting Krohn.

declination from this will involve a proportionate lessening in force of all the other epithets attributed to it. Any being other than pure reality will have or be to some degree non-reality, and any being other than the totally incomposite will proportionately risk being decomposed.[8] To *associate* soul and the Idea of Life, as happens in the final argument of the *Phaedo* (105C9 ff.), does little to resolve the difficulty; to *be* the Idea of Life, not simply to be associated with it, is essential if the soul is to be demonstrated to be immortal.[9]

Plato himself seems to have realized the weakness of the argument. At 79D9–80C1 he concludes:

> Very well, then, in the light of all that we have said, both now and before, to which class do you think that the soul bears the closer resemblance and relation?
>
> I think, Socrates, said Cebes, that even the dullest person would agree, from this line of reasoning, that the soul is in every possible way more like the invariable than the variable.
>
> And the body?
>
> To the other.
>
> Look at it in this way too. When soul and body are both in the same place, nature teaches the one to serve and be subject, the other to rule and govern. In this relation which do you think resembles the divine and which the mortal part? Don't you think that it is the nature of the divine to rule and direct, and that of the mortal to be subject and serve?
>
> I do.
>
> Then which does the soul resemble?
>
> Obviously, Socrates, soul resembles the divine, and body the mortal.
>
> Now, Cebes, he said, see whether this is our conclusion from all that we have said. The soul is most like that which is divine, immortal, intelligible, uniform, indissoluble, and ever self-consistent and invariable, whereas body is most like that which is human, mortal, multiform, unintelligible, dissoluble, and never self-consistent. Can we adduce any conflicting argument, my dear Cebes, to show that this is not so?
>
> No, we cannot.

8 See J. B. Skemp (1) 9; A.-J. Festugière (3) 111–12.

9 A.-J. Festugière and others go the whole way and conclude that soul *is* an Idea (see above, 30n19). At *Lg.* 959B3 the ὄντως ὄντα ἕκαστον is called the ἀθάνατον ψυχήν, and the apparently technical language leads Müller to criticize the description, no doubt on the grounds that soul is nowhere else described as an Idea (G. Müller 106). But the fluidity of Plato's supposedly "technical" terms is notorious, and in the context he seems to be stressing the "genuine" (ὄντως ὄν) self – i.e., the soul – as distinct from the apparent self (i.e., the body).

Very well, then, in that case is it not natural for body to disintegrate rapidly, but for soul to be quite *or very nearly* [ἐγγύς τι] indissoluble?

Certainly.

The italicized phrase is the clearest of admissions that we have been dealing with a suasion, rather than a demonstration. But it is a suasion which dies hard, and we have many reminders of it in the *Republic*. The most striking passage is at 490AB:

> Will it not be a fair plea in his defense to say that it was the nature of the real lover of knowledge to strive emulously for true being and that he would not linger over the many particulars that are opined to be real, but would hold on his way, and the edge of his passion would not be blunted nor would his desire fail till he came into touch with the nature of each thing in itself by that part of his soul to which it belongs to lay hold on that kind of reality – the part akin to it, namely – and through that approaching it, and consorting with reality really, he would beget intelligence and truth, attain to knowledge, and truly live and grow, and so find surcease from his travail of soul, but not before?
>
> No plea could be fairer.

In the *Phaedo* the entire soul was seen as noetic; here only a part or aspect of it. But the argument is similar. The soul is akin to the Ideas, and cannot rest till it contacts them. The relationship between soul and the Ideas is one of love (490B2), and the powerful sexual imagery describing it can be paralleled in a number of mystical writers.[10] Mental contact is not enough; the sensation of *presence*, of total union with the beloved, is an integral part of the experience.[11]

IV IMMORTALITY

A notable proof of immortality in book ten touches on important points about the nature of soul, and must be discussed at some length. Plato begins

---

10 In the writings of John of the Cross and Teresa of Avila the soul or self is invariably seen as the female element in the mystical union with God, and much of the language they use, drawing its inspiration from the Song of Songs, is frankly sexual. Among many examples one might instance the well-known poem of John of the Cross beginning "Oh llama de amor viva" and the comments of Teresa of Avila on the Kiss of God (*Interior Castle* VII 5).

11 Cf. *Phd.* 65B9, 66A6.

by positing the usual neat dualism of soul and body (609C5–D4), and then, on the grounds that "practically everything has its own congenital evil and disease," asserts that the soul itself is subject to the same law.[1] But there is a difference. The "congenital evil" of anything other than soul is said to kill and destroy that thing; the "congenital evil" of soul, summed up as "injustice, licentiousness, cowardice, and ignorance," is affirmed to do nothing of the sort.[2] The "soul" in question seems to be the tripartite one of *Republic* 435A ff., since the vices here adduced are the exact counterparts of the four cardinal virtues "justice," "restraint," "bravery," and "intelligence" which are there explained in terms of the tripartite psychology. However, this has not stopped a number of scholars from maintaining that only a part of soul is being shown to be immortal, and that the ratiocinative part.[3] But is this the case? If one resists the temptation to import doctrine from the *Phaedrus* (246A ff.) and *Timaeus* (41CD), the important passage 611B–612A, taken by itself, can be understood far more plausibly as affirming the immortality of the entire soul, three parts and all. What Plato wants to say, if I am right in my interpretation, is that one cannot judge the true nature of the soul if one merely looks at that degraded state which it endures *ici bas*; what one must contemplate is the "soul when it is purified" as distinct from the "soul when it is marred by communion with the body and other nuisances."[4] This distinction is clearly brought out by the comparison of the soul we know to the sea-god Glaucus encrusted with barnacles and bits of stone. (611C7–D7) To call these unwelcome accretions the two "lower" parts of soul is less plausible than to see them as the blemishes necessarily resulting from any

1 609A3–4, 609B9–10.

2 609A8–B1, 609B11–C1, 609D4 ff. It should be noted that Plato is saying here that "injustice" (ἀδικία) and the rest do not *destroy* (i.e. *kill*) the soul, as the words εἰς θάνατον (609D6) make clear. This should be carefully distinguished from an earlier assertion at 445AB, where it is urged that ἀδικία and κακία do involve the "disruption" or "corruption" (διαφθειρομένης 445B1) of the soul. To translate διαφθειρομένης in this latter passage as "destruction" would certainly make it look as though Plato is contradicting himself flatly; ἀδικία either does or does not kill the soul, but hardly both. However, such a translation can be shown to be incorrect by reference to the context, where the *body's* constitution is clearly thought, not to be actually destroyed, but simply to have "gone to wrack and ruin" (διαφθειρομένης 445A7). Since the constitution of soul (ἡ τούτου ᾧ ζῶμεν φύσις) is here drawn as a very precise parallel (μὲν/δὲ) to that of body, one can safely take it that the phrase ταραττομένης καὶ διαφθειρομένης (445A9–B1) used to describe it will mean something like "is disordered and corrupted" (Shorey) or "is deranged and corrupted" (Cornford).

3 E.g., J. Adam (2) *ad loc.*; A. E. Taylor (3) 496; W. K. C. Guthrie (1) 6–7.

4 611B10–C2; 611C3. (See P. Frutiger 92)

association with the body and the bodily.[5] Among such blemishes will be the four vices outlined at 609B11–C1. In the *Gorgias* the evildoer is seen after death as marred, defiled, and scarred by his vices in a former life. (524D ff.) Here, too, Plato seems to mean that blemishes and vices, brought on no doubt by a preoccupation with the bodily and its needs, distort and mar the soul or person; he is not living at that level of pure intellection and moral perfection of which he would have been theoretically capable had he not been joined to a body. The vicious soul is the soul at its most tainted and un-recognizable; but *any* soul still attached to a body – including that of the true philosopher – is to that degree "tainted," in at least the minimal sense that the cares and distractions of the bodily generally divert its attention to some degree from those activities which are claimed to be the natural ones of soul in its pure state. In book five a distinction is drawn between pure being, absolute non-being, and an intermediate state, the objects of "know-ledge," "ignorance," and "opinion" respectively. (477A ff.) The object of "opinion" is stated to be the world known to us by sense perception; it is a world of fluid and shifting existence, with only a fleeting hold on reality, a world opined rather than known. (478A8 ff.) This seems applicable here. The soul on earth is to a greater or lesser degree involved in the cares, worries, frustrations, irritations, etc., caused by body and the bodily, and the point seems to be that, to the extent to which it is itself *involved* with realities whose status is somewhat unreal, its own attitude to and appreciation of them is unreal; the genuine cognition of the soul in its pure state is "knowledge" (of the Ideas), and the "opinion" which is the most it can achieve concerning realities other than the Ideas has the same dubious status in the world of cognition as material objects have in the world of ontological existence. The same might be said of the soul's desires; the genuine desire of the pure soul is for intelligence (*Phd.* 66E3), but the presence of the body tends to divert its attention to desires of a less elevated nature, and in the same way as before such desires are somewhat unreal so far as the soul's true nature is concerned, dealing as they do with objects in a world of sense perception which is itself somewhat unreal. In other words the soul, however good, which we see on earth is never its fully real or genuine self; perhaps one should say that it never fully *realizes itself*, and indeed cannot, till it is separated from the body. The genuine state of soul is "what it is in reality," "what it is in its purified state." (611B10–C3) The soul bound in a body is by that very fact "untrue"

5 P. Frutiger, *ibid.* In defending this point of view he follows Blass, Raeder, Von Arnim, and Robin. For the references see 92 n1.

(cf. τῇ ἀληθείᾳ 611B) to its own genuine nature; and the deeper it involves itself in the body and the material the more it defiles itself and distorts its own true nature out of all recognition, just as Glaucus becomes covered with barnacles. To this degree we are back to the position of the *Phaedo*, where the body is definitely an "evil." (66B6) But the differences are much greater. In the *Phaedo* the soul which was bound to the "evil" which was the body was (in that particular context, at any rate) very much an intellectual principle, and hardly to be distinguished from what comes to be called the "rational principle" (λογιστικόν) in the *Republic*. (435E ff.) This soul was seen as exhausting the plenitude of psychic activity in pursuing and loving intelligence: passions and emotions were confined to the body, and moral conflict was considered to be a dispute between soul and body. In the *Republic* (435E ff.) conflict within the soul itself is admitted, and passions and emotions are promoted to the status of psychic activities. It is *this* (tripartite and more than simply intellectual) soul which is said to be "in a mutilated state" here below. That it *is* the tripartite soul which Plato has in mind is hinted at by a phrase like "dissolve and destroy" (609C2) and by the important sentence: "It is not easy, said I, for a thing to be immortal that is composed of many elements not put together in the best way, as now appears to us to be the case with the soul." (611B5–7)

If the central phrase "not put together in the best way" be omitted, this is simply a restatement of the *Phaedo* position, where it is argued that the soul's indivisibility is a suasion of its likelihood to be different in kind from divisible (and hence destructible) physical objects.[6] But if one accepts the central proviso it becomes clear that Plato, having reconsidered the problem, has concluded (if only by implication) that a composite *can* very well be immortal, provided that its composition be of the "best" sort. If this is so, the short proviso seems to represent an important change of view. It is not *easy* for the composite to be immortal, but it is not claimed that it is impossible. The composition of the soul's constituent elements in this life can never hope to be perfect; the best approximation will presumably be found in the soul of the philosopher, who canalizes his energies into the pursuit of intelligence, thereby lessening the cravings of the "spirited" and "desiderative" elements. (586D4–587A2) A process of purification in this life will bring about the nearest thing to a perfect synthesis achievable here and now, but the clear conclusion, as in the *Phaedo* (66E–67B), is that only death itself will

6 78C1 ff., especially προσήκει (c2, c3) and εἰκός (c7). W. K. C. Guthrie (1) 7 feel that even here Plato is "attributing probable, not certain mortality to the composite."

provide the indispensable element which makes it *truly* the "best" synthesis and so indestructible.

Not that Plato is particularly concerned to affirm as a dogma that soul is tripartite, here or in any other world. We have already seen his uncertainty in book four, and the same indecision seems to reappear here in the phrase: "And then one might see whether in its real nature it is manifold or single in its simplicity, or what is the truth about it and how."[7]

Adam may be right in claiming for this quotation that "Plato seems clearly to imply that soul in its true nature is μονοειδής,"[8] but this is not to say that such a soul is simply a ratiocinative principle. What Plato seems to be doubting is his own artificial tripartition of soul; while serving a practical purpose when we talk of the soul here and now, it may turn out to be useless when applied to the soul "as such," that is, soul in its discarnate state. True soul may be an undifferentiated unity, and its apparent fragmentation into parts just the result of association with the bodily. Be this as it may, the "soul in its purified state" is the *same soul* as the "marred" soul: it has the same gamut or extension. Whether it be simple or manifold it is recognizably a purified version of that entire substance summed up as a combination of ratiocinative, spirited, and desiderative elements.

If this analysis is correct, the view of soul in *Republic* x is in a very vital respect different from that expressed in the *Phaedo*. At the same time it is not a revision of the psychology of *Republic* iv, but simply a more candid expression of doubts which at that stage were hinted at rather than stated. (See 443D3–7, 435D1–3.)

---

7 612A3–4. Cf. 443D3–7 and 435D1–3.

8 J. Adam (2) n. *ad* 612A3. *Phdr.* 271A5 ff. may possibly refer to this same problem, but Hackforth (7) 147 n1 is probably right in referring it to "types" or "characters" generally. One should compare *Epin.* 992B2–7, where a man's unity, rather than multiplicity, after death is asserted. If I have interpreted the passage about Glaucus the sea-god correctly, Plato (or some Platonist) is here repeating with conviction an opinion voiced a little less trenchantly at R. 611B–612A. W. Theiler (3) 353, not accepting this view, takes it that any "unity" is that which is achieved in philosophic contemplation now, and as *totus ratio* hereafter; that is, to say that soul is a unity is to say it is purely λογιστικόν. For a similar view see A.-J. Festugière (1) 214. He, however, apparently sees no contradiction between this and Plato's views on contemplation expressed elsewhere, whereas Theiler feels that in such a view of man after death we are wandering "unendlich weit von Plato weg." (*Ibid.*) J. B. Skemp (3) 38 takes R. 612A2–6 as "an almost explicit denial of tripartition in the ψυχή." He continues, "This whole passage exhibits most clearly the tensions which the *Republic* has in its making – man in himself and man in society; man in this life and man *sub specie aeternitatis*." (*Ibid.*)

V SOUL, DESIRE, AND PLEASURE

We have seen that two of the most signal features of Plato's psychology in the *Republic* are the tripartition of soul and the recognition of conflict within the soul, rather than between soul and body. Important by-products of this reassessment are much more sophisticated views about the notions of desire and pleasure. In the more rarefied atmosphere of the *Phaedo* pleasure, like the body itself, is looked upon with suspicion and distaste. In the context this is understandable enough; the body and its desires are seen as a hindrance and a nuisance, if not a downright evil (66B6), and when pleasure in general or particular pleasures are mentioned they too, being considered to be of bodily provenance, incur the same suspicion. (65C5–8) But even in the *Phaedo* hints appear which suggest that the problem is being over-simplified. At 64D3–4 the bodily pleasures of food and drink are dismissed as only "so-called" pleasures, and we are left to infer that there are pleasures which more fully deserve the name. At 65A7 we read of "the pleasures that come by way of the body," and again we can infer that there are others which do nothing of the sort. As for the soul, this has definite pleasures of its own, if all the talk about the yearning for the vision of, and contact with, the Ideas is to have any meaning at all.[1]

At first sight, much of the *Republic* suggests that the extreme dualism of the *Phaedo* is not yet out of Plato's system. Even though the "bodily" desires of the *Phaedo* are now more rightly seen as belonging to the soul, albeit its least respectable part (439C ff.), on a number of occasions Plato talks as though this has hardly improved their status in his eyes. One might instance the constant use of evaluative language, like that of 431A4–5, in which he claims that "in a man's soul, one element is better, one worse." Or the unfortunate term "desiderative element" (ἐπιθυμητικόν 439E5, and *passim*), suggesting as it does the bodily and suspect desires of the *Phaedo*. This suspicion is corroborated at 588C6–10, where the ἐπιθυμητικόν is compared to a multi-coloured, multi-headed beast, while throughout book eight it shows its constant nuisance-value as a wrecker of the equilibrium of the soul.[2]

But important changes are in the air. As early on as 328D2–4 a distinction is drawn between "the pleasures of the body" and "the pleasures of good talk," and later on the "parts" of soul, bipartite or tripartite, are expressed

1 *Phd.* 65C9, ὀρέγηται τοῦ ὄντος; 65B9, 66A6.
2 See especially the accounts of the oligarchic, democratic, and tyrannical man.

as φιλο-compounds, and in their new guise of "wisdom-loving" part (φιλόσοφον 581B9), "victory-loving" part (φιλόνικον 581B2), and "money-loving" part (φιλοχρήματον 581A6) are probably better described as "drives" of the soul, rather than parts.[3] Again, the mystical passage at 490B1 ff. can only be explained as the satisfaction of an immense longing in the soul of the contemplative; his yearning, we must presume, is different in kind from the cruder yearnings of the non-philosopher. As for the account of the decline of the soul in books eight and nine, this only makes sense if we accept the notion of disruptive tendencies in both "spirited" part and "desiderative" part; in the timocratic man in particular that aspect of the "spirited" part which is characterized as "victory-loving" and "honour-loving" has full scope to indulge its desires, while in the oligarchic, democratic, and tyrannical man some or all aspects of the "desiderative" part are given free rein.[4] But perhaps the most clear indication of a change of view is to be found at 485D1–2, where a distinction is drawn between pleasures enjoyed by the soul independently (i.e., pleasures of knowledge) and those pleasures "of which the body is the instrument."[5] The latter point is important because it combines elements drawn from both *Phaedo* and *Republic* and reconciles them; the pleasures dismissed as "bodily" in the *Phaedo* are now seen to have an important function in the soul, though their *instrument* is still considered to be the body. In Cornford's words, the whole passage suggests "that desire is a single fund of energy which can be turned from one object to another 'like a stream diverted into another bed,' "[6] and the same view seems to lie behind passages at 580D and 581C, where for the first time we are explicitly told that each "part" of soul has its own specific pleasures, desires, and principles. It is worth noticing that it is at this point in the dialogue that the soul's tripartition in terms of "drives" is introduced (580E ff.), in keeping with the assertion that each part of soul has its own form of desire.[7] Most important is the substitution of the terms "money-loving" part and "gain-

---

3 See F. M. Cornford (2) 219. Here, without offering a defence of tripartition as such, he mentions how different elements of Plato's tripartite psychology have been stressed by twentieth-century psychologists. Freud's interests lie in τὸ ἐπιθυμητικόν (the libido), Adler's in τὸ θυμοειδές (the *Wille zur Macht*), while Jung, thinks Cornford, is "admitting something in our nature answering to the true self, or divine Spirit." (*Ibid.*) For a comparison between Plato's views on tripartition and Hindu beliefs see J. Ferguson ad 595A7.
4 550B5–7, 553B7 ff., 560B7 ff., 573A ff.
5 Cf. *Phd.* 65A7.
6 F. M. Cornford (4) 295; R. 485D7–8.
7 However, the dangers underlying the colourful social and political metaphors applied to the three parts of soul in R. VIII–IX, where each part is in fact personified, have been seen by W. F. R. Hardie 140, who writes, "the yielding by the self to its own desire will be

loving" part for "desiderative" part, to clear any remaining doubts. (581A6) As for the desires of this lowest part of soul, they are examined in much greater and more painstaking detail than before, being finally distinguished into necessary desires, unnecessary desires, and those which are unnecessary and illicit. The oligarch gives rein to the first group, the democrat to the first and second indiscriminately, and the tyrannical man to the third. (558D–571B) This distinction alone is considerable progress over the global condemnation found in the *Phaedo*. But now we are told that when the entire soul is just and in harmony, with the two lower parts submitting themselves to reason, all three parts achieve the best and truest pleasures of which they are capable, and in thus contributing to making the soul just are themselves acting justly. (586E4–587A1) The contrast with the *Phaedo* could hardly be more complete, and, like the new psychology itself, can only come from a more sober appraisal of the facts of moral experience.[8]

The treatment of pleasure runs parallel to the treatment of desire. Here, too, the extreme dualism of the *Phaedo* is never far from the surface. At 442A8 we read of the "so-called" pleasures associated with the body, a comment already noted at *Phaedo* 64D. "Bodily" pleasures are scarcely candidates for the title of "pleasures" at all, and the pleasures of all men other than the truly intelligent man are dismissed as "phantoms" (586B8) and "shadow-sketches" (586B8; cf. *Phaedo* 69B), depending as they do on their balancing with some antecedent pain. But, as in the case of the *Phaedo*, to call "bodily" pleasures "so-called" pleasures is to suggest that there are pleasures other than bodily. At 584C4–5, for example, the "so-called" pleasures are now no longer dubbed simply as bodily, but are called "the pleasures that find their way through the body to the soul," and this is already a move in the direction of the notion of purely intellectual or spiritual pleasure. However, in the final analysis even these psychosomatic pleasures still seem beneath his consideration, and all are (with the exception of pleasures of smell, 584B) written off as merely "in some sort releases from pain." Pleasure in the truest and fullest sense of the word, it transpires, can only be that of the philosopher when he enjoys the vision of true Being. (581D10 ff.)

---

represented as the victory of a foreign foe. The bad will is not my will." A good example of such an interpretation can be found in Th.-H. Martin (II 299–301), who is so impressed by Plato's language that he thinks he believed in three souls, and it comes as no surprise to find him arguing that Plato was from start to finish a fatalist and determinist. (II 365 ff.) For a modern believer in the "three souls" theory see V. Martin 126.

8 On the whole question of a development in psychology between *Phd.* and *R.* see M. Pohlenz 232–4; H. Raeder 214–16; R. Hackforth (6) 49. For a notable disagreement see J. Moreau (1).

This rather alarming language stems from a long analysis of the notion of pleasure in book nine, in which pleasure and pain are seen as states of completion and emptiness, opposite poles from an intermediate state called "satisfaction." (585A ff.) A further set of distinctions classes them as true and false, pure and impure, and a mixture of both. (583B ff.) All this is a study in itself, but for the moment the important thing to notice is that *all* pleasures, however mean or exalted their status, are now seen to be psychic, or at any rate psychosomatic, rather than simply bodily. This in itself, like his fresh view of desire, is a notable advance on the position adopted in the *Phaedo*.

The further distinction of pleasures into those which are more truly and genuinely such and those less so, with the assertion that some pleasures are in fact more pleasurable than others, leads to the conclusion that the different sorts of pleasure are different because of their different relationship to reality and truth. (585B ff.) The old distinction between the world of true Being and the world of Becoming lies at the heart of the argument, and a powerful image shows the depth of Plato's commitment to it. Men without intelligence and virtue, he says, are like cattle, their eyes always on the ground and never looking up to see: "Bent over their tables, they feed like cattle with stooping heads and eyes fixed upon the ground; so they grow fat and breed, and in their greedy struggle kick and butt one another to death with horns and hoofs of steel ..." (586A7–B2)

The pleasure of the soul which is involved in contemplating the Ideas is stable and pure because they, too, are stable and pure. As for men without intelligence and virtue, they kick and butt one another to death, since "they can never satisfy with unreal nourishment that part of themselves which is itself unreal and incapable of lasting satisfaction." (586B2–4) This reads very like the Myth of the Watercarriers in the *Gorgias*, where the desiderative element in the soul is likened to a "pierced vessel." (493A7) The lower part of the soul is in either case seen as bottomless and insatiable, although, as we saw, in the *Gorgias* tripartition is probably not involved.

At this stage one would have liked some further analysis of the pleasures of the lowest part of soul, similar to the division of desires into necessary, unnecessary, and illicit. As it is, we are left with two apparently opposing viewpoints: that the "money-loving" part is an "insatiable vessel" and obviously to be looked upon with distrust; and that the "money-loving" part in the balanced soul has a necessary and valuable part to play, and in the process enjoys a pleasure and satisfaction of its own. The dilemma is thoroughly Platonic.

4

The Timaeus
27A – 47E

The *Timaeus,* one of the two or three most influential of Plato's dialogues, is also the one which has lent itself to the most contradictory interpretations. Many of the problems which it raises are only peripheral to our present purposes, but since they all have some influence or other on one's final interpretation of soul in the dialogue, one must indicate a number of *partis pris* at the outset. These will necessarily be somewhat dogmatic; discussion of them will be confined to footnotes, to avoid extending the text of the chapter to unmanageable proportions.

As far as dating is concerned, I shall argue that it makes slightly more sense of the development of the notion of soul in Plato's writings if we take the dialogue as following closely upon the *Republic*.[1] I accept that the work is couched in mythological terms, but feel that *any* analysis of its contents, be it literal or interpretative, compels us to conclude that Plato felt that he was saying something of prime importance.[2] The "literalist" analysis of, say, Plutarch,[3] and the "interpretative" analysis of, say, Proclus,[4] both seem to me to be extremes, and any chance of understanding Plato's meaning will lie in a close attention to the Greek text, and a willingness to accept whatever

1 See G. E. L. Owen (1) 79–95. For extended criticisms of this view see H. Cherniss (6) 225–66, and J. M. Rist (2) 207–21. See also the postscript in J. B. Skemp's translation of the *Politicus*. For a startling piece of statistical evidence in favour of Owen's thesis see D. R. Cox and L. Brandwood, "On a discriminatory problem connected with the works of Plato," *Journal of the Royal Statistical Society*, series B, XXI 1 (1959) 195–200.

2 In this I disagree with the burden of A. E. Taylor's edition of the *Timaeus*. I cannot believe that the views expressed in the dialogue are simply those of a fifth-century Pythagorean more than a little interested in Empedoclean biology.

3 In his essay, *De animae procreatione in Timaeo*. For a translation and useful analysis see M. Thévenaz.

4 In his (unfinished) commentary on the *Timaeus*. The most recent edition, in the Teubner series, is by E. Diehl (Leipzig 1903–6, 3 vols.).

interpretation seems most plausible in any particular context. Finally, I want
to maintain that the views expressed in the dialogue are Plato's own views,
and that they are meant to be his considered opinions on cosmology at a
particular time in his life.[5]

Of the many important cosmological and psychological questions
raised in the *Timaeus* one of the most absorbing is that of World Soul, first
hinted at in the *Republic*.[6] But prominence has little to do with clarity of
meaning, and the problem of World Soul, good or evil, rational or irrational,
pre-cosmic or cosmic only, has been a topic to divide students of Platonism
from the beginning.[7] This is hardly to be wondered at. Knowing, as we do,
Plato's views on the degree of reality enjoyed by this world and the world
of Ideas respectively,[8] it is no surprise to be told at the outset that any account
of the sensible cosmos will be at best a "likely story" (29D2), not a scientific
analysis beyond dispute. In either case the problem of communication
presents itself most forcibly. In talking of the world of Ideas, seat of authentic
existence, he had been compelled to use the language of mysticism;[9] similarly,
when discussing the world known to us by sense perception, a twilight
domain of semi-existence with only a fleeting and shifting hold on reality,
he is aware that the medium of scientific language can only carry him so far.
So he employs the language of myth. This is only a *pis aller*, no doubt, but
it has at least two advantages. It compels the reader himself to play an
important part in the act of communication; he is flattered and stimulated to
find himself both contributor and beneficiary at the same time. It also gives a
fair indication that the matter under discussion is seen as vitally important to
Plato himself. For the myths tend to be about man and the divine, conduct
in this world and bliss or punishment in another, free will and destiny, birth
and death: ideas, in a word, which *engage* a man, and form the wellsprings
of action, for better or for worse.[10]

Warned thus, at the outset, by Plato himself of the non-dogmatic

---

5 See above, 59n2. I stress the phrase "at a particular time in his life" because I should like to
argue that the cosmologies of the *Timaeus*, *Politicus*, and *Laws* are distinct from one another,
and reflect a definite development in Plato's thought.

6 R. 546B3, where the world is a θεῖον γεννητόν.

7 The two "camps," roughly speaking, were those of Aristotle, Plutarch, and Atticus on
the one side, and the neo-Platonists, particularly Proclus, on the other. Details of the
controversy will emerge as the chapter progresses. A complete list of references to all
notable parties in the debate can be found in P. Frutiger 200 nn. 1 and 2.

8 See *Phd.* 78B–80C, R. 490B5–7, 540A7–9.

9 R. 490AB, *Phd.* 78B–80C.

10 See J. A. Stewart 98 ff.

nature of his account, we might now turn to the text. What we see is what purports to be an account of the formation of the universe by a divine Craftsman or Mason,[11] using as his model a conglomerate Idea (30CD), described as the perfect and eternal Living Creature. (30D2, 37D1) For the sensible world is seen as a living creature (30D3), and *a fortiori* the eternal model of such a world will have the same characteristics, though in a more perfect form. This world is said to receive a soul from the Craftsman or Demiurge (δημιουργός), and we are given an account of its composition from what purport to be the contents of a celestial mixing-bowl. (34B3 ff.) The Demiurge also forms the divine element in human souls, using a recipe similar to that used in the fabrication of World Soul, though this time it seems to be of a rather inferior nature, like the lees of wine at the bottom of the jar. (41D4–7) The Demiurge is also, it seems, the author of the existence of the celestial gods, and to these he delegates the formation of non-human souls, and the non-divine elements of human souls. (41A3 ff.) In other words, their task is to complete the work of making the world, *qua* living creature, as perfect an imitation of the archetypal Living Creature as possible. (41B7–C2)

So far, with one notable exception – the account of World Soul – the whole story has been couched in terms of temporal succession. But this may eventually turn out to be misleading, for Plato himself makes it clear at the start that his account of the cosmos is by its very nature compelled to be somewhat schematic and artificial; the (temporal) formation of the cosmos is seen to be itself only one element in a *series* of activities labelled "what was brought about by Intelligence" (47E4), and they in turn find their important correlate in what he terms "what happens as a result of Necessity." (47E4–5) This "Necessity" appears to have just as large a part to play as the Demiurge himself in the formation of the cosmos, and is, like him, eternal (47E5–48A5); its activities and those of the Demiurge are clearly meant to be simultaneous (*ibid.*), and for this reason there can be no temporal division between them, whatever their position of anteriority and posteriority in the dialogue. In other words Plato, for purposes of exposition, is making a large and artificial distinction of a purely logical nature. The question is, must we assume that the *totality* of his account is of such a logical and artificial nature?

The reply will be important for anyone considering the question of the eternity or temporality of the cosmos in the dialogue, and the bearing that this will necessarily have on Plato's cosmic and individual psychology. From the beginning the problem has divided Platonists into two broad camps,

11 *Ti.* 28A6. The idea had already been broached at *R.* 507C6–7 and 530A6.

owing their allegiance to the colours of Plutarch and Proclus respectively. For Proclus the world is eternal, and in a state of becoming without beginning or end.[12] For Plutarch the world was created in time;[13] when Plato affirms that time and the world began together there is no contradiction involved, for there was some sort of duration *before* time began. In this pre-cosmic time (for want of a better word) soul held sway, but it was irrational soul, the "soul in accompaniment with folly" and the Evil World Soul of the *Laws*.[14] The intelligent World Soul of which the *Timaeus* speaks is simply the original irrational soul reduced to a state of order and reason by the Demiurge.[15] By this argument Plutarch solves a number of "problems" at a stroke. For example, the *Phaedrus* holds that soul is eternal (245C5), while the *Timaeus* states that it was fashioned by the Demiurge. (35A ff.) The apparent discrepancy is resolved by stating that in the two cases Plato is talking of two different stages of development of the same "eternal" soul. As for the notion of precosmic time, this, too, presents no difficulties. For time is *ex hypothesi* the *ordered* measurement of the heavenly bodies; it is "the image of eternity moving *according to number* . . . the πέρας imposed upon an ἄπειρον of duration."[16] The "Necessity" and "Wandering Cause" and "Distributed Being" of the *Timaeus* (48A1–2; 35A), the "Evil World Soul" and "soul in accompaniment with folly" of the *Laws*,[17] and the

---

12 *in Ti.* 89B (Diehl I 290/30–291/3). In this view of the world as eternal he follows the opinion of the first-generation Platonist Xenocrates and Xenocrates' pupil Crantor. According to Proclus this was the view which largely prevailed till his own time, the only notable adversaries being Plutarch and Atticus (though there were others, too, he admits). He might have mentioned Aristotle himself as a notable "literalist" expositor of the *Timaeus*. For a summary of the different opinions on the matter in antiquity see Taylor (3) 67 ff. For a review of the *status quaestionis* till 1942 see R. Hackforth (2) 17–22. In the nineteenth century Th.-H. Martin set the fashion by his general adherence to Plutarch in interpreting the *Timaeus* (see especially I 371–3), but this was largely reversed in modern times by the editions of Taylor and Cornford, with their respect for Proclus. Of recent interpreters Cherniss tends to follow Proclus to a large degree, while Meldrum, Hackforth, and Vlastos follow Plutarch at least insofar as the world's creation is concerned (H. Cherniss (3) 204–16; M. Meldrum 65–74; G. Vlastos (1) 71–83; R. Hackforth (2) 17–22). J. B. Skemp (1) 76 follows Plutarch's interpretation of the irrational, pre-cosmic ψυχή, but sees it rather as an element of the (eternally existing) cosmos. Vlastos, Meldrum, and H. Herter ((1) 327–47) are united in thinking that Plato's views on the eternity or temporality of the cosmos are not immediately coherent.

13 *de An.* 1016CD.

14 *Ibid.* 1014DE. See *Lg.* 897B3 and 897D1.

15 *de An.* 1014C.

16 J. B. Skemp (1) 111, Plu. *de An.* 1014D f. See also *Phlb.* 16C, 24A.

17 897B8–C1. On the problem of Evil World Soul see below, 149ff.

"Unlimited" of the *Philebus* (16C ff.) are all one and the same pre-cosmic "irrational" soul.[18] Final loose ends are neatly tied up by identifying Space with Aristotle's "matter" ($\ddot{v}\lambda\eta$),[19] and by describing it as the sphere of activity of irrational soul before the cosmos began.

The two points of view might be described as those of thorough-going monism and mitigated monism, and both seem to me misleading. This, as far as I can judge, is to be attributed largely to the unfortunate attitude, shared by most scholars in antiquity and far from dead even now, that the writings of Plato are a sort of Bible or Koran, divinely inspired and guaranteed free from error. Any apparent contradictions are no doubt the fault of the interpreter, and the true Platonist will exercise all his skill and patience to show that they can be explained away. The idea that Plato might have developed in some way; that in old age he might have been less sure of things dogmatically asserted in youth; that he might even have contradicted himself on occasion; seems to have been an idea that, like the putatively evil Demiurge or the putatively evil cosmos, it was impious even to contemplate. The result is that interpreters have felt free to pick and choose indiscriminately from any and every part of Plato's writings, with often fantastic results; given sufficient ingenuity, and a determination not to contemplate the context from which one adopts one's quotations, one can "prove" that Plato is a determinist or a voluntarist, a monotheist or a polytheist, a monist or a dualist, a communist or a fascist. The list could be extended; but it is long enough to make one suspicious of an attitude which can lead to such odd and contradictory conclusions.

The patient work of a number of nineteenth-century scholars in particular has shown, I think convincingly, a definite chronological order in the writings of Plato. Much remains and will remain obscure, but the general lines I accept as well established.[20] This, however, has not stopped a number of scholars from trying to get the best of both worlds. While accepting that one dialogue can be safely asserted to be anterior or posterior

18 *de An.* 1014D f., 1015DE.

19 *Ibid.* 1024C.

20 The researches of L. Campbell and W. Lutoslawski are outstanding in this field. Most scholars would now accept, I think, that the dialogues fall into the following number of groups: (a) the so-called "Socratic" dialogues, (b) the central "metaphysical" dialogues, (c) the "critical" dialogues, (d) very late dialogues. Till recent times the *Timaeus* had been presumed to belong to (d) or late (c), but I tentatively follow G. E. L. Owen ((1) 79–95) in seeing it rather as the crowning work of the *Republic* group, followed closely by the *Phaedrus*.

to another, they feel free to interpret the earlier dialogue in the light of the later, and supposedly "new" ideas professed in the later dialogues they see as "implicit" in the earlier, even though there is little in the natural sense of the Greek text to support the assertion. Let us concede the obvious before we go any further; clearly Plato is bound by the laws of grammar, syntax, temporal succession, and the like, and cannot be expected to say everything all the time. The purpose of a particular dialogue will govern its subject matter, general layout, and illustrative material; it would be absurd to expect Plato to introduce irrelevant ideas just because we know that they have been of central importance to him till that date. But here we must draw what seems to me a crucial distinction. It is clearly true that silence on Plato's part does not mean ignorance, and in a matter of *peripheral* importance he may be prepared, for a particular purpose, to suppress an idea completely in one dialogue, while using the same idea in a more meaningful context in a later one. But would he be at all likely to do this in a matter of *central* importance? A good example presents itself at *Timaeus* 52E, where we have a description of a supposedly pre-cosmic chaos in which there is no explicit mention of the operation of soul. In the *Laws*, however, which most would admit to be a posterior dialogue, soul is said to be the source of *all* movement. (896B1–3) I submit that here in particular it is a mistake in method to interpret the earlier by the later dialogue, as the matter is one of such deep importance; monism and dualism apart, the whole problem of evil is apparently involved.[21] It seems to me extraordinary that Plato should suppress the notion of soul as the source of all movement "for purposes of the Myth,"[22] when by doing so he leaves himself open to radical misinterpretation on a point of cardinal importance. It seems hardly likely that he will simply "suppress" an idea so important that it is the ruination of one or a number of things which in the text he seems to be asserting as basic cosmological fact. Minor incoherencies in a man's thought one may expect; but hardly an incoherency of so all-embracing a nature.

We have strayed some distance from Plutarch and Proclus, but inadequacies in some modern interpretations of Plato, particularly of the *Timaeus* and *Laws*, seem to me to spring directly from their influence. This should become clear as particular parts of these two dialogues are discussed. For the moment let us return to the question of the temporal or non-temporal formation of the cosmos. Whatever Plato may have meant, he

21 See A.-J. Festugière (1) III xiv.
22 H. Cherniss (3) 24 n26, and (5) 428–9.

certainly *speaks* of the beginning of the world as though it took place in time. "It came into being" (γέγονεν 28B7) is unequivocal enough, and in the passage at 27D5–28B7 we have the phrases γένεσιν σχεῖν, γενέσεως ἀρχήν, and γιγνόμενα καὶ γεννητά. However, one must concede, with Cornford, that words like γένεσις and γίγνεσθαι can have a definite *double entendre* in Plato's writings, so that to opt for any one of the two possible interpretations without further evidence would be arbitrary. This further evidence is provided by the use of the word "produced" (γεννητά 28C2) and the phrase "in *process* of becoming" (γιγνόμενα 28C2) in one and the same sentence, and seems to clinch the issue; whatever Plato may *intend*, he is certainly *talking* in terms of the *temporal* sense of γένεσις.[23] But, since the rest of the account of the world's formation is so schematized, one seems hardly justified as yet in taking this particular section literally. And yet, it seems to me, one *is* justified, and on the following grounds. The realities described as "what was brought about by Intelligence" (47E4) and "what happens as a result of Necessity" (*ibid.*) are admitted by Plato himself to be correlative and of equal importance in the genesis of the cosmos (47E3–48B3), so that it matters little if, for the sake of the discussion, they are considered in the text one after the other. Again, at 34BC, he tells us that the soul, although anterior and superior to the body, is being discussed *after* the body. But, on consideration, how could one intelligibly do otherwise? In a matter of such complexity as the body-soul relationship, it seems natural enough to proceed from the better known to the less well known, from the seen to the unseen, from the simple to the involved. If this is true, it would appear fair to assume that Plato felt that he had good reason for treating *certain* topics in the *Timaeus* in a schematic manner, but may have wished to be taken literally in other respects. In both instances of schematization cited above, for example, he makes it quite clear that it is being done deliberately. This being the case, I take it that the only safe rule to follow is to accept the text at its face value, unless there is compelling evidence to the contrary.[24] It may be that one completely misunderstands the point of the *Timaeus* as a result; this is an unfortunate risk that one must run. But at least such a method has the advantage that it deals all the time with what Plato purports to say, rather than with what on other grounds we should like to think he is saying.

We have seen how at 28B7 the world was said to have come into being

---

23 See R. Hackforth (2) 18–19, who stresses the same points. See also F. Solmsen (2) 268–82.
24 For examples of instances in which such compelling evidence seems to be present, see below, 67, 75, 80, 82.

(γέγονεν), and this assertion is corroborated by an epistemological argument, some of it already used at 28A and in the *Republic* (477A1 ff.). The two stages of the argument are as follows: (a) The world is a thing that can be seen and touched, and possesses body, and all such things are sensible (αἰσθητά 28B8); (b) (1) Sense-objects we apprehend by a combination of thought (δόξα) and sensation, and (2) "They are obviously of the class of things which come into existence and are produced." (28C1-2)

A second argument follows closely on the heels of the first. Again it has two stages, though this time the relation between the two is less clear: (a) that which comes into being must necessarily do so "by the agency of some cause" (28C2-3); (b) it is a difficult task to find the "maker and father" of this universe, and, "even if we found him to tell of him to all men would be impossible." (28C3-5)

The translation "by the agency of some cause" is Cornford's, and is carefully chosen. For, while the noun αἴτιον can obviously mean simply a cause, there is a danger of taking the word in too arid and Aristotelian a sense, thus losing the notion of "personal responsibility" which Plato seems to have found in the adjective αἴτιος.[25] If this is true here, the transition to the notion of father does not seem too severe. Certainly in the *Republic* the being described as guiltless for man's fate was a (personal) divinity. (617E4-5) The present additional step from person to father makes sense in view of Plato's vision of the world as a living being, a notion far from new in the history of cosmological speculation. As for a word like "produced" (γεννητά 28C2), the sexual overtones hardly need stressing.

The notions of "maker" (28C3) and "Demiurge" (introduced already at 28A6) change the metaphor, but are introduced, it would seem, with much more in mind than literary variation. For the Theory of Ideas, crucial to earlier dialogues in the most basic respects – ontological, epistemological, and ethical[26] – and introduced here again in unmistakeable terms,[27] receives new significance by reason of them. For the Ideas are now unequivocally portrayed as the everlasting model of an everlasting Artisan,[28] and in *this* way the origin of the being of all that has any claim to existence; they are

---

25 See R. 617E4-5: αἰτία ἑλομένου. θεὸς ἀναίτιος. On the whole question see A. E. Taylor (3) 63-4, and J. B. Skemp (1) 71.

26 See H. Cherniss (4) 445-56.

27 30C3 ff., 31A4 (παράδειγμα). Cf. R. 500E3-4, 592B2.

28 One might already have drawn this conclusion from hints in the *Republic*, where the Theory of Ideas is put forward in conjunction with a clear assertion of the existence of a "Craftsman of the universe." (530A6)

for the eternal Craftsman on a cosmic scale what they were for the truly just man on an individual scale. (See *R.* 500C9 ff.) Their role as ultimate true existents is still not questioned, but Plato is now making it clear that their causality is of an exemplary order only. For efficient causality he looks to a "father of this universe" (28C3–4), who will account for a world endowed with, among other things, the qualities of a living being. This is an important clarification of the position adopted in the *Republic*, in which the Ideas themselves were credited with "generative" causality (e.g., at 508B12, where the Idea of Good is said to beget its offspring, the Sun).

After supposing, for the sake of argument, that there might be two models, one eternal, one generated, to which the Demiurge might have looked, Plato concludes that he looked to the eternal, on the (for him incontrovertible) grounds that this world is the best of things that have come into being, and the Demiurge the best of causal agents. (29A1–6) A certain incoherence is evident here; at 29A3 it was simply a question of the world's being "excellent" and the Demiurge "good." Of these propositions the first, at any rate, might have been defended with some show of plausibility by a series of a posteriori arguments, as Proclus saw.[29] But with the next breath Plato is asserting that the world is the *best* of all things that have come into being, and the Demiurge the best of all causal agents, on the grounds of the eternity of the model. This goes rather further than his more minimal assertions at 28AB, and is not readily intelligible. For nowhere else in the dialogue is it suggested that there have been *other* worlds preceding this one, such that the present one can be described as the finest or best (κάλλιστος 29A5). One solution would be to suggest that Plato foreshadows Leibniz here, and that he is really maintaining that this is the best of all *possible* worlds; in this way one will not be obliged to posit the existence, in the past or future, of other ones. Another, perhaps more plausible solution, would be to suggest that the distinction between this world and other worlds is a hypothetical one only, like the distinction between an "eternal" and a "generated" (γεγονός) model to which the Demiurge might have looked (28C6–29A2). Just as in the latter example the "generated" model is a patent fiction, inserted merely for purposes of argument, so, too, in the present instance the other worlds that have been "generated" (γεγονότων; cf. γεγονός above) are probably fictitious, and likewise inserted merely for purposes of argument.

At 29D–30C we are given an account of the likely motive underlying

29 *in Ti.* 100D (Diehl I 329/17–18) and 101D ff. (Diehl I 332/18 ff.).

the world's fashioning, and in the process receive some of our most valuable information on Demiurge, intelligence, and soul. The Demiurge, we learn, being good and without jealousy, wanted the world to become as like as possible to himself. The principle, taken over from "men of intelligence," is stated, not proved. (29EI–30A2) Desiring all things to be as good as possible, and feeling that order was better than disorder, "the god took over all that is visible – not at rest, but in discordant and unordered motion – and brought it from disorder into order." (30AI–5) Whatever Plato wants us to understand by this sentence, the Demiurge is clearly not meant to be a *creator ex nihilo*. Something visible, and in disorderly motion, is stated to be there "before" he "took it in hand" and reduced it to order. A later passage (52D4 ff.) has been offered as an explanation of this assertion, and this will be discussed in due course.[30] For the moment let us watch as Plato continues with an account of the implications of such "order." After stating that "he who is best" could not do anything but "the most excellent" (compare his similar statement at 30AI–7), he makes the further assertion that no work devoid of intelligence could be fairer than one which has intelligence. (30BI–3) But nothing, he argues, can possess intelligence without the presence of soul.[31] So the Demiurge fashioned a soul within the body of the universe, and reason within the soul. Then the world we know came into being as a "living creature truly endowed with soul and intelligence by the providence of the god." (30B4–CI)

So far there seems to be no particular reason for writing off either the Demiurge or the primeval chaos as "symbolic." It is true, of course, that for Plato it is still the world of Ideas that enjoys authentic existence, and the sensible world only a quasi-existence; and an interesting facet of their differing ontological status is the assertion that the one enjoys eternal existence, the other merely an existence in time, "the moving likeness of eternity."[32] But this is hardly evidence that the world had no temporal beginning. The rela-

---

30 See below, 94ff.

31 30B3. See also *Sph.* 249A4–8, *Phlb.* 30C9–10.

32 37DI, 37D5–7. The use of the adjective ἀΐδιος to describe both the model and the everlasting gods is confusing, as F. M. Cornford ((5) 98 n1) sees. But G. E. L. Owen (2) 333 is correct in stressing that αἰώνιος certainly does mean "eternal," and rightly castigates Cornford's efforts to emend the text. However, as he admits, Plato himself finds a better word, διαιώνιος, at 38B8, and the picture is thereby clarified considerably. The world, whose formation constituted the first moment of time, will continue forever *in* that time. In a word, the Ideas are eternal (i.e. outside time and so without beginning or end), while the world is *sempiternal* (i.e. in time, of the same duration as time, and consequently with a beginning but without an end).

tionship between the Ideas and the sensible world discussed at 27D–28A is an epistemological and ontological one only, and adds nothing to the *Republic* account (477A1 ff.); there is little to show that Plato wanted to corroborate this doctrine by indicating a *further* parallelism between the timeless eternity of the Ideas and the temporal everlastingness of the sensible cosmos.[33] On the contrary, as I hope later evidence in the dialogue will substantiate, Plato's earlier doctrine still stands, but he is now adding to it the further cosmological assertion that the world we know came into being with (ordered) time. The two views do not seem *prima facie* incompatible. For the ontological and epistemological accounts of the *Phaedo* and *Republic* were presumably dealing with the ordered world we know; any further (cosmological) assertion of a pre-cosmic chaos could hardly be said to impinge upon them, dealing as it does with a quite different realm of reality, and Plato's basic dualism will stand unimpaired.

Pages 31B–34A deal with the ostensible formation of the world's body by the Demiurge. The argument is largely Eleatic and Empedoclean, and is concerned to show the rationality, uniformity, and harmony which the world's body possesses. More to our present purposes is the section beginning at 34A, where Plato discusses the formation of World Soul. He offers no explanation for treating this after the world's body, but I have already suggested that a number of practical and intelligible reasons offer themselves.[34] All that Plato says here is that, whatever the order he himself has chosen, the Demiurge "made soul prior to body and older than it in origin and in excellence, to be the body's mistress and governor." (34C4–35A1) The language is not new; we have heard it in the *Phaedo*.[35] It is easy enough to discount words like "origin," "prior," and "older" as purely metaphorical, but the fact that precisely the same things are said of individual soul in the *Phaedo* makes this look a little hazardous, unless better evidence than recourse to a posterior dialogue is offered.[36] For purposes of exposition it would be no doubt difficult, if not impossible, to *describe* World Soul before the world's body; but Plato, I suggest, is saying that World Soul is *in fact* anterior to the world's body in some way, as well as being its mistress and

---

33 See Procl. *in Ti.* 87D ff. (Diehl I 285/17 ff.). He concludes that the cosmos had an ἀρχή, but not a temporal one; it is a "final" one rather, which he identifies with the Good (*ibid.* 26 ff.).

34 See above, 65.

35 See *Phd.* 94B ff. for the notions of ἄρχειν and δεσπόζειν, and 69E–72D and 72E–78B for soul's pre-existence to body.

36 F. M. Cornford (5) 59.

ruler. The notion is a difficult one to appreciate, but so is that of individual soul's anteriority in the *Phaedo*. It also means, I think, that, whatever else Plato wants us to understand by World Soul, he expects us to see a parallelism between it and individual soul in the matter of anteriority to the body. Whether there are any further similarities will remain to be seen.

Before describing the composition of World Soul, Plato offers a description of how it was set in the world's body. "In the centre he [i.e., the Demiurge] set a soul and caused it to extend throughout the whole and further wrapped its body round with soul on the outside [ἔξωθεν]." (34B3–4) The somewhat "physical" description is not surprising to one who remembers some of the similar images used to describe the human soul in the *Phaedo*.[37] ἔξωθεν is curious, and Cornford may be right in thinking that we are meant to understand that World Soul only reaches the circumference of the world's body.[38] It is difficult to see what Plato could have had in mind if he had wanted us to understand that World Soul stretched *beyond* the world's body, unless perhaps that a greater "sphere of influence" was seen as an indication of superiority. Whatever the truth, World Soul clearly extends throughout the entirety of the world's body, from centre to circumference (or further), and we are left in no doubt that in the world there is no place where soul does not operate.[39]

The sentence which tells of the composition of World Soul has been well described as "one of the most obscure in the whole dialogue."[40] This is understandable enough when one considers the highly abstract nature of the contents. Solutions have been many and various, but the one which seems to me to do most justice to the text as we have it and to make some sort of philosophical sense is that of Proclus, championed in recent times by Grube and Cornford.[41] According to this particular exegesis World Soul is composed of three ingredients:

A. An "intermediate" form of Existence, formed by a mixture of that Existence which is "unchangeable" (and to which Plato adjoins the addi-

37 Especially 67C7–8, 84C4 ff., 80E2 ff.

38 F. M. Cornford (5) 58. For a different explanation, based upon the notion that the soul is a κινητικόν τι, see A. E. Taylor (3) 105, and F. Solmsen (4) 155.

39 See J. B. Skemp (1) 84–5.

40 F. M. Cornford (5) 59. The passage in question is 35A1 ff.

41 Procl. *in Ti.* 176C ff. (Diehl II 119/29 ff.); G. M. A. Grube (1) 80–2; F. M. Cornford (5) 59 ff. This explanation has won wide acceptance among English-speaking scholars, but is apparently not accepted by A.-J. Festugière ((1) II 103, 257). For a criticism of his view see H. Cherniss (3) 208 n5. A review of other explanations, ancient and modern, can be found in A. E. Taylor (3) 106–27.

tional epithet of "indivisible"), and that Existence which is "distributed among bodies" (and to which he adjoins the additional epithet of "divisible"). (35A1–3)

B. An "intermediate" "Different," formed on the same principle as the intermediate Existence above: that is, a mixture of that kind of Different which is indivisible and that kind which is distributed among bodies. (35A4–6)

C. An "intermediate" "Same," again formed on the same principle as the intermediate Existence: that is, a mixture of that kind of Same which is indivisible and that kind which is distributed among bodies. (*Ibid.*)

There follows a brief description of the Demiurge combining the three ingredients: "Then, taking the three, he blended them all into a unity, forming the nature of the Different, hard as it was to mingle, into union with the Same, and mingling them together with Existence."[42]

If we examine the ingredients in turn, the first (in order of exposition: there is no hint that Existence is in any way "superior" to Same or Different), intermediate Existence, seems readily intelligible. The "unchangeable" form of Existence can only be the Existence enjoyed by the Ideas, and the Existence which is distributed among bodies will be the quasi-existence enjoyed by the world of sense-objects. The former will be "undivided" because, though the Ideas may be more than one in number, each is in itself incomposite; objects of sense perception, by contrast, are composite. So far, nothing new. But what of the "intermediate" form of Existence? If the metaphor of mixture has any meaning at all, it will be a form of Existence which enjoys the characteristics of *both* the other forms insofar as the combination is possible. Here we can review what we already know of soul, from earlier dialogues and in the *Timaeus* itself. It has two basic elements, the one immortal and in some sense divine – intelligence – and the other mortal and bound up with bodily existence only. The former shares with the Ideas the characteristics of divinity, eternity, and (if we understand the soul in much of the *Phaedo* as meaning to all intents and purposes *intellective* soul) incomposition. The affinity between the characteristics of intellective soul and the Ideas Plato uses as a suasion for soul's immortality. To this extent one can say that soul possesses the Existence of the world of authentic existence. By contrast, the "mortal" soul possesses the characteristics of that body and environment which it inhabits for this life. The upshot is that in the one soul we have two types of Existence, the one which we associate with the world of Ideas, the

---

42 35A6–B1. For the whole passage I have followed the text adopted by F. M. Cornford, following G. M. A. Grube.

other with the world of sense. Here, at any rate, we seem to have a candidate for the possession of that "intermediate" Existence of which the *Timaeus* speaks, formed by a combination of two very different types of Existence.

If this is true of individual soul, it seems not unfair to think that it will be largely, if not totally, true of World Soul. For so far, in talking of World Soul, Plato has given no hint that the soul of which he is speaking is in any way different in *kind* from the soul which he has discussed in earlier dialogues. Both are bound up with a body (e.g., *Ti.* 31B ff.; *Phd.* 82E2–3, 92A1), and both have an element of intelligence in them. (*Ti.* 35A; *Phd.* 65A ff.) Both, *qua* intelligent, are immortal. (*Ti.* 36A4–5; *Phd.* 77CD) Both of them function as life-principles.[43] Whatever may be the differences in detail, such points of similarity suggest that Plato does not mean us to see a difference in kind between the two types of soul, and to this extent it looks as though the notion of intermediate Existence can be applied equally meaningfully to both.

The notions of "intermediate Sameness" and "intermediate Difference" are less easy. Cornford saw them as being unintelligible to readers un-acquainted with the *Sophist*;[44] Taylor, by contrast, wanted to claim just the opposite, on grounds peculiar to his own view of the man Timaeus, and of what the latter was likely to have known and not to have known.[45] Thanks to a basic misinterpretation of the passage at 35A, Taylor took it that the three elements of World Soul were the Same, the Different, and the blend of the two, and that the Same and the Different were identical with two other notions introduced later in the dialogue, namely the Indivisible and the Divisible respectively. His defence of his position is neat and succinct, but it cannot make up for the fact that he misreads the text and upholds a position which Plato never affirmed. However, this does not mean that Cornford's view has won universal acceptance. The reason for this is that, in the eyes of a number of modern scholars, the *Timaeus* clearly propounds the "classic" version of the Theory of Ideas. Since, in their view, this same classic version suffers a mortal blow in the *Parmenides* and is interred in the *Sophist*, the *Timaeus* must consequently ante-date the *Sophist*, if Plato is not to be accused of intolerably naive philosophical tergiversation.[46] Cornford forestalls the

---

43 *Ti.* 30B8 (the world is a ζῷον ἔμψυχον ἔννουν τε) and *Phd.* 69E–72D.

44 F. M. Cornford (5) 61.

45 A. E. Taylor (3) 128.

46 For the arguments see G. E. L. Owen (1). He is followed by J. Gould 202 n3; D. W. Hamlyn 290 n3; D. A. Rees (2) 113 n29; C. Strang 147–64. W. G. Runciman 4, while still somewhat diffident, feels that Owen has at any rate tested the accepted dating of the *Timaeus*. For criticisms of the view see the references to Cherniss, Rist, and Skemp above, 59n1.

objection by taking the "Greatest Kinds" of the *Sophist* to refer to the Ideas; in this way the Theory of Ideas is retained, except that Life and Soul are conceded to have some share in reality as well; the latter is no longer exhausted by the Ideas.[47] On this analysis the *Timaeus* is not an act of retrogression, but a lengthy amplification of the nature of that Soul and Movement first asserted as "real" in the *Sophist*, aided by a number of concepts (Existence, Sameness, and Difference) elaborated in that same dialogue. If Cornford is right in this regard, the *Timaeus* might reasonably be placed after the *Sophist*; if he is wrong, one must contemplate the possibility either that the *Timaeus precedes* the *Sophist* or that as a piece of ontological analysis it is an act of retrogression to the naive realism of the *Phaedo* and *Republic*. For many, as was mentioned above, the latter alternative is unpalatable, and they would prefer to date the *Timaeus* before the *Sophist*. However, this is not the place to investigate the merits of the two cases in that particular controversy. Suffice it to say that, in the opinion of the present writer, it seems clear that, whatever the status of the "Greatest Kinds" in the *Sophist*, the notions of Same and Different (as applied to the Ideas) *could* be inferred from the *Republic*, as Owen has indicated;[48] that the *Sophist* can provide the only clue to the passage is not as self-evident as Cornford thought.[49]

Whatever their provenance, the terms Same and Different have received their most cogent analysis so far from Cornford. Of any Idea one can say that it has authentic existence, is the same as itself, and different from every other Idea. This seems hardly very profound, but it is at least some sort of solution to the problem of the individual specification of the Ideas. If each entails those of Existence, Sameness (as itself), and Difference (from every other Idea), one has given some sort of answer to the problem of individuation in the world of authentic existence. But even if one concedes that the logical distinctions of Existence, Sameness, and Difference can be applied to the Ideas, what can Plato have meant by talking about the "indivisible and divisible kinds" of Sameness and Difference? The context may help here. We noticed that in the text there is no hint of any *subordination* of Existence, Same, and Different; all three seem to have equally important parts to play in the composition of soul, and Plato is at pains to show how it is a particular version of each – the "intermediate" one – that the Demiurge chooses. The Theory of Ideas proved a meaningful explanation of the indivisible and divisible forms of Existence. If this is true, may it not help in our explanation

47 *Sph.* 254D; F. M. Cornford (5) 61–6.
48 G. E. L. Owen (1) 88.
49 F. M. Cornford (5) 61.

of divisible and indivisible Sameness and Difference also, in view of the careful textual parallelism of all three? "Indivisible Sameness," for example, might be applied to any individual Idea, in the sense that the Idea is numerically one and atomic; it exhausts the totality of our concept of it, while at the same time being indivisible into any further parts. It is single, simple, and unique. And if this logical attribute of Sameness can be applied to the the Ideas, it may equally well be applied to their counterpart in the world of sense. Whatever one's views on the problems of perception and the identification of objects, there is a case for saying that a particular object, such as a radio, is, for all its unseen molecular change, *for practical purposes* one and the same as itself and different from other objects. Nobody will expect this Sameness to have the stability of the Sameness of the Ideas, in view of the different degrees of reality enjoyed by the two worlds; but the affinity is still there, and seems to be just as meaningful as the affinity between model and image which underlies the whole Theory of Ideas. Much the same might be said of the notion of Difference, in the one world and the other.

How would all this, if true, be applied to soul? Plato himself hints how at 37AB, where we are informed that it is by virtue of the elements of Sameness and Difference in itself that soul can appreciate in what respect in the world of indivisible Existence (i.e., the world of Ideas) one existent (or Idea) is to be classed as the same as or different from another, and similarly in the world of divided Existence (i.e., the world of sense). In other words, in introducing the notions of Same and Different Plato seems to be offering an explanation of the *cognitive* faculties of soul. Not that this is a far remove from a discussion of soul's essential characteristics; given Plato's conviction of the close relationship of being and intelligibility, and the affinity of knowing instrument and object known,[50] it is not surprising to find soul here endowed with the requisite instruments for appreciating whatever degree of reality (i.e., of knowable content) there is in both the worlds to which, by reason of its amphibious nature, it belongs.

At this stage we seem to have come full circle, for Plato appears to be attributing to World Soul the same essential and cognitive characteristics that he attributes in earlier dialogues (and later in this same dialogue) to individual soul. (Cf. *Phd.* 65A ff., 80B ff.; *R.* 490AB) As yet, however, there has been no explicit mention of any "non-rational" element in World Soul. On the contrary, all the stress for the moment is on its ordered, reasonable, and

---

50 See esp. *R.* 477A1 ff. on the objects of δόξα and ἐπιστήμη and the distinction between the two faculties.

harmonious nature. At 35B–36B, for example, we are given a description of its division into harmonic intervals, each with that blend of Existence, Sameness, and Difference which is characteristic of the whole; reason and attunement, like being and intelligibility, are taken as a doublet.[51] The desirable state of the individual soul, that is, justice, turned out in the *Republic* to be one of "attunement,"[52] and such seems to be true of World Soul here, though the whole account at this stage takes a much more figurative turn than hitherto. Since Plato has opted to express his cosmology in terms of demiurgic construction, he now begins to present soul as a supply of soul-stuff, in the hands of the mason, marked off first into harmonic intervals and then manipulated and moulded into a certain shape.[53] We know, however, that World Soul, being distinct from the body of the world, is immaterial, so the figurative nature of the passage can be taken for granted.[54] Nonetheless, certain clear lines of thought emerge. The first characteristic with which the soul-stuff is endowed by the Demiurge is a series of harmonic intervals. (35B–36B) These may or may not have an ultimate significance; it goes without saying that they were a happy hunting-ground for neo-Platonist commentators.[55] Whatever the truth, one can offer the minimal observation that World Soul, already characterized as intelligent by its very composition, enjoys "attunement" or harmonic proportion in some sense. However, it can hardly be that attunement of the three parts of individual soul spoken about in the *Republic* (443A ff.); for, while we may be correct in interpreting 35A as meaning that World Soul has ontic constituents corresponding to the cognitive states of "knowledge" and "opinion," there is as yet no evidence of that purely irrational *appetition* which one associates with the "desiderative" part, or of that more elusive amphibian, the "spirited" part of soul. Whatever else Plato wants us to understand by "attunement"

51 36E6–37A1: λογισμοῦ δὲ μετέχουσα καὶ ἁρμονίας ψυχή.

52 *R.* 433A ff. Cf. 443DE, where the "parts" of the soul are compared to the νεάτη, μέση, and ὑπάτη of the musical scale. See A. E. Taylor (3) 497–8.

53 *Ti.* 36B ff. This aspect of ψυχή as a type of stuff or psychic force interpenetrating the universe is the one stressed in *Laws* x. See below, 147ff.

54 For the methodology here, see above, 64–5. The fact that a material structure would make World Soul a part or aspect of the *body* of the world seems to me to be a piece of "compelling evidence" in favour of the view that World Soul is meant to be nothing if not immaterial; otherwise, Plato's careful distinction between World Soul and the body of the world can only be regarded as meaningless. (A second, but not secondary, consideration in favour of World Soul's immateriality is, of course, all that has been said about the immateriality of *human* soul in earlier dialogues.)

55 For the interpretations of such commentators as Amelius, Porphyry, and Iamblichus, see Procl. *in Ti.* 205A ff. (Diehl II 212/9 ff.).

here, he himself seems to take it as a constituent of a World Soul which he
thinks of as purely rational. In other words, even if both the rational and the
non-rational world fall within the competence of World Soul, its approach
and activity in either case will be one that manifests intelligence; though the
elements in it that appreciate the worlds of "knowledge" and "opinion"
may be of an essentially different make-up, the activities of both will be
canalized and co-ordinated to serve the purposes of intelligence. If this
interpretation is correct, the parallelism with the individual soul in the
Republic (586D ff.) is still a close one, but the difference remains that in the
earlier case the appetitive nature of part of the soul was accepted, while here
World Soul looks purely cognitive. From the point of view of the virtue
of justice, the good man was the one who canalized the appetites of the lower
areas of soul to serve the ends of the higher. The lower appetites were seen
to have their value, but only insofar as they served the purposes of intelligence. (586E4 ff.) Similarly here, World Soul can be seen to possess the virtue
of intelligence because both *cognitive* constituents operate in such a harmonious way as to manifest intelligence. (ἔμφρονος 36E4) In either case
"attunement" of constituent parts, cognitive or otherwise, is an important
mutual characteristic, and this may have been one reason why Plato introduced the notion at this stage. A further reason can be gathered from later
comments in the dialogue: World Soul will be seen as an exemplar for
individual souls. Virtue for them will consist in a state of attunement of their
constituent elements, and for an example of this they will look to the
attunement of World Soul, at least in its external manifestation in the
movements of the heavenly bodies. (47BC)

   The importance of attunement in World Soul is vouched for by the
extreme care with which Plato describes its composition by the Demiurge.
The terminology used is that of geometrical progression and musical
harmony, but it soon becomes clear that Plato is not out to propound any
theory of musical harmony as such, or to construct any new musical scale.
The series of twenty-seven notes which Plato brings in is simply a section of
the diatonic scale, which could in theory be extended indefinitely in either
direction. If practical musicologists opt for another section, this is because
their aims are quite different; that section of the scale which interests them
is the one that falls within the range of the human voice and ear. The commentator Adrastus saw that Plato's real interest lay in the numerical proportion of the harmonic intervals rather than in the harmonic intervals as such;
for, at any rate to one group of people – the Pythagoreans – there was a

direct relationship between numerical proportion and the composition of the universe.[56] Already at 31C3, when talking of the composition of the world's body, Plato talks in Pythagorean terms, telling us that the best sort of bond, the one that makes connected terms into a unity in the completest sense, is "proportion" ($\dot{\alpha}\nu\alpha\lambda o\gamma\dot{\iota}\alpha$). But such are precisely the questions at issue in the dialogue – the composition of the universe, the nature of its soul and body, and in what sense, if any, World Soul acts as a bond[57] holding together the elements which go to make up the world's body. In the light of this, ancient commentators saw clearly that Plato could only have had the *cognitive* function of World Soul in mind when he extended his progression as far as the so-called "solid numbers." For to the Pythagoreans the cube was the symbol of three-dimensional body.[58] In a word, if World Soul is to be united to the world's body in perpetuity, and if it is to have as a large part of its sphere of influence the world of three-dimensional objects, then it will in some sense have to contain within itself the cognitive counterpart of such objects. The terminology may be Pythagorean, but the principle is still the old Empedoclean one of "like knows like" that plays so central a part in Plato's thought. The notion of "attunement," on this interpretation, is introduced with the same intention as that which underlay the introduction of the terms Same and Different: it is an attempt to show that the ontological gap between a non-material soul and the material environment in which it dwells is not unbridgeable, at least insofar as cognition is concerned.

Up to this point Plato has spoken as though the Demiurge is working with a sort of soul-stuff, which he cuts up into pieces in such a way that they form a scale or ratio. At this point the picture changes a little. We must imagine that the pieces are placed together contiguously, so that the Demiurge now has a long band or strip of soul-stuff with the marks of the junctures of the particular sections still visible. This strip is then split length-wise into two halves. In the case of each half he joins the extremities together, so that a circle is formed from each. One of the circular strips he places inside the other – but not in the same plane. (36c ff.) We are informed that

---

56 For this section, with the references to Adrastus and the Pythagoreans, I am indebted to F. M. Cornford (5) 68 ff.

57 38E5 ($\delta\epsilon\sigma\mu\dot{o}s$). Cf. 37A4, $\dot{\alpha}\nu\dot{\alpha}\ \lambda\dot{o}\gamma o\nu\ \mu\epsilon\rho\iota\sigma\theta\epsilon\hat{\iota}\sigma\alpha$. For the notion of $\delta\epsilon\sigma\mu\dot{o}s$ as a "principle of continuity" see E. Ballard 34–5. This principle, he argues, underlies Plato's introduction of soul as a bridge between the Ideas and sensible things, between reason and irrationality, and is directly derived from the assumption that the universe is a perfect and coherent whole.

58 F. M. Cornford (5) 68.

the movement of the outer circle (which he calls the movement of the Same) revolves "around by the side to the right" (36c6), while that of the inner circle (which he calls the movement of the Different) revolves "diagonally to the left." (36c7) Whatever the meaning of the phrases "to the right" and "to the left," the notions of "side" and "diagonal" are readily explicable if one thinks of a geometrical drawing representing the celestial globe, the sidereal equator, and the tropics of Cancer and Capricorn.[59] If the two tropics are shown as parallel to the sidereal equator, lines joining the two easternmost points of each and the two westernmost points respectively will produce a rectangle. The movement "round by the side" will be that of the sidereal equator, the "sides" in question being those of Cancer and Capricorn, which run parallel to it. The "diagonal" movement will be that of the Ecliptic, which touches the tropic of Cancer at the easternmost point in the diagram, and the tropic of Capricorn at the westernmost point. Movement "round by the side" had been described as "to the right," and this is clearly going to be movement from west (left) to east (right). "Diagonal" movement was qualified as "to the left," and this will be movement from east (right) to west (left). However, it is movement by reference to the diagonal of the imaginary rectangle, not to the parallel sides which were the tropics of Cancer and Capricorn; in brief, since such a diagonal is the diameter of the Ecliptic, this movement will be the movement which takes place in the plane of the Zodiac. So we have two motions, that of the Same in the plane of the sidereal equator, moving from west to east, and that of the Different in the plane of the Zodiac, moving from east to west.

But there is little evidence to show that the circle of the Same is meant to be in any way "superior" to that of the Different, in spite of Cornford's contentions.[60] While it is true that in the traditional tables of opposites Same and Right stood in the column of things superior, and Different and Left in the column of things inferior,[61] it is by no means clear that Plato must necessarily use the words in such a sense. Like the words εἶδος and ἰδέα, they can be used in a quite neutral and non-committal fashion. For example, when talking of the Same and the Different as components of World Soul earlier

59 *Ibid.* 73–4.

60 *Ibid.* 76, 96, 144 n2, 118–19, 208. Cf. A. D. Winspear 332, who also like Cornford assumes that the circle of the Different is "irrational," L. Robin (1) 228, and G. Morrow (1) 162–3. For the opposite point of view see J. Gould 199, and H. Cherniss (3) 208–9 n5, who lay stress on the fact that the composition of inner and outer circles is identical. See also J. B. Skemp (1) 78.

61 See Procl. *in Ti.* 219F (Diehl II 258/20 ff.), and F. M. Cornford (5) 74.

on, Plato treated them in parallel fashion; no hint of the superiority of the one or the inferiority of the other was offered. In saying that any Idea or sense-object was the same as itself and different from all others he was making two statements of equal importance and of equally universal application. The most we are told is that the Demiurge gave "supremacy" (κράτος 36C7) to the circle of the Same, and the explanation of this, given immediately afterwards, is that this particular movement was left "single and undivided," while that of the Different was subdivided into several movements. (36D1 ff.) In other words, the movement of the Same has no *inherent* supremacy; any supremacy it possesses comes from the fact that it is not allowed to dissipate its strength by being fragmented into a *number* of movements. If one prescinds from the fragmentation introduced into the circle of the Different by the Demiurge there is little reason to think that the two movements are not of equal importance. The fact that one circle is spoken of as being "inside" the other proves little, since the whole description from 36C onwards is in terms of an armillary sphere, where "inner" and "outer" circles form part of the chosen model of description. This being the case, I take it that the motion of the Different is in no way inferior to that of the Same, and that if the circular movement of the latter is meant to express the operation of intelligence, the same will be no less true of the former. Plato puts the matter succinctly at 36E4–5 when he tells us that World Soul, endowed with its *two* motions, "made a divine beginning of ceaseless *and intelligent* [ἔμφρονος] life for all time."

The details of the particular planetary motions have been sufficiently discussed by others;[62] suffice it for the moment to realize that Plato is treating the movements of the heavenly bodies, and with them the circles of Equator and Ecliptic, as movements of World Soul, and that these movements are rational.[63] All this talk about heavenly movements, however, must not be taken as indicating that the οὐρανός in the sense of "the heavens" is the unique province of World Soul. No doubt this is where its kinetic operations and their rationality are most evident, but Plato makes it clear that its activity is

62 E.g., F. M. Cornford (5) 105–17, and A. E. Taylor (3) *ad loc.*
63 Aristotle sees this point clearly enough, and goes so far as to equate World Soul with νοῦς (*de An.* 407A3–5). A.-Ed. Chaignet 87, thinking along the same lines, identifies κίνησις and thought. But this seems to me to over-spiritualize the highly physical language which Plato uses of ψυχή, here and elsewhere. (See G. S. Claghorn 110, R. K. Gaye 92 ff., 101, and A. E. Taylor on *Ti.* 86E3–87A7, *ad loc.*) The dangers of over-stressing *this* aspect of soul's make-up, however, can be seen in the view of A. Rivaud who maintains ((1) 335–6) that for Plato there is *no* substantial difference between ψυχή and σῶμα.

ubiquitous in the universe when he talks of it as "being everywhere inwoven from the centre to the outermost heaven." (36E2, see also 34B3–4) If this is true, the movement of the Same will have to be imagined as governing that of the entire universe, not merely that of the planets (whose movements are in fact the fragmented movements of the Different). Nothing escapes the influence of the universe's total rotation, and if this rotation is a movement of soul and intelligence, then nothing will escape *their* activity and influence either.[64]

At 36E–37C we have another important account of the cognitive activities of World Soul, and the whole passage should be compared with 35A, where Proclus, it will be remembered, interpreted intermediate Being, Sameness, and Difference in terms of cognition. Prominent in the new description is the Empedoclean principle of like knowing like that we have seen already, for the blend of Being, Sameness, and Difference is expressly given as the *reason* for the soul's ability to pass judgments of sameness and difference both about objects in the world of Ideas and about sense-objects.[65] This much emerges with clarity, but the language which follows could be a little confusing. For although Plato has told us above that soul is to be found throughout the totality of the world, he now says that World Soul, whenever she "contacts" anything possessing either "dispersed" or "indivisible" existence (that is, either Ideas or sense-objects), is "set in motion all through herself," and it is in this state that she then makes "statements" ($\lambda \acute{\epsilon} \gamma \epsilon \iota \nu$) about the logical attributes of sameness and difference belonging to what she has just "contacted."[66] In other words, the imagery is now that of temporal succession, and World Soul here seems to be viewed as something like the brush which cleans the gramophone record as the latter revolves upon the turntable; the brush is guaranteed to miss no speck of dust, but it only reaches each speck in temporal succession. The image, however, is seen for what it is by the earlier clear assertions of the simultaneous ubiquity of soul and the ceaselessness of its motion. (34B3–4, 36E2–5) Plato goes on to say that the statement ($\lambda \acute{o} \gamma o s$) of World Soul is always a true one, whether affirming similarity or difference,[67] but a distinction is drawn between two

---

64 See F. M. Cornford (5) 136. A notable exponent of the view that for Plato World Soul is in fact only a *celestial* soul is N. Almberg, in his book *Platons världssjäl och Aristoteles gudsbegrepp* (Lund 1941). See Axel Dahl, *Theoria* 7 (1941) 268–70.

65 37A2. For the same Empedoclean principle see 41C2–3, 30A6–7 and Arist. *de An.* 404B16.

66 36E2, 34B3–4 (soul ubiquitous); 37AB (soul's "statements").

67 F. M. Cornford (5) 96 refers to the *Sophist* as an aid, where, he says, "all philosophic discourse is regarded as consisting of affirmative and negative statements about Forms."

different types of truth. If the statement concerns something in the sensible world, it is the circle of the Different which "moving aright carries its message throughout all its soul," and the result is "opinion" and "beliefs" which are "secure" and "true." (37B8) If it concerns something in the world of authentic existence, however, it is the circle of the Same which "running smoothly declares it," and the result is necessarily "knowledge and intelligence." (37C2) Here, in a sentence, we have a succinct statement of the epistemology which at an earlier date found its most elaborate statement in the central books of the *Republic*. Genuine knowledge is and can only be obtained in dealing with the world of authentic existence; all our own world can yield us is opinion or belief, which may or may not be "true." "True opinion," however, even if unable to give completely adequate grounds for itself, is at any rate factually correct, and so in this sense can be said to be the nearest possible equivalent to "knowledge and intelligence" that one will ever have in this world of quasi-reality. This being the case, there seems no evidence here, either, for the idea that the circle of the Different is in some way "less rational" than that of the Same. True, both have different provinces, different spheres of influence. The Same has to do with the eternally stable world of Ideas, a world only penetrated by pure intelligence. The Different, by contrast, deals with the sub-rational world of sense-experience.[68] But it still approaches the world of sense in the most rational manner compatible with that exiguous amount of reality which such a world enjoys, and compatible with such a world's inherent inability to be fully comprehended by rational analysis. Given the nature of the subject matter, the Different will never come to conclusions other than "opinions" and "beliefs": but its *rational* activity is made clear by the way it can guarantee that any such opinions and beliefs will be factually correct. We learn soon enough that the intractability of his materials is a limitation even upon the powers of the Demiurge. (47E ff.) So too, here, the limitations of the sensible world restrict the conclusions of the circle of the Different to statements of "belief" and "opinion." But this seems to be no reflection upon the latter's inherent rationality, which is made manifest by its approach.

One important sentence in the passage has been left till last. Plato talks of statements (whether about the world of Ideas or of sense-objects) as

---

This is misleading, for the *Timaeus* has only mentioned assertions of identity and difference (27B3-5, 44A1-5); the *Sophist* is making a rather different logical point, and one of no small importance, by analyzing negation in terms of difference. See G. E. L. Owen (1) 89.

68 See J. B. Skemp (1) 78.

being "carried on without speech or sound within the thing that is self-moved." (37B5–6) The first point is readily intelligible; a statement need not be uttered in words to perform its function. Some have assumed that the phrase "in that which is self-moved," refers to soul, but it seems equally possible that the reference is to the universe.[69] We have been informed already that world and soul are co-extensive, and the whole passage is dealing with the cognitive relationship between the two. The universe, we have been told, is a living creature, as an image of the Eternal Living Creature, and the self-motion of living things is a commonplace. This being the case, there is as much sense in saying that the *world* is moved by itself as there is in saying that *any* living creature is moved by itself. There seems to be no compelling evidence here for the later, more sophisticated philosophical doctrine that soul as such is autokinetic. It seems more reasonable to take the text as stating as a commonsense truth the notion that the world, *qua* living being, is moved by itself. The idea of the world as a living being has its roots deep in Greek thought; as for the idea that living things are self-moving, this can be accepted for the commonplace that it is, without reference to doctrine of a more elaborate nature propounded elsewhere.

So far all stress has been laid on the rational nature of World Soul, seen in the circular motions of Same and Different. Now the Demiurge is described as setting out to make all the other types of living creature, so that the likeness of model and copy may be as close as possible. (39D8 ff.) (Some of these living creatures – the planets – were already described, along with their movements in the Different, at 38C–39D. This anticipation of the natural order is readily understandable, since the planets are said to be the instruments of time; as Plato puts it, they were made "to define and preserve the numbers of time." [38C6] He had himself just been discussing the notion of time, and time needs the celestial clock for its measurement and consequent usefulness to mankind. [47A4–B2] Hence the mention of the planets immediately afterwards. It is another indication of Plato's willingness to abandon the temporal sequence of the Demiurge's activity if a plausible reason presents itself.) These living creatures fall into four classes: the heavenly race of gods, flying creatures, land animals, and those that live in water. (39E ff.) The first group consists of the stars, the planets, and the earth. The planets have been already described as living creatures (38E5–6), and the language there used makes it clear that each possesses intelligence as well as life-soul:

69 For the first point of view see A. E. Taylor (3) 182, and H. Cherniss (2) 26 n4. For the second see F. M. Cornford (5) 95 n2.

"As bodies bound together with living bonds, they had become living creatures and learnt their appointed tasks."

Plato accordingly confines his description to the stars, and we read that the Demiurge, after making them, set them "in the intelligence of the most powerful."[70] The combined notions of control and intelligence make this a clear reference to the circle of the Same.[71] The stars are said to be an adornment set in the outer heaven, accompanying the Same as it everlastingly imparts its own motion to the rest of the universe. (40A5–7) They have the forward motion of the Same and their own axial rotation; the individual motions of the planets they do not have. (36D2–7; 38C3–39E2) Here it is interesting to see the reason which Plato proffers for their axial rotation. At 34A2–3, when talking of the axial rotation of the world's body, he had described such motion as the one which "above all belongs to reason and intelligence," as distinct from the other six (rectilinear) motions. An explanation of this is now offered; it is that each star "always thinks the same thoughts about the same thing." (40A8–B1) If a body is to have intelligent motion, it must have circular motion, this being of all motions the most stable and the most uniform. For intelligence has dealings solely with the stable, unchanging, and uniform – i.e., with Ideas. In either case stability and uniformity are seen as integral to intelligent activity. The stars have the circular motion of the Same and their own circular axial rotation (40A7–B2); the planets, too, have the circular motion of the Same, in addition to that of the Different, and they also have their own proper circular motions.[72] Whether they have their own axial rotation as well is not mentioned explicitly, but some commentators have inferred it.[73] Whatever the truth of this, it is clear that both stars and planets possess movements which are a compound of circular, that is, intelligent movements. Whatever their difference of function in the universe, both groups of heavenly bodies are by their movements shown to be equally rational. If it eventually transpires that World Soul does have an irrational element within it, one will be compelled to look for such an element elsewhere than amidst the operations of the heavenly bodies.

70 40A5, εἰς τὴν τοῦ κρατίστου φρόνησιν.

71 Cf. 36C7 (κράτος). Taken by itself, φρόνησις could equally well apply to Same or Different.

72 36C2 ff., 36D, 38D1–7, 39A4 ff.

73 See F. M. Cornford (5) 119 and 137. Proclus seems to have been the first to make the inference, in Ti. 278CE (Diehl III 127–8), and was followed by Th.-H. Martin 85 and A. Boeckh 59. For a denial see A. E. Taylor (3) 225–6.

Plato now passes to a description of the formation of the other types of living creature, in particular human beings, and here the old problem of the relationship between the world of uniform Ideas and this world of change presents itself anew. How can the totally real produce the half-real? For one would expect like to produce like.[74] With this as his axiom Plato attempts to solve the problem by multiplying intermediaries. The first of these is the personal intelligent Demiurge himself, whose creative intelligence is the counterpart of the perfect but uncreative rationality of the Ideas.[75] The second is World Soul, whose rational nature is the counterpart, on a lower plane, of the rationality of the Demiurge. The heavenly bodies, too, divine compositions of the Demiurge, enjoy this rational life of World Soul, as well as the privilege of sempiternal existence, counterpart of the Demiurge's eternal existence.[76] But we are still a long way from the world of birth, change, and death. The Demiurge has produced what is most like himself, but another intermediary is still called for to bridge the gap between this essentially stable world and the world of change. So Plato talks of the Demiurge as delegating the task of forming the lesser living creatures – including human beings – to the gods whom he himself has formed, that is, to the astral bodies. (41C3 ff.) All that he himself will form will be that one element in human souls – intelligence – which is most like himself, and man's link with the world of authentic existence. (41C6–D1) This introduction of intermediaries is hardly very satisfactory, but, given the impossible type of problem which Plato has set himself to solve, it does make some sort of sense. For the two characteristics of this world are the fact of change, associated with life, and the fact that many biological processes which we see going on around us are apparently teleological, in that they seem to follow their own laws of internal finality. If this is true, one way of accounting for the facts as they appear to us is to posit soul as the source of the change associated with life and a personal intelligence as the ground of teleological activity. However, *ex hypothesi* soul and intelligence are not to be found among the Ideas. They must therefore be imagined as intermediaries, operating as the efficient causes of change and teleological activity, while exemplary causality can be left to the Ideas. In this way one can hope to

---

74 41C2–3. A direct product of the Demiurge would have the perfections of the Demiurge, Timaeus claims. For other applications of the same principle see above, 80 and n65.

75 "Le Dieu du *Timée* est bien l'intelligence organisatrice, que Platon a reçue d'Anaxagore, et qu'il achève de spiritualiser et de diviniser." A. Diès (1) II 551.

76 38B6–C3. For the notion of sempiternity see above, 68n32.

preserve the Theory of Ideas in its pristine state and "preserve the phenomena" at the same time. But this answer is hardly more satisfactory than the undiluted Theory of Ideas first encountered in the *Phaedo*; whatever the multiplication of intermediaries, the basic epistemological error underlying the whole theory has not been corrected, and this must wreck any coherent solution to the problem. But the recognition that a place must be found for the operation of soul and intelligence is evidence that Plato has now seen some of the more disturbing implications of the Theory of Ideas in its simplest form. (41D4–6)

At this point we are given an account of the formation of the immortal part of the human soul by the Demiurge. It is made with the same ingredients, and blended in much the same way as the ingredients which had gone to form World Soul: intermediate Existence, Sameness, and Difference. This time, however, the mixture is "no longer as pure as before, but second or third in degree of purity." (41D6–7) This description, like its counterpart at 37A to be interpreted in terms of cognition, is another indication of the affinity which Plato wishes us to see between World Soul, which is totally rational, and the rational part of the human soul. The mixture which forms World Soul is "pure" in the sense that the rationality of World Soul is total, inviolable, and everlasting; that of the human soul is less pure in the sense, perhaps, that its rational judgments can be clouded and perverted by that irrational element with which it is inevitably associated while living an embodied existence. It can hardly mean that human intelligence is at a greater remove from true reality than World Soul, since both are direct creations of the Demiurge, and "like produces like." It is divine, as the heavenly bodies are divine (41C2–3); its activity, however, is intermittent rather than continuous, and it operates under conditions which must hinder and distract, if nothing worse.

The mixture the Demiurge next divides up into individual souls, equal in number to the stars, and then distributes each soul to a star.[77] That is to say, the number of individual souls is a *finite* one, and no doubt it is no accident that this finite number is equal to that of the stars, each of which is itself said to possess a soul. Whatever this number might be, it is clearly meant to be yet another manifestation of the rational structure of the universe. The idea that the number of souls might be just *any* number, or one hap-

---

77 41D8–EI. As I argue in the text, this seems to mean that the number of souls is finite. Plato clearly took the whole matter seriously, since at *R.* 611A5 he again implies the same thing.

hazard number rather than another, runs counter to the notion of a universe governed by divine providence. Plato is perhaps thinking of each star as being the starting-off point for one individual human soul, from which it enters into the Orphic wheel of birth and death, for at 42B4–5 he talks of the soul that has lived well in this life journeying back to its star to enjoy a life which is "blessed and congenial." This sounds at first like a reward for virtue, and an escape from reincarnation. But it could also mean that the star is an *interim* habitation for the soul before reincarnation. The first interpretation has affinities with the account in the *Phaedrus* myth (249A1–4), and both interpretations could find some corroboration in Pindar's account.[78] Whatever the truth, the star begins by exercising a purely practical function; it offers each soul a "bird's eye view" (the phrase is Taylor's)[79] of the nature of the universe and is the place where they learn the laws of Fate from the Demiurge. (41E2–3) The whole account is very similar to that in the *Phaedrus*, where the souls are carried round the rim of the universe, and are granted a vision of the eternal Ideas, and afterwards spend their incarnate life trying to recapture the lost vision by the exercise of memory. (247C ff.) In the *Timaeus* account they are granted a vision of the true nature of the ordered and rational cosmos, and from other parts of the dialogue we can infer that in their incarnate state they must try to reproduce this state of balanced order in themselves. (42C4 ff., 47B6 ff.) Recollection is not mentioned, but the parallelism is clear enough; in either case the rational pattern and activity of a superior world serves as the model and incentive for life in this. Again, at 42A5–B2 we are told that justice in a man involves the control of "perception" and "love" and "fear" and "anger"; in other words, by that harmony which results from control of the lower by the higher elements in the soul (cf. *Republic* 430E ff., 433A ff.). An important aid to this is said to be the contemplation of the rationality and harmony of the cosmos. (47B6–C4) In the *Phaedrus* myth the Ideas themselves are the pattern (247C ff.); in the present myth the intermediate universe, an image of the Ideal Living Creature, is the pattern. But in learning the "nature of the universe" the soul sees the cosmos for what it is, an image of the Ideal, so that the result is in either case the same.

The "laws of destiny" (41E2–3) are far from clear. We learn that the first incarnation is one and the same for all, to exonerate the Demiurge from any charge of unfairness (cf. *Republic* 617E5). They are first sown in the

78 P. O. II 65–7 and 68–9, with Farnell's commentary *ad loc.*
79 A. E. Taylor (3) 257.

"instruments of time," that is, in the planets, each one in the particular planet which is "suitable" for it. (41E3) Perhaps we are meant to understand that each planet is associated with a particular temperament, just as in the *Phaedrus* myth each soul takes its temperament from that of the god whom it had as guide in its previous life. (252E5 ff.) For the planets, too, are gods.[80] After this the souls are to be born as "the most god-fearing of living beings." (42A1) This is elucidated in the next sentence: human nature is two-fold, and the "better sort" is what will from then on be called "man." (42A2–3) How far this is meant to be taken seriously is hard to judge. For at first sight, if we take the text at its face value, we must conclude that the first generation of souls was entirely male. This is odd, but not totally unintelligible. For, one could argue, the "allotted span" (42B3) of each soul varies, as we see from everyday observation, and some souls can be imagined as dying and being reincarnated as female while members of the original generation of (male) souls still enjoy life. But if 42B4–5 is interpreted as meaning that good-living souls of the first generation escape from the Wheel of Birth to the bliss of their particular star, while the rest are reincarnated as female, then sooner or later all *male* souls will die out, and the new position is even odder than the first. If, however, one interprets the passage as signifying an "interim period" for the soul this difficulty is obviated, for *good* male souls will be reincarnated as *male*, and only the bad as female. In this case the phrase "failing to attain this" (σφαλεὶς δὲ τούτων 42B6) will have to be interpreted as meaning both failure to achieve moral goodness in this world and failure to obtain those pleasures which might have been its reward in the interim world before reincarnation. On either interpretation the first generation will be male, unless one accepts Cornford's interpretation of the passage, according to which the first generation of human beings is male *and* female, the male being the "better sort" than the female.[81] This, however, is hard to square with the statement in the previous sentence that the Demiurge made the first incarnation one and the same for all, "so that none might suffer disadvantage at his hands." (41E4) Also, to be incarnated as female is mentioned as a *punishment* to the male. (42B3–C1) If this is true, one can only conclude that any female souls of the first generation had committed some pristine sin to warrant their incarnation as female. Some such notion does

---

80 This seems to be implied clearly enough at 40B6–8, and Proclus takes it for granted, *in Ti.* 278D (Diehl III 127/27–8). For the evidence of Albinus see F. M. Cornford (5) 119 n2.

81 F. M. Cornford (5) 145.

underlie the doctrine of Recollection in the *Meno* (81BC) and *Phaedo* (82E5, 81D7–9), but there seems to be no hint of it here. On the contrary, we are much nearer to the Myth of Er in the *Republic*, where one's previous life *on earth* plays an important part in the choice of one's next reincarnation. (609B ff.) The two points of view seem essentially different. In the *Meno* and *Phaedo* the incarnated soul is a fallen soul, enduring the prison-house of this life as a punishment for sin in a previous one.[82] In the *Timaeus*, however, the souls are specifically formed by the Demiurge for the perfection of the universe: they help to complete it as a living creature, image of the Ideal Living Creature. (30D1–31A1) The notions of fall and previous sin appear out of the question, and the whole account of the human soul seems much more optimistic.[83] Not that the difficulties presented to the soul by body and its passions are not stressed. At 42B, for example, we learn that justice for the soul will consist in mastery of such passions; failure to do so will lead to reincarnation first as a woman and then in some subhuman form in keeping with one's character. Though the latter point is stated in the *Phaedo* (81E2 ff.; cf. *R.* 620A2–3), the whole picture of justice and injustice presented here is more like a restatement of the position adopted in *Republic* IX, where passions and the bodily, for all their nuisance value, are seen as having a part to play in true virtue, if they are carefully controlled. (*Ti.* 42A5–B2, *R.* 586D ff.) There is no reason to think that Plato may not have been attracted to one or the other point of view at different times, and varied the myth accordingly.

The more optimistic viewpoint of the *Timaeus* is best seen, I think, at 42B–D, where Plato does not seem to envisage any *escape* from the Wheel of Birth. In the first place, we have seen how the "blessed and congenial" life makes most sense if seen as applying to an interim period between one incarnation and the next. And then at 42CD we are told how changing from one beast to another constitutes "trouble" for the soul. This will never cease till the soul allows its circle of the Same to control by reason the irrational turmoil introduced into itself by earth, air, fire, and water (i.e., the corporeal or material in general).[84] Only then will the soul "return once more to the

---

82 *Phd.* 82E5 (εἰργμοῦ), 81D7–9, *Men.* 81BC.

83 The best study of the "optimism" of the *Timaeus* which I know is the chapter on that dialogue in A.-J. Festugière (1). For a different view see J. Gould 203, who finds "articulate despair" in the dialogue, and H. Cherniss (3) 204–16.

84 In this the account seems to differ from that in the myths of the *Phaedo* and *Phaedrus*. See *Phd.* 81A4 ff., *Phdr.* 249A, 256B. F. M. Cornford (5) 144 n2 takes the passage as implying that the human soul, like World Soul, has one rational (circular) motion, and several irrational (circular) motions, corresponding to the Same and Different as he interprets

form of its first and best condition." (42D1–2) In other words, Plato is apparently not here envisaging an escape from the Wheel of Birth to a world of rewards or punishments. On the contrary, any "escape" from the "trouble" of the Wheel will be a return to the optimum *human* condition, where one's rational activity and control over one's lower self is the microcosmic counterpart of the eternally rational activity of World Soul. This is the raison d'être of the human soul, and it is its own reward, for here the soul knows that it is contributing its uttermost to that perfection of the cosmos desired by the Demiurge. In a word, the soul in human form, acting with rationality and virtue, exemplifies and epitomizes the goodness and rationality of the universe. A viewpoint more directly opposed to that of the *Phaedo*, for example, could hardly be imagined.

The immortal soul is next spoken of as being "sown" in one of the planets till such time as the lesser gods have fashioned its mortal part and body. (42D4 ff.) When these are ready they are joined to the immortal soul, and we are given a long description of the early effects of such a conjunction. (43A6 ff.) It is a reply to the question: if the immortal soul is supposed to be rational, why is it that human beings demonstrate little or no rationality for many years after their birth? Plato replies by insisting upon the different conditions under which World Soul and individual soul labour. Both are rational, and this rationality is certified by the circles of Same and Different which both possess (44D), as well as by that "attunement" to which we were first introduced at 35B4. The difference is that the regular motions of the human soul are exposed from birth to the haphazard and irrational motions of either external bodies or the particular body in which it is housed. These buffetings hamper the Same from performing its task, stopping it from "going on its way and governing,"[85] and the revolution of the Different is dislocated as well. (43D3–4) The harmonic intervals are twisted and deformed, and the soul's revolutions, while continuing to exist, are anything but regular. The result is that the soul has no genuine powers of cognition; judgments of sameness are expressed when they ought to have been those of difference, and vice versa. Everything is seen awry, like the world looked at by a man standing on his head. (43D4 ff.) World Soul, by contrast, can never

---

them. But anything which disturbs the rationality of the infant soul is said to come from *outside* the soul (ἔξωθεν, 44A1, A5), be it the ἐπίρρυτον σῶμα καὶ ἀπόρρυτον (43A5–6) or τὰ τῶν προσπιπτόντων παθήματα (43B7). There is no hint of any intrinsically irrational element in the infant soul itself equivalent to an "irrational" circle of the Different. See G. Vlastos (1) 78 n2, and J. B. Skemp (1) 78.

85 Cf. 81E2 ff., with 43D3 and 36C7 (κράτος).

suffer this fate, for the Demiurge gave it a spherical body which had no part in those six motions (forward-backward; right-left; up-down) which, being rectilinear, will tend to disorganize any circular motion they contact. (43B2–5) The upshot of all this is that there is no difference in kind between World Soul and the rational element in the human soul; the different conditions under which they act account for their varying degrees of success in rational activity. The whole passage is a perceptive piece of child psychology, and at the same time a confirmation of that close parallelism of World Soul and the ratiocinative human soul which Plato is at pains throughout to establish.

The section on the intelligent part of the human soul is concluded with an account of its placing in the body. It is placed in the head, says Timaeus, because this is spherical, and so in some sense a copy of the round-shaped cosmos (44D), and also because the head, like the immortal soul, is seen as "the divinest part of us and lord over all the rest." (44D5–6) If the immortal and divine soul is to contact the material world at all, it will do so at just that point where the material is most like the divine, however remote this likeness may be. As soul is superior to body, so head is said to be superior to the rest of the body, which exists only to serve the head and its divine charge. (44D ff.) The soul, however, must have means of communication with the world, and this is achieved through the senses, two of which – sight and hearing – are stressed here. The mechanism of vision is described in some detail, but we are soon told that this gives us merely an account of the indispensable *conditions* (συναίτια) which the Demiurge uses as aids towards putting into execution, as far as possible, "the Idea of the best." (46C7–8) Mankind may consider these the *sole* causes (αἰτίαι) of everything, acting by heating, cooling, rarefaction, etc. But this is impossible, says Timaeus, for such (material) things cannot possess any plan (λόγος) or intelligence (νοῦς) for any particular end. Intelligence can only be found in soul, which is something invisible. (46D2–6) One must look first for the causality which belongs to the "intelligent nature" – the soul – and only later for that causality "which belongs to things that are moved by others and of necessity sets yet others in motion."[86] In a word, the only *serious* explanation of

---

86 46D8–E2. In taking the "intelligent nature" as soul I follow F. M. Cornford (5) 157 n1. For a notable disagreement see J. B. Skemp (1) 77–8. He takes the αἰτίαι τῆς ἔμφρονος φύσεως as meaning that (psychic) causality which serves a rational end (46D8), by contrast with that (psychic) causality which does not (46E1–2). In this he seems to take the genitives κινουμένων and κινούντων (E1–2) and φύσεως (D8) as objective, while others would take them as possessive. (See R. Hackforth (2) 21 n1.) For Skemp the αἰτία/συναίτιον

anything is a teleological one. Both kinds of causality are summed up at 46E3–6: "We must speak of both kinds of cause, but distinguish causes that work with intelligence to produce what is good and desirable from those which, being destitute of reason, produce their sundry effects at random and without order."

Stress has been laid on the use of the term "causes" (αἰτίαι), rather than "indispensable conditions" (συναίτια), in both sections of the latter half of this sentence, and it has been taken, along with passages at 52E and 30A, as indicating the existence of a non-rational World Soul.[87] However, it seems more likely that this is a case of philosophical jargon ceding to popular usage for a while. In the phrase "those [causes] that are deprived of intelligence" (46E5) we simply have a restatement of the earlier description of accessory causes (συναίτια 46C7, D1) as "incapable of reason or intellect." (46D4) In similar fashion the phrase "the random and haphazard" (τὸ τυχὸν ἄτακτον 46E5) parallels "lack of plan" (λόγον οὐδένα 46D4).[88] That Plato meant no new information is shown, I think, by his immediate return to his more technical terminology (συμμεταίτια 46E6) in the next sentence when concluding his discussion of the indispensable conditions of sight. His previous careful description of what an indispensable condition was (46C7–D4), and his description here of causes which could only be categorized as such indispensable conditions, no doubt led him to think it safe to speak loosely of two "causes," following popular usage. That Plato is liable to do this sort of thing is sufficiently shown, I think, by the technical and non-technical usage of such terms as εἶδος and ἰδέα in different contexts.

The true (i.e., teleological) causes of sight and hearing are discussed at 47A ff. Sight lets us contemplate the intelligent circuits of the heavens, which are akin to those of our own intelligence. We gradually learn to know these heavenly circuits and compute them, and use them as a model for ourselves, in an attempt to reduce to like order the "wandering" circuits in ourselves. (44D, 90CD) Hearing serves a similar purpose. It is given us "for the sake of

distinction is not between a rational ψυχή and an irrational, nonpsychic ἀνάγκη; rather, all συναίτια, mechanical as they are, serve the purposes (ὑπηρετοῦσι 46C7–8) of two equally "psychic" agents, one of which (νοῦς) aims at rational ends, the other of which (ἀνάγκη) does not.

87 J. B. Skemp (1) chapter six. He follows Plutarch in thinking such an irrational World Soul to be the World Soul which instigates the random κινήσεις described as a pre-cosmic chaos, and which is itself reduced to rationality by the Demiurge when the (organized, temporal) cosmos is formed, thus becoming the (rational) World Soul. See Plu. de An. 1016CD and Ti. 30A5–6.

88 For the distinction between αἰτία and συναίτιον see Phd. 99A4 ff.

harmony ... [which is] an ally against the inward discord that has come [γεγονυῖαν] into the revolution of the soul, to bring it into order and consonance with itself." (47D1–6) For by hearing we are introduced to speech, artistic activity (μουσική), and rhythm.[89] The tense of γεγονυῖαν recalls the recent discussion about the effects of birth, where the buffetings caused by the processes of feeding, excreting, etc., throw the rational circuits of the soul out of gear. It is noticeable again how Plato loses no opportunity to stress his favourite image of model and copy, and the close parallelism of World Soul and human intellective soul.

89 47C6–E2. For the importance of μουσική and ῥυθμός in the balanced personality see R. 400C ff.

5

The Timaeus
48A – end

Having completed his account of the products of Intelligent Causation to be found in the universe, Plato now turns to that which owes its being to what he had called "Necessity." Here we find that the familiar dualism of the world of Ideas and the world of sense-objects is significantly modified. A new factor is introduced, and its nature, being extremely hard to grasp, is only elucidated by stages. It is first described as a Receptacle of all Becoming, that "in which" the qualities we associate with earth, air, fire and water "are always coming to be, making their appearance and again vanishing out of it." (49A5–6, 49E7–50A2) The notion that objects of sense perception can be reduced to qualities might well have been inferred from the quasi-existence attributed to them in the *Republic*. (477A ff.) Here it is more openly affirmed. The Receptacle does not "contain" anything at all, it would appear; certainly it would be hard to envisage that which "contained" qualities only. This is no doubt the reason why the Receptacle is further described as though it were a mirror. (49E7–8) If the Ideas are the models, and sensible qualities a reflection of these, the Receptacle will be the mirror in which they are reflected.

At 50AC the simile changes, and the Receptacle is likened to a piece of gold, which can be moulded into a number of shapes, though always remaining gold. The Receptacle, like gold, takes its shape and appearance from the qualities it possesses at any particular instant. (50B1 ff.) It acts like a matrix, which takes on the shape of whatever is impressed on it, without ever becoming itself the stamp or seal. (50C2, 50D3) But the image is inadequate, since any matrix we know of is already qualified to begin with, and will inevitably contribute something of its own character to that which it contains. If the Receptacle is to receive frequently and over its entire extent *all* the likenesses of the Ideas in question – that is, those of earth, air, fire, and water – it must itself be free from any trace of such, or of their compounds. So at 51A7–B1 Timaeus further describes it as "a nature invisible and characterless, all-receiving, partaking in some very puzzling way of the intelligible and very hard to apprehend." It is invisible; that is, not perceived by the senses, since it has no shape of its own, and its function is to be "all-receiving." It "partakes of the intelligible in some puzzling way;" we are also told at 52B2 that it is grasped only "by a sort of bastard reasoning." This may mean that the Receptacle, while being itself neither an Idea nor a sensible, has in some way the characteristics of both. For it is everlasting and indestructible (52A8–B1), like the Ideas, while at the same time playing its part as a vital factor in the becoming of the world. Its similarity with the Ideas will qualify it, perhaps, as a candidate for apprehension by reason, while its part in becoming will characterize such an act of reason as to some extent spurious.

In another attempt to describe the Receptacle Plato calls it Space. (52A8) But this, too, compels us to think of room or place in which "objects" are "contained," while in reality he seems to want to maintain that it is only qualities that are in question in this pre-cosmic state. Attempts to identify Space with Descartes' "extension" fall down before such an obstacle.[1] An even bigger obstacle is introduced at 52E1–5, where Space is said to be in a permanent state of motion, moving the "forces" ($\delta\upsilon\nu\acute{\alpha}\mu\epsilon\iota\varsigma$) within itself, and itself being "swayed and unevenly shaken" by them as well. The use of the word "forces" looks like another attempt to avoid giving the impression of any sort of material objects inside a container, or even of material particles. All that one has are "traces" ($\check{\iota}\chi\nu\eta$)[2] of what will later be earth, air, fire, and water. At this stage words are clearly starting to break down under the strain. Faced with the thesis that soul is anterior to body, Plato took the easy path and described body first. Faced with the thesis that the "powers" or "qualities" of the basic forms of matter were in some way anterior to these forms, he declines to follow the easier path. The first method, while being practical, had hardly produced very satisfactory results; for all his efforts, Plato was still left at the end with the bald (and unexplained) statement that World Soul was anterior to the world's body, and we were little the wiser. This time the description itself is in terms of anteriority. That qualities

---

1 See C. Bäumker xiii, for whom matter is simply "der leere Raum, d.h. die blosse Ausdehnung" (i.e., matter = space = extension), and L. Robin (3) 257, with his references *ad loc.* Robin further agrees with Zeller and Bäumker that $\chi\acute{\omega}\rho\alpha$ is equivalent to Aristotle's $\pi\rho\acute{\omega}\tau\eta$ $\ddot{\upsilon}\lambda\eta$. But on this latter point see J. B. Skemp (4) 206–12.
2 53B2. On Taylor's attempt to introduce "particles" into the Receptacle see F. M. Cornford (5) 199–202.

should precede things qualified is a curious notion to grasp, but it is little odder, I suggest, than that soul should precede body. What is more, it is not Plato's own invention, but has a fairly respectable ancestry in pre-Socratic thought.[3]

The doctrine of the *Phaedrus* and *Laws*, that soul is the principle or origin of all motion, has been adduced in explanation of this whole section.[4] For at 53A2 in particular we read how the Receptacle, itself in motion, moves the four "kinds" which it has received into itself, thus separating the "unlike" kinds farthest from one another, and bringing "like" kinds close together; so that even in this pre-cosmic world there is *some* sort of organization, some region to which each kind gravitates. Before that they are "without plan" (or "without pattern" or "without proportion," ἀλόγως) and "without measure." (53A8) It is the action of the Receptacle itself, apparently, which gives them some sort of primitive organization. It is when they are in this *latter* state – a state qualified as "what one would expect from a thing when divinity is absent from it" (53B3–4) – that the Demiurge intervenes. The point at issue is whether the power of motion here expressly attributed to the Receptacle indicates the presence of soul or not. One can begin by saying that in the *Phaedrus* and *Laws* the argumentation is very generalized and schematic; no reference is made to pre-cosmic states, and understandably so, since the context does not demand them.[5] In addition, the reader coming new to the text can be forgiven for assuming that in these two dialogues the movement referred to is that which he sees operating in the world around him, and that the "bodies" in question are those with which he is acquainted

3 F. M. Cornford (5) 53, 199.
4 J. B. Skemp (1) 77–8 and H. Cherniss (2) 25. Both use the same notions of πρωτουργοί and δευτερουργοί κινήσεις at *Lg.* 897A4–5 to prove rather different things. For Skemp the δευτερουργοί κινήσεις are the συναίτια of *Ti.* and *Phd.*; that is, they are the purely mechanical *sine quibus non* of the (psychic) actions of νοῦς and ἀνάγκη. In this way the *Lg.* are used to bolster a view of ψυχή, rational or irrational, as the *direct* (πρωτουργοί) causes of all κίνησις. For Cherniss (rational) ψυχή is the *indirect* (though ultimate) cause of all κίνησις; this is based on his assumption that the πρωτουργοί and δευτερουργοί κινήσεις of *Lg.* 897A4–5 stand for "primary" and "secondary" causation respectively, and that they find their exact parallel at *Ti.* 46DE in the causes which (a) μετὰ νοῦ καλῶν καὶ ἀγαθῶν δημιουργοί (εἰσιν) and (b) μονωθεῖσαι φρονήσεως τὸ τυχὸν ἄτακτον ἑκάστοτε ἐργάζονται. (b), on his analysis, are the side-effects of (a), and, while serving no directly rational end, find their *fons et origo* in rational ψυχή all the same. The point to notice is that ψυχή is taken to be rational; Cherniss will not concede that there is an irrational World Soul (Skemp) or part of World Soul (Cornford (5) 208), represented by ἀνάγκη (Skemp) or by the Different (Cornford). See also H. Herter (1) 332.
5 See G. Vlastos (1) 78.

in the world of everyday experience; in a word, the movement which is to be found in an (already) organized universe. How far it would apply, if at all, to a pre-cosmos is hard to see. It was argued by Plutarch that it definitely does apply to the pre-cosmos;[6] by most modern scholars, following Proclus, that it applies to that element in the cosmos which talk of a pre-cosmos is meant to symbolize;[7] by Herter that it ought logically to have applied to the pre-cosmos (real or metaphorical) but that it does not appear to do so.[8] Certainly the passage 52E–53C (like 30A3–5) offers no hint of the presence of soul, rational or irrational. While it must be admitted that the *argumentum e silentio* is often a foundation on quicksands, in this particular instance it seems to have more cogency than usual. If the pre-cosmic chaos did possess soul, that soul is part of what the Demiurge "took over"; he did not create it. It will also be an irrational soul, since it does not possess the exclusively rational circular motions with which (rational) World Soul is endowed.[9] These conclusions combined lead one to doubt any thesis that such an irrational soul is to be included within World Soul as outlined in the *Timaeus*, since it is apparently both distinct from it and different in kind from it.[10] If, however, one still accepts the notion of soul as the motive force of the pre-cosmic chaos, though not as "part" of World Soul, one is left with the conclusion that there are or were two distinct psychic forces in the universe, one rational, one irrational. But in the *Politicus* myth Plato rejects the notion of two opposing divinities in the universe (270A1–2), and one could argue that the notion of two opposing "psychic agents" would be open to the same objection. (On the other hand, there is no particular reason why Plato should not have changed his mind; the problem is sufficiently puzzling to give pause to the most confident.) The most basic objection to the theory, however, seems to be as follows: the notion of a soul other than that created by the Demiurge is so crucial in its implications that it seems incredible that Plato should not have given clear indication of its presence. To say that one

6 *de An.* 1016CD.

7 Procl. *in Ti.* 323B (Diehl III 273/31–2); J. Moreau (2) 25 ff., 39 ff.; W. F. R. Hardie 152; A. E. Taylor (3) 115 ff., 352 ff., 390 f.; F. M. Cornford (5) 207.

8 H. Herter (1) 343 n55, 346.

9 See above, 80–1.

10 No doubt this is one reason why Aristotle (*Metaph.* 1072A1) says that Plato's αὐτὸ ἑαυτὸ κινοῦν is only ἐνίοτε ἀρχήν: as he goes on to say (A2), ὕστερον γὰρ καὶ ἅμα τῷ οὐρανῷ ἡ ψυχή, ὡς φησίν. See H. Herter (1) 329 n6, and A. Rivaud (1) 337. T. Gould 29 suggests that the pre-cosmos is described as in chaotic motion to make the most complete contrast with the static permanence of the Ideas, where intelligence is supremely manifest.

can "infer" its presence from the evidence of the *Phaedrus* and *Laws* is not enough. For, if Owen and others are right, both *Phaedrus* and *Laws* may well have been written *after* the *Timaeus*,[11] and if this is the case one would be engaged in the dubious task of interpreting an earlier dialogue in the light of later ones. But even if, for the sake of argument, one granted that the *Phaedrus* pre-dates the *Timaeus*, it is still far from evident that both are talking about the same thing. In the *Phaedrus*, for example, it is natural to assume that the movement in question is that which obtains among bodies in the fairly organised cosmos known to us by sense experience; to infer that it also applies to the pre-cosmic world where duration is not time and the bodily (i.e., organised bodies which we can recognize) is as yet non-existent, is less easy. The *Phaedrus* seems to be saying that soul is the cause of all movement in an organised world, a world measurable by time. In a *non-*organised world *not* measurable by time it is debatable whether the movement in question has anything to do with this.[12] Plato is compelled to give *some* description of the pre-cosmic chaos, and talk of movement in such a world is no more and no less intelligible than phrases like "before this" (πρὸ τούτου 53A8) in the same passage, when time has been admitted to be absent. So Herter seems right in saying that the doctrine of *Phaedrus* and *Laws* is not to be applied to the *Timaeus*, but perhaps unjust in saying that logically it ought to have been. Plato, as far as I can see, is dealing in two instances with two completely different types of motion, the one accepted and universally admitted, and operating in an organised world of temporal succession, the other a reality in every sense different, and almost beyond description. If this analysis is correct, there seems no reason to reproach Plato here with lack of logic, though on points of clarity he may leave a lot to be desired.

---

11 See above, 72–3.

12 F. M. Cornford (5) 205 finds "bodily changes" in the pre-cosmic chaos, and so argues (from the *Phaedrus* and *Laws* x) to the presence in it of an (irrational) soul. In this he seems to stress the wrong alternatives in the two ambiguous terms "change" and "bodily" which Plato is using. It is true that the Demiurge is said to "take over" all that was *visible* (30A3–4), but one need hardly conclude, with Proclus, that the bodily must therefore be present in the pre-cosmic chaos, if only in some minimal way. Plato himself only talks about ἴχνη and δυνάμεις, and there is no reason to think they necessarily obey the same rules as organised σώματα. The word "visible" is probably used loosely for "non-spiritual" or "non-psychic," in much the same way as in the *Phaedo* soul is called ἀόρατος where one might have said "non-material." See *Phd.* 79A6 ff., where reality is divided into τὸ μὲν ὁρατὸν τὸ δὲ ἀιδές, the objects of δόξα and ἐπιστήμη respectively, and 79B12 ff., where soul is said to be more of the class of things ἀιδῆ than ὁρατά.

It is noteworthy that Plato, in conclusion to this section, speaks of the victory of Intelligence over Necessity as taking place "in the beginning" (48A5); the reign of Necessity (which he also calls the Wandering Cause, 48A7) is pre-eminently in the pre-cosmic world. To talk of this world as that of mechanical causality is misleading, because of the modern overtones of the word "mechanism."[13] Plato himself offers the best, if somewhat negative, description at 53B3-4, when he talks of the "traces" of the pre-cosmos as being "in such a condition as one would expect when divinity is absent from it." That is, it is a world of *some* sort of cause and effect, but such cause and effect as is aimless and purposeless. In other words, the stress is not so much upon a mechanistic view of nature, in which particular effect stems from particular cause, but rather upon the fact that the entire complex of such cause-effect relationships is not teleologically orientated. This aimlessly moving world of Necessity is a reality over and against Intelligence until the Demiurge begins the formation of the universe, when we are told that Intelligence "over-ruled" Necessity and "persuaded" her to "guide the greatest part of the things that become towards what is best." (48A2-3) If we take this word "persuaded" seriously, it seems at first sight to add strength to the argument of Plutarch: only if Necessity is an irrational World Soul will it make sense to talk of its being "persuaded" by the Demiurge. However, it seems not implausible to argue that Plato was thinking here of the hypostatized Necessity particularly favoured in Orphic circles, and so to talk of her as being "persuaded" would hardly have surprised his hearers. But even were this true, it would be rash to take the word "persuaded" as serious evidence for something personal (i.e., possessing soul) in the pre-cosmos. The genuinely Orphic Necessity, introduced in her true guise in the Myth or Er, " 'presides' over the destinies of all things and is an unmistakable symbol of intelligent divine purpose and providence,"[14] whereas the Necessity of the *Timaeus*, the very antithesis of this, has closest affinities with Chance ($\tau\dot{v}\chi\eta$, or $\tau\dot{o}\ \tau\upsilon\chi\dot{o}\nu$),[15] and seems in no sense describable as personal. A hint of this is to be found at 47E4-5, where the works of Reason are described as "produced" ($\delta\epsilon\delta\eta\mu\iota\upsilon\rho\gamma\eta\mu\acute{\epsilon}\nu\alpha$), while those of Necessity simply "come about" ($\gamma\iota\gamma\nu\acute{o}\mu\epsilon\nu\alpha$); the change of verb in itself seems to indicate

---

13 E.g., G. Vlastos (1) 77, 82 n3. He qualifies himself, however, by adding (82 n3), "We must never forget that Plato thinks of mechanism as disorderly, except in so far as it is teleologically ordered." For less guarded statements see L. Robin (3) 241, and M. Guéroult 41.

14 A. E. Taylor (3) 299.

15 F. M. Cornford (5) 163 ff.; E. R. Dodds (1) 21.

the difference between the personal and the non-personal, the one endowed with soul, the other devoid of it.

So far Plato seems to be saying that in the pre-cosmos a blind and aimless non-psychic causality, called Necessity or the Wandering Cause, held sway. To start off the organised cosmos, this Necessity had to be tamed, "persuaded" by Intelligence to guide the majority of things that become towards what is best. This victory took place, as we have seen, "in the beginning." (48A5) So from the beginning of time, that is, from the beginning of the organised cosmos, causes orientated towards a rational end have dominated causes of an aimless and non-teleological nature. But they have never fully controlled them. How this is so Plato tries to demonstrate when he discusses the formation of the human body. Whatever excellent intentions the Demiurge may have, he is faced with the "inevitable" ($\dot{\epsilon}\xi$ $\dot{\alpha}\nu\dot{\alpha}\gamma\kappa\eta s$)[16] truth that dense bone and a large quantity of flesh are incompatible with keenly responsive sensation. For Plato the point and purpose of the various parts of the human body are clear enough, and the operation of Intelligence in their making beyond dispute. At the same time there are certain built-in and "inevitable" ($\dot{\epsilon}\xi$ $\dot{\alpha}\nu\dot{\alpha}\gamma\kappa\eta s$) disadvantages, and this is an indication of the extent to which Necessity has not been mastered. On this interpretation, Necessity, when operating in the world we know, will be the equivalent of the "indispensable conditions" ($\sigma\upsilon\nu\alpha\dot{\iota}\tau\iota\alpha$) of the *Phaedo*, which answer "how" questions rather than "why" questions, and tell us of operation rather than of ends. It is harder, however, to talk of $\sigma\upsilon\nu\alpha\dot{\iota}\tau\iota\alpha$ in the pre-cosmos, since the rational causes to which they might have served as prerequisite conditions were not in operation. $\sigma\upsilon\nu\alpha\dot{\iota}\tau\iota\alpha$, while not in themselves orientated towards a rational end, do at least follow certain generalized "laws" in the cosmos known to sense experience; their "causality," even if for Plato it indicates no self-evident rationality as such, is at least reliable and organised, and upon this organisation we depend in our everyday existence.[17] The "causality" operating in the pre-cosmic chaos, however, is *neither* rational *nor* organised, but is something as blind and haphazard as the non-temporal, non-bodily world in which it operates. Hence the use of the phrase Wandering Cause; in both senses – non-rational and non-organised – the causality is aimless and wandering. The most one will get from this chaos is

16 75A7. This is another indication that the Demiurge is not omnipotent.

17 To this degree we *can* talk of "mechanism" in the *organised* cosmos, where Intelligence can utilize the different cause-effect conjunctions for its own ends. It is upon the general *reliability* of such cause-effect relationships that we base our everyday lives. See G. Morrow (1) 153.

a certain conjunction of like with like and disjunction of what is dissimilar. (53A2–7) The συναίτια of the *Phaedo* can be classed as those "mechanical" conjunctions of cause and effect which we take for granted as *conditiones sine quibus non* of purposive activity. (98c ff.) At *Timaeus* 74B ff., however, Plato is considering a similar group of mechanical conjunctions from the point of view of their power to *hinder* purposive action. If Socrates is sitting on the bed, it is because the joints and muscles of his body are flexed in such a way as to allow him to do so: such is the συναίτιον seen as an indispensable condition. The same Socrates, if he has too large a lunch, will be in no condition to carry on philosophical conversation afterwards, however firm his intentions. This is really the obverse of συναίτιον – a condition to be *avoided* if ... In a word, different chains of cause and effect can be looked upon as now helping (*Phaedo*), now hindering (*Timaeus*), purposive activity. If this is true, the phrase Wandering Cause seems to cover two different manifestations of non-rational causality, in the pre-cosmos and formed cosmos respectively. In the former, the emphasis is upon its non-rationality and haphazardness, though it is granted some minimal order (attributed to Chance at 69B5–6); in the latter, while it produces its effects in an organised and predictable way, so much so that one can draw up "laws" about relations of cause to effect and can rely upon them for practical living, its activities are still totally different in kind from those initiated by Intelligence, since their causality can never be teleological as such, but merely mechanical. The fact that the Wandering Cause is considerably more organised (and hence predictable) in the finished cosmos indicates no basic change in its nature, but simply a change in the surroundings in which it operates. So the distinction between cause and indispensable condition drawn up in the *Phaedo* still stands, though the cosmological question has considerably widened its scope and introduced a number of nuances and shifts of emphasis: the province of Intelligence is that of αἰτίαι ("final causation originating in a responsible agent"), while that of Necessity accounts for συναίτια ("causation which, whether acting haphazardly or in an organised and predictable manner, is seen to be different in kind from final causation, and which can on occasion cause insuperable obstacles to plans formulated by Intelligence"). *Both* are indispensable elements in any purposive action, and what had been seen as an ethical truth in the *Phaedo* is now stressed as a cosmological one in the *Timaeus*.

Some have seen in the Demiurge a mere doublet of World Soul,[18] or,

18 W. Theiler (1) 72; A.-J. Festugière II 104; P. Frutiger 206; G. S. Claghorn 119, among others.

as in Cornford's case, a doublet of the rational element in World Soul.[19] Similarities there are: both are non-material, rational, and divine. But the differences are more significant. World Soul is spoken of as fashioned by the Demiurge, while he himself is eternal and uncreated. (34B3 ff.) In language popularized by the Schoolmen, the Demiurge is non-contingent, and World Soul, like the world's body, is contingent. That alone is enough to indicate a radical difference in kind between the two; the eternal existence of the Demiurge as distinct from the sempiternal existence of World Soul is another aspect of the same truth. Again, World Soul may be rational, but it is not a person, as the Demiurge is represented as being. It is hard to see why many are so prepared to explain away this personal Demiurge.[20] From the beginning thinking men have seen the operations of nature as inexplicable without recourse to the notion of a ruling Intelligence;[21] the analogy between the works of human intelligence and those of a higher Intelligence was not looked upon as naive. On the same grounds it seems not unreasonable to conclude that such a higher Intelligence will be personal, as we ourselves are personal. Whether the analogies are fair or coherent is another matter; that they are often used is a matter of everyday observation. Need Plato be an exception? Unless he is to be accused of complete cynicism, the constant references to θεός, ὁ θεός, οἱ θεοί, τὸ θεῖον, etc., in the dialogues must surely be taken as indicating that he believed in divine agency in the universe. In the *Phaedrus* we read that it is proximity to the Ideas that makes the gods to be divine, that is, eternal (249C5–6); in the *Timaeus* the Demiurge contemplates the Ideas, is eternal, and is described in a way we would expect a

---

19 F. M. Cornford (5) 361.

20 For Cornford he is a symbol of rationality ((5) 176); for Theiler and Festugière a doublet of World Soul; for Th.-H. Martin (II 60–1), P. Frutiger (206–7), J.-M. Lagrange (*Revue thomiste* n.s.t. IX, 39 (1926) 196–9), U. von Wilamowitz-Moellendorff (597–8), and others he is the Idea of Good. Taylor, however, takes the Demiurge as "a really self-existing being, the 'best ψυχή,' God" ((3) 71). (For controversy on this see *Mind* XLVII (1938) 180–99, 321–30.)

21 According to Plato, νοῦς plays an important part in the cosmology of Anaxagoras, but the accounts he gives of it are considerably different. At *Phd.* 97B ff. νοῦς is seen merely as a *deus ex machina*, dragged in to help out when no physical explanation is available; at *Cra.* 413C5–7, however, νοῦς is described as though it were immanent in the world, and its description bears remarkable comparison with that of the Demiurge: αὐτοκράτορα γὰρ αὐτὸν ὄντα καὶ οὐδενὶ μεμειγμένον πάντα φησὶν αὐτὸν κοσμεῖν τὰ πράγματα διὰ πάντων ἰόντα. See also 400a: καὶ τὴν τῶν ἄλλων ἀπάντων φύσιν οὐ πιστεύεις Ἀναξαγόρα νοῦν καὶ ψυχὴν εἶναι τὴν διακοσμοῦσαν καὶ ἔχουσαν; In both these passages, particularly the latter, it looks as though the contingency of the world (by contrast with the non-contingency of the divinity) is being stressed. See also DK[12] B 25–6 (Xenophanes), where divinity operates through mind.

personal god to be.[22] In either case Plato sees at least two factors which must be taken into account in any attempt to describe the sum total of reality – the eternal exemplary Ideas and personal divinity of some sort, coeternal with them and distinct from them. To try to show that both are simply aspects, personal and impersonal, of the same reality, seems to me to misinterpret him here, and to confuse his Demiurge with the Prime Mover of Aristotle.[23] There is no indication that the Ideas are the thoughts of the Demiurge; they are existents distinct from and over and against him.[24] They are, in fact, still the same static realities which we first met in the *Phaedo*, but now their inadequacy to account for the changing, living world of everyday experience has apparently been recognized, and the mediating factors of personal soul and intelligence have been introduced. It may be inferred, no doubt, that the personal Intelligence, or Demiurge, is himself a soul,[25] but it is his nature as a person, I suggest, which is to be stressed. In another dialogue, the *Phaedrus*, it is stated that soul in all its forms has as its job the care of the soulless in all its forms (246B6), but this seems a long way from that over-all providence which Plato here sees in the universe, where a personal planner is at pains to persuade Necessity to guide the greater part of things that become towards what is best. That soul should care for body seems to fall into place as part of this more general personal providence. The delegation

22 30C2 ff., 29E1 ff., esp. ἀγαθὸς ... οὐδέποτε ἐγγίγνεται φθόνος. Cf. *Phd.* 63B7, *R.* 379BC, *Phdr.* 247A7. For unequivocal references in other dialogues to the Demiurge and his activities see *R.* 507C6–7, 530A6, *Sph.* 265CE, *Plt.* 273B.

23 A. Diès (1) II 553–4. For the phrase most likely to support his case see 29E3 (παραπλήσια ἑαυτῷ).

24 30C2 ff. For a history of the notion that the Ideas are the thoughts of God, see A. Rich 123–33.

25 See the whole powerful passage 29E1 ff., esp. 29E1–3. For emphasis on the Demiurge as a ψυχή see A. E. Taylor (3) 71. One must also consider the three passages *Ti.* 30B3, *Phlb.* 30C9–11 and *Sph.* 249A4–8, where it is said that νοῦς cannot come into being without ψυχή. For those, like Cornford and Cherniss, for whom the Demiurge is simply a symbol of νοῦς, the problem does not arise; a symbol as such can hardly be said to have a ψυχή (though what it symbolizes may). In recent times, however, R. Hackforth (following Zeller and, more remotely, Proclus) has argued that for Plato νοῦς is a more "ultimate" principle than World Soul ((1) 4–9). Perhaps the clearest quotation in his favour is *Phlb.* 28D, where a distinction is drawn between τὰ ξύμπαντα καὶ τόδε τὸ καλούμενον ὅλον and νοῦς καὶ φρόνησίς τις θαυμαστὴ συντάττουσα. All three passages mentioned above are explained as references to the universe, i.e., to "that which *has* νοῦς, not that which *is* νοῦς." This distinction between immanent and transcendent Reason he draws from Procl. *in Ti.* 122E (Diehl I 402/15 ff.), and he concludes that "if God is to impart his goodness to the world ... if Reason is to penetrate this world of κίνησις and γένεσις, it must be through ψυχή, the principle of movement." For a criticism of this position see H. Cherniss (5) app. II and J. B. Skemp (1) 114.

of responsibility to the lesser gods of his fashioning is another indication that ultimate control belongs to the Demiurge; he can delegate power precisely because it is his to dispense. Finally, while one could readily admit that the Demiurge and World Soul both display intelligence and that both are souls, a distinction must be drawn between the intelligence and soul with which each is endowed. In the case of the Demiurge his soul and intelligence are uncreated and thus one assumes non-contingent, while World Soul, along with its intelligence, is created (by the Demiurge) and thus contingent. The distinction is one of kind rather than degree, and seems evidence enough that Demiurge and World Soul are not to be confused.

As I have mentioned in another context, there seems to be no conclusive evidence in this dialogue for the specialized doctrine of soul as a source of motion expounded in the *Phaedrus* and *Laws*.[26] This, of course, would in itself be no proof that Plato had not already formulated such a doctrine. However, the account of soul, cosmic or personal, in the *Timaeus* seems readily explicable in terms of what we already know about the nature and operations of soul from the *Phaedo* and *Republic*. It may be conceded that all talk of soul as a life-principle is an embryonic assertion that it is a source of motion, since life and motion go hand in hand.[27] But at this stage the specialized doctrine does not seem to have been formulated in any clear terms, and the notion of soul as a life-principle and a cognitive principle accounts adequately for its different descriptions. In any case, as was mentioned above, the theory of soul as a source of motion would make little sense if applied to the pre-cosmos. In the *Phaedrus* and *Laws all* motion is caused by soul, as will be seen, but this seems to mean the motion known to us in the formed cosmos. However, even if we confine the discussion to the problem of the *formed* cosmos in the *Timaeus*, we still seem to be talking about two different types of motion. For in the *Timaeus* World Soul, being purely rational, accounts only for the rational, circular motions of the heavenly bodies; other motions are non-rational and initiated by Necessity. By non-rational, however, Plato seems to mean "in themselves not ordered by Intelligence to some end": they can obey, particularly in the formed cosmos, quite intelligible mechanical laws of their own. The neat difference between the two points of view is that in the *Timaeus* such non-teleological motions are in no way to be attributed to soul, while in the *Phaedrus* and *Laws* they are. If one retains the traditional order of the three dialogues

26 See above, 95ff.
27 On this see H. Cherniss (2) 24 n26 and H. Cherniss (5) 428–9.

Phaedrus–Timaeus–Laws, one must conclude, it seems, that there is a certain incoherence on this point in Plato's mind. One solution, as we saw, was to combine the doctrine of the *Phaedrus* and *Laws* that soul is a source of motion with talk of "soul in accompaniment with folly" and "soul helped by wisdom" from *Laws* x and use both to explain what is "implicit" in the *Timaeus*.[28] The main objections to this were the evidence of the text of the *Timaeus* itself and the more general objection of the dangers of interpreting an earlier dialogue in the light of a later one. A second and more radical solution has been to reinstate the *Timaeus* in that place among the dialogues where it purports to be, that is, immediately after the *Republic*.[29] This is, of course, a highly controversial move, but I have tentatively adopted it, on the grounds that it seems to make for greater coherence in the development of Plato's views on cosmic soul. The latter point, it must be admitted, is a suasion rather than an argument; Plato has no self-evident claim to total coherence, on matters of psychology or anything else. But one can at least extend to him the benefit of the doubt, when totally conclusive evidence one way or the other is hard to come by. And this (at any rate as far as cosmic psychology is concerned) is what Owen's redating succeeds in doing.

The *Timaeus* has much to say about the individual soul, and the tripartition outlined in *Republic* IV is still Plato's basic position. As we have already noticed, the intelligent part of the soul, immortal and divine, is the direct creation of the Demiurge, while the two lower parts are made by the lesser gods of his creation, on the same Empedoclean principle that necessitated the introduction of soul as an intermediary between the Ideas and the sensible world.[30] We noticed, too, how the separate and special mixture of the immortal individual soul in the celestial mixing-bowl indicates its essential disjunction from World Soul, in spite of their close affinities in most respects.[31] But we omitted for the moment discussion of the assertion in the same passage that its mixture is "less pure" than that which went to form World Soul, in fact only "second or third in degree of purity." (41D6–7) What this means is not explained, but it is hard to believe the neo-Platonist interpretation expounded by Robin, whereby individual souls are like fallen angels, debased copies of the archetypal World Soul.[32] This would appear to stem from a conflation of two myths, those of the *Phaedrus* and *Timaeus*,

28 See above, 95ff.
29 See above, 72f., and *Ti.* 17A1–2.
30 41C6–D7, 42D7–EI and 42E6 ff.; 41C2–3, 81A3–4 (the Empedoclean principle).
31 See above, 85.
32 L. Robin (1) 203 (and in his *Phèdre*, cxxiii), followed by M. Thévenaz 41 ff.

which are in fact saying two very different things. In the *Phaedrus* the souls have fallen from an original state of happiness, in which they contemplated the Ideas, though there is hope that after experience of the Wheel of Birth they will regain that state.[33] In the *Timaeus* the human soul is deliberately created to *perfect the universe*; its final end, apparently, is not necessarily to escape from the Wheel of Birth, but to fulfil its function in the divine plan by living a life of rational human existence. (41B7–C2) Robin's answer, while trying to do justice to both myths, in fact does justice to neither. The passage is probably better explained by taking "less pure" to mean "less perfectly rational." For the outstanding characteristic of World Soul is its rationality, whereas the immortal human soul is forever distracted by the importunities of the two "lower" parts and bodily sensation generally. At 44B4–C4 a return to rationality is equated with a return to purity, and the use of language of the Mysteries is reminiscent of the *Phaedo*, where true purification was seen as the life of intelligence.[34]

The damage which the body and its sensations can do to the infant noetic soul is outlined at 42E–44D, but we have to wait till 69A ff. for a more detailed description of those "lower" parts of soul which we first saw at *Republic* 435C ff., and which are here described as a "necessary" adjunct to soul when it is united with body, and mortal, by contrast with intelligence (69C8–D1, 69D5–6, 69C8). The adverse results of bodily influence on intelligence are worth quoting in full:

> ... first pleasure, the strongest lure of evil; next, pains that take flight from good; temerity moreover and fear, a pair of unwise counsellors; passion hard to entreat, and hope too easily led astray. These [the lesser gods] combined with irrational sense and desire that shrinks from no venture, and so of necessity compounded the mortal element. (69C8–D6)

This passage should be compared with 42A5–B2, where a similar position is expressed, and where such difficulties encountered by the immortal soul are likewise seen as a "necessary" concomitant of conjunction with a body. If the Demiurge chooses to make the soul incarnate, there are certain conditions which Necessity will demand, and she will not be persuaded out of them. The somewhat pessimistic view of the body and its sensations and inclinations is strongly reminiscent of the *Phaedo*, but the following passage (69D–72D)

---

33 *Phdr.* 247C ff., 248E ff. In asserting that the fall is "original" I follow the accepted tradition, as outlined by D. D. McGibbon 56–63. For a different view see R. S. Bluck (1), (2).

34 *Phd.* 67C2–3, 69A6 ff., esp. 69B8–C3.

makes it clear that it is still the tripartite psychology of *Republic* IV which is in question. Not only does the individual soul possess three "parts," but, if we are to take the text at its face value, each part is to be situated in a special section of the body, the immortal reason in the head, the spirited part between the neck and diaphragm, and the appetitive part in the belly. (69D6 ff.) There seems to be no particular reason why we should not take this seriously. Whatever the views of Empedocles and Aristotle, one hardly needs to be a skilled physician to guess that there is some close connection between damage to the brain and impairment of reasoning ability, and a little personal observation would suffice to conclude that passionate feelings seem to stem disturbingly frequently from the pit of the stomach. It is possible to explain away the three "parts" of the *Republic* account as the inevitable materialistic language which one is compelled to use when describing the non-material, since only the material world can supply us with our instruments of description. Here, however, Plato seems to be suggesting that there are a number of practical reasons, based upon observation, for saying that not only has the soul three distinctive "parts" but that these can be shown from observation to be localized in different parts of the body.

The similarities of language used in describing the three "parts" of soul in both the *Republic* and *Timaeus* will be mentioned elsewhere.[35] One notable difference, however, is the categorical ascription of mortality to the two "lower" parts of soul in the *Timaeus*. This means, in effect, that the parallelism of World Soul and individual soul is a remarkably close one, since the genuine, immortal individual soul is seen as pure intelligence.[36] The individual soul, on this view, embodies characteristics of soul outlined in both *Phaedo* and *Republic*; its essence, pride, and supreme virtue is intellectual (*Phaedo*), though its make-up during human embodiment can be expressed as tripartite (*Republic*).

That in the *Timaeus* soul is meant to be seen as definitely localized within the body is corroborated by the views of sense perception which are put forward. For example, when talking of vision, Plato answers the question in terms of passing-on of "movements" (κινήσεις). These "movements" pass *through the body to the soul* (45D1–3). The same point emerges at 73B ff. and 75A, where the marrow is seen as the life-substance which is the root or anchor of the soul; once more we have soul as an "internal" substance. At

---

35 See below, 120ff.

36 69CD, 41CD. Some have seen a reference to this view at *R.* 611B ff., but I have argued against this. See above, 50–4.

75A3 he talks of "paucity of soul within marrow," and at 74E1 bones are called "ensouled" (ἔμψυχα). Some marrow has more soul and intelligence than other marrow, it appears: for example, that marrow which is the brain, as distinct from that in the bones of the arms or legs. All this, if taken seriously, must slightly qualify the neat localization of all soul in the brain, chest, and belly. That the soul is seen as localized in the body is still true, but now the marrow to be found throughout the body's bone structure is regarded as its sheet-anchor. From the description in terms of tripartition one might have thought that the legs, say, were devoid of soul, but the new description does away with this possible misunderstanding. It also brings us back to an idea found in several passages of the *Phaedo*: if the soul is supposed to be a life-principle, it can be expected to occupy the same spatial volume as all the parts of the body as are reckoned to be "alive,"[37] and this will be much more than head, chest, and belly.

Before leaving the *Timaeus* one must examine a notable passage at 86B ff., which treats of those diseases of the soul which are caused by things physical, whether this be a defective bodily constitution or faulty education. Taylor has interpreted the passage as determinism pure and simple, and, thinking that this has nothing to do with serious Platonic doctrine, has written it off as the viewpoint of Timaeus only.[38] It must be conceded that much of the language in the passage does read like determinism. In particular, two passages, 86DE and 87AB, taken out of context, seem to be blunt enough assertions that no man who is bad is willingly so, and that his badness is to be attributed either to a "defective bodily constitution" or to "faulty education." (86E1–2) Blame for such badness, in other words, must be attributed to parents rather than children, to educators rather than the educated. The more guarded phrase "generally speaking" (καὶ σχεδὸν δὴ πάντα 86D5–6) hardly counteracts the apparent determinism of such passages. One attempt to absolve Plato from the charge has been to lay stress upon the general context. He has spent some time discussing bodily diseases, and it is natural enough to pass from this to those diseases of the soul which stem from physical causes. The context is a biological one, and Plato's views on the *moral* implications of the problem can only be known, thinks Cornford, by reference to other dialogues.[39] This may be true, but Plato still seems to

---

37 *Phd.* 67C7–8, 84C4 ff., 80E2 ff.
38 A. E. Taylor (3) 613–14. In thinking that the passage involves determinism, he is preceded by Th.-H. Martin II 365 ff., and followed by W. F. R. Hardie 134.
39 F. M. Cornford (5) 347.

allow his biological interests to lead him into some very compromising statements. "It is not stated," writes Cornford, "that *all* mental disorders are *solely* due to bodily states."[40] It is indeed not stated; but who could be blamed for seeing it as assumed in a sentence like the following?

> No-one is willingly bad; the bad man becomes so because of some faulty habit of body and unenlightened upbringing, and these are unwelcome afflictions that come to any man against his will. (86D7–E3)

Or

> ... besides all this, when men of so bad a composition dwell in cities with evil forms of government, where no less evil discourse is held both in public and private, and where, moreover, no course of study that might counteract this poison is pursued from youth upward, that is how all of us who are bad become so, through two causes that are altogether against the will. (87A7–B4)

The "two causes" would appear to be the "faulty habit of body" and "unenlightened upbringing" mentioned above.

On examination, however, the two statements are much less trenchant than they at first appear. Essentially, they say that no man chooses his bodily make-up or upbringing, and that if either of these is imperfect, the sufferer will have tendencies towards badness which more fortunate men will be spared. They stress, too, that if any man *is* found to be bad, those two causes will be found to be at the root of the matter. All of this makes much sense, provided one does not take the terms "bad" and "badness" as referring to overt and calculated moral viciousness. "Evil" (κακία) means any declination, great or small, from that standard of bodily beauty and spiritual goodness which makes the good man good. It can be used to describe a state just as much as an attitude, or, in more scholastic terminology, material evil as well as formal.[41] In no sense does it necessarily and universally involve the imputation of open-eyed and willing viciousness. It is of κακία in this broad sense that Plato seems to be speaking here. This is shown, I think, by the statement

---

40 *Ibid.* 346.

41 One might say, for example, that the violent, unmerited and unexpected death of an innocent person is an evil. This could be brought about by an assassin's bullet or by a motorcar accident. The act of the assassin would be formally κακόν in this case; that of the man who caused the car accident (presuming he was not to blame) materially κακόν, in the sense that the state of affairs unwittingly resulting from his action was one of κακία.

at 87B7–8 that "a man must use his utmost endeavour by means of education, pursuits and study to escape from badness and lay hold upon its contrary." If a man is *completely* mastered by physical causes, such a statement is meaningless. What it presumably indicates is that the (material) κακία to which a man is unwittingly subject by defects in birth and education can be remedied, partly if not totally, by his own moral effort. If he becomes (formally) κακός – that is, overtly and willingly vicious – this will mean that he has made no effort to master such defects. On this interpretation, they are the two "unwilled causes" (ἀκουσιώτατα 87B4) underlying all κακία, material or formal, and in neither case do they imply the doctrine of determinism. In the case of material κακία the problem of moral choice does not arise, so that the question of determinism is not involved; in the case of formal κακία freedom of moral choice is affirmed, so that determinism is rejected out of court. In a word, the two statements quoted above, the one (87A7–B4) apparently affirming determinism, the other (87B7–8) freedom of moral choice and effort, make sense if they are seen as complementary rather than contradictory. Taylor, underplaying the second statement, and taking κακία solely in its material sense, seems to misunderstand the whole passage. If determinism is to be found anywhere in Plato's writings, it is much more easily seen in *Republic* x, where Plato is discussing the choice of lives. In spite of the much-quoted "responsibility lies with the chooser – God is guiltless" (617E4–5), the fact remains that in the choice of lives the souls are deprived of a small but crucial amount of information, so that any supposedly "free choice" turns out to be a blind leap into the dark.[42]

Perhaps the most convincing argument against determinism in this passage is to be found in the assumptions underlying the pages that follow (87B–90D). Here a series of remedies are offered to correct the undue influence of soul on body and body on soul, with a view to instituting a right balance and proportion between them. This, together with a stress on "care of the soul," particularly of the divine and immortal element, adds nothing to what we do not already know from the *Apology*, *Phaedo*, and *Republic*, but it implicitly assumes that it is *in man's power* to apply the necessary remedies to himself and effect some sort of readjustment. How this is to be done is reiterated at 90C7–D7; the eternal intelligent motions of the heavens are to be the model whereby man corrects the wandering motions in himself and reduces them to order.

42 See Th.-H. Martin II 366–7. For Aristotle's discussion of the problem of free choice and moral responsibility see *E.N.* III, 5, 1113B2 ff.

From all this one must conclude, I think, that at certain points Plato's conviction of the important part played by non-psychic factors in the (at any rate early) formation of character has led him to overstate his case somewhat misleadingly. However, an examination of the context, together with statements of a very different nature in the same general passage, must lead us to the conclusion that for the Plato of the *Timaeus* man is, in spite of all obstacles, ultimately a free moral agent.

6

The Phaedrus

One of the most condensed and abstruse arguments for soul's immortality is to be found at *Phaedrus* 245C–246A. It is not even clear whether "soul" here is meant to refer to soul collectively[1] or to individual souls;[2] perhaps it refers to neither, but simply to "soul in all its forms."[3] Certainly the very general form of the argument which follows would lead one to the latter conclusion, though "soul" must still be understood as "rational soul" or perhaps rational *part* of soul if one is to abide by the limiting characteristics outlined at 245C2–4: "Our first step ... is to discuss the nature of soul, *divine and human*, its experiences and its activities." If this description has any meaning at all, "all soul" (πᾶσα ψυχή) can hardly be World Soul (as Posidonius took it to be), nor can it include the souls of flies (as Harpocration seemed to think). It must be the noetic soul, as Hermias saw,[4] the θεῖόν τι common to gods and men. (*Ti.* 41C7, 69C3)

Until recent times it was thought that this argument for soul's immortality stemmed from an assertion that it was "eternally moving" (ἀεικίνητος 245C5). The discovery of an Oxyrhynchus papyrus, however, which read "self-moving" (αὐτοκίνητος)[5] convinced Robin that this reading made much more sense of the argument, and he duly incorporated it into the Budé text. The move has found a number of champions, notably Vollgraff, Bignone, Pasquali, Müller, Ross, and, more recently, Ackrill.[6] It is certainly true that with this reading one can reduce a complicated argument to the neater lines of an Aristotelian first-figure syllogism, but this in itself ought perhaps to be grounds for suspicion. As Diano has pointed out,

---

1 A.-J. Festugière (2) 21, like Posidonius, takes the argument to refer to World Soul.
2 See P. Frutiger 130–4.
3 See J. B. Skemp (1) 3 n1, and A.-J. Festugière (5) 496.
4 Herm. *in Phdr. ad loc.*
5 *Ox. Pap.* 1017.
6 For the references and comment (both on these and L. Robin) see C. Diano 189–92. For J. L. Ackrill's comment see *Mind* LXII (1953) 278.

αὐτοκίνητος is a word found nowhere else in Plato;[7] the first incontrovertible instance of its usage is at Aristotle, *Phys.* VIII, 5, 258A2. Plato tends rather to use phrases like "that which moves itself" (τὸ αὐτὸ ἑαυτὸ κινοῦν). It is at least possible that αὐτοκίνητος is the gloss of some commentator interested in reducing Plato's looser arguments to a more terse and respectable logical format. Be this as it may, the original reading, "eternally moving," ought, I think, to be defended. The diffuse series of arguments will then run as follows:

Introduction (= the thesis in a nutshell): All soul is immortal, because it is eternally moving, and anything eternally moving is immortal (245c5).

The meaning and implications of the phrase "eternally moving" are then brought out in two arguments:

1

i To call anything eternally moving is to call it also self-moving (c5–9).

ii For (a) if it were *not* self-moving there would be a cessation of life and movement (c6–7); (b) if it *is* self-moving there will never be any cessation from moving, since what is self-moving never "breaks contact" (c8) with itself (c7–8).

iii Unstated conclusion: self-moving and eternally moving are one and the same, and presumably immortal. Cf. the phrase "never ceases from movement" (c7–8).

2

i The eternally moving is also ungenerated, for it is a principle (or source – ἀρχή) of movement (D1). (D3: explanation of why the notion of a "principle" should imply this.)

ii *Qua* principle it is also indestructible (D3–4). (D4–6: explanation of why the notion of a principle should also imply this.)

A third argument links together the results of 1 and 2, corroborating

---

7 C. Diano 190 ff. For a number of recent comments on the subject see H. Cherniss (1) 137. The most telling criticism of Robin's arguments for αὐτοκίνητος is that of Diano, who is followed by W. J. Verdenius (3) 276. Robin had made the first lines into an Aristotelian syllogism, taking δέ at c6 as adversative, and δή at c7 as consecutive (see his translation *ad loc.*, Budé edition). Diano points out how δέ can equally well be progressive, and δή emphatic, thereby changing the character of the argument considerably. At c5 the words τὸ γὰρ ἀεικίνητον ἀθάνατον are really a definition, as Diano sees (191). As such, it is the argument's conclusion, rather than its starting point. It gains by being placed startlingly at the beginning, in the manner of a textbook definition; what follows is an *explicatio* and *probatio* of what it contained succinctly.

them with a number of *per impossibile* considerations for good measure. It runs as follows:

3

i The upshot (οὕτω, D6) is that "principle of movement" and "that which moves itself" are one and the same (since both are identical with what is eternally moving) (D6–7).

ii This means that (a) it is imperishable; (b) it never came into existence (D7–8). Cf. D1–4 above.

iii Consider the odd results if it did *not* entail this! (D8–E2).

These results are now applied to the notion of soul itself, and the final argument runs as follows:

4

i It has already been seen that the self-moving is immortal (i.e., by implication at the end of the argument 1 above) (E2–3).

ii This will mean that soul, too, is immortal (E3–4). For (a) body, whose movement is from without, is soulless (E4–5); (b) soul has as its nature movement which is from within (E5–6).

iii One must therefore conclude that the self-moving and soul are one and the same, and also (from D1–4 and D7–8) that soul will be thereby necessarily "ungenerated and immortal" (E6–246A2).

While Hackforth defends the original reading "eternally moving," he can hardly be right in assuming that it is an ἔνδοξον,[8] serving as a major premiss, since the greater part of the argument is spent in elucidating it and outlining its implications. In Ackrill's words, "[the major premiss] can perfectly well express a proposition required for the main proof though itself needing to be established by a subordinate proof."[9] This "subordinate proof," he thinks, follows three stages: (1) the eternally moving is self-moving (C5–8); (2) the self-moving is immortal (C5–E2); (3) soul is self-moving, and thereby immortal (E5 ff.). In my own interpretation of the passage, the first two arguments are apodeictic, each one sufficient of itself to establish the immortality of the self-moving and the eternally moving. But Plato chooses to stress their cumulative rather than their individual plausibility (argument 3 (i–ii)), adding what Hermias calls an argument *per impossibile* for good measure (3 (iii)).[10] The results are then applied to soul.

The argument, as many have pointed out, has much in common with

8 R. Hackforth (7) 65.
9 J. L. Ackrill 278.
10 Herm. *in Phdr. ad loc.*

the final argument for immortality in the *Phaedo*.[11] But whereas that of the *Phaedo* sprang from a metaphysic of Plato's own creation, the *Phaedrus* argument is of a more empirical cast, and has its roots deep in the pre-Socratic tradition.[12] It also goes a long way towards solving difficulties presented by the psychology of the *Phaedo*. There the soul had been assimilated to the Ideas, and the hiatus between the unmoving Intelligible World and that of sensible things subject to motion had meant an inadequate explanation of the soul as we experience it in the world of movement. In the *Phaedo* he had found himself compelled to run in the face of all philosophic tradition, as part of his defence of his newborn metaphysic; the elementary attribute of all living things, movement, was quietly shelved, and the static, homogeneous, unchanging entity whose immortality he was left to prove was recognizable only to himself. Now soul is seen as the source of motion or activity, and a more balanced appreciation of its true nature is possible. This is not to argue, of course, that the notion of movement appears like a bolt from the blue in the *Phaedrus*. It was there by implication in both *Phaedo* and *Republic* when soul was seen as a principle of life, or bound up with the

11 On the affinities between the two arguments see R. Hackforth (7) 68, who refers to Skemp, Frutiger, and Bury. Add H. Cherniss (5) 435–8, and H. Cherniss (3) 208. These scholars take it for granted that Plato got his idea of psychic movement from the observation of living things. A.-J. Festugière, however, has argued that he took it from " la découverte purement grecque de la régularité des mouvements célestes" ((2) 21). In this he is followed by V. Martin 116, who also allows some cogency to the accepted explanation (117). If this guess is correct, the line of reasoning seems to be as follows: (a) the κυκλοφορία of the heavenly bodies manifests the operation of νοῦς (*Ti. passim*); (b) νοῦς cannot arise apart from ψυχή (*Ti.* 30B3, *Sph.* 249A4–8); (c) ψυχή, with νοῦς, is consequently responsible for the movement of heavenly bodies; (d) by analogy, the same reasoning will be applicable to all λογικαὶ ψυχαί, celestial or otherwise. The strength of this argument, if it genuinely represents Plato's thought, is that it accounts for the motive power of the λογικὴ ψυχή (see above, 111n4) – that is, the only ψυχή apparently in question in the *Phaedrus* argument. In the *Laws*, however, the ψυχή which is the source of movement is something much wider than the λογικὴ ψυχή; it is in itself neutral, only taking on ethical colour when seen as νοῦν προσλαβοῦσα or ἀνοίᾳ συγγενομένη. This seems to lay stress on the nature of soul as a vital principle, the *sine qua non* of all activity, good or bad (see V. Martin 120), rather than on ψυχή as essentially characterized by νοῦς and ἐπιμέλεια (the *Phaedrus* position), and here Festugière's explanation hardly fits.

12 For a study of the doctrine of κίνησις in Empedocles, Alcmaeon, and the Pythagoreans see J. B. Skemp (1). (His views on Alcmaeon are criticized by A.-J. Festugière (5) 59–65.) H. C. Baldry 27–34 has shown, I think convincingly, that Anaximander saw the world as a living creature, in many ways like a foetus. For an account of soul as source of motion in Alcmaeon, Anaxagoras, and Diogenes of Apollonia see A. Diès (1) II 536. For Aristotle's views on ψυχή as κινητικόν among pre-Socratic thinkers see *de An.* 403B24 ff. and 405A4 ff., and compare *Ph.* VIII, 9, 264B17–266A5.

Idea of Life;[13] unfortunately this notion was allowed to stand on equal terms with others barely compatible with it – such as that of soul's likeness to the static Ideas[14] – and one is led to conclude that Plato was not then fully aware of the implications of what he was asserting.

Following the claim that soul in all its forms is eternally moving we read: "All soul has the care of all that is inanimate, and traverses the whole universe, though in ever changing forms." (246B6–7) The denotation of the phrase "all soul" presents the same difficulties as before. It would be convenient if Robin were right in taking it as a reference to individual human souls,[15] for the whole of the passage which follows seems to describe them in their individual state.[16] Others, like Frutiger, have assumed that ψυχὴ πᾶσα is used here in a collective sense: the sum total of soul "cares for" the sum total of what is inanimate.[17] But it is not clear that Plato is particularly interested in distinguishing between collective and distributive senses of soul: as at 245C his argument seems to be completely generic, and ψυχὴ πᾶσα, here as there, is probably best translated by "soul in all its forms."[18] If this translation is correct, Plato is saying that it is a characteristic of any soul that it should care for that which is deprived of soul. This is new. In the *Phaedo* the soul was seen as the dominant partner in the body-soul complex, and any co-operation with the body was a grudging one. The sharpness of this dichotomy was lessened in the *Republic*, where a legitimate place for the cruder desires was found in the soul, and one could say that the state of justice in the soul, in which all the parts performed their own tasks and operated in harmony, was one in which the intellective element exercised care and forethought for the good of the whole complex. But such care is confined to the human soul and is inward-looking, whereas in the *Phaedrus*

13 H. Cherniss (5) 435–8, seems to me to go beyond the evidence when, in seeing a connection between the final proof of the *Phaedo* and that in the *Phaedrus*, he identifies the "idea of life" with the "idea of motion." Compare H. Cherniss (3) 208, where he makes the point that the notion of self-motion is to be found as early as *Chrm.* 168E. To have a notion, however, is not necessarily to see its implications. If, at the time when he wrote the *Phaedo,* Plato really did see all the implications of the notion of the "idea of life," it is hard to think that he would have painted the very static portrait of ψυχή that he did. For a different viewpoint see G. Müller 79–80.

14 E.g., *Phd.* 80B1 ff.

15 Budé translation: "c'est toujours une âme qui a charge ..." etc.

16 246C1 ff. This view is evidence of Robin's own perplexity, for elsewhere he takes πᾶσα ψυχή and πᾶν τὸ ἄψυχον to refer to World Soul and the world's body respectively (L. Robin (2) 139).

17 P. Frutiger 130–4.

18 J. B. Skemp (1) 3 n1, and A.-J. Festugière (5) 496–7. See also O. Regenbogen 204.

it is said to be a characteristic of any soul, and is clearly outward-looking and universal in its scope. Again, however, "soul" is apparently to be taken as noetic soul only; if plants and animals are included, they are not brought into the discussion.

This stress on soul's "care" has much in common with a statement at 246E5-6 that Zeus "orders and cares for all things." This may seem un-startling, but the corollary which Plato draws is significant. If soul shares in the gods' divinity, it also shares in their care. (246B6-7) The idea is of im-portance for a right understanding of the *Timaeus*,[19] and will be developed in the *Laws*.[20] At *Cratylus* 400A the notion is attributed to Anaxagoras, where psychic intelligence is said to conserve and uphold and order all things.

The view of soul as a principle of movement is a milestone in Plato's thought, and the direct ancestor of the cosmological argument *ex motu* first outlined by Aristotle[21] and followed by Aquinas.[22] It is perhaps better be-cause it contains within itself some notion of providential care guarding and sustaining the sum of things.[23] But if these ideas are new, it does not mean that earlier ones are necessarily discarded. In the *Phaedo*, for example, soul was an incarcerated intellect; here it is seen as bound like an oyster in its shell (*Phd.* 82E3, *Phdr.* 250C6). In the *Phaedo* the stress on the soul's intellective aspect resulted in its equation with intellect; in the *Phaedrus* the same thing happens on a number of occasions.[24] The distinction between philosophic and popular virtue still holds good (249A, 256E), as does the doctrine of Recollection (249E), and there is the same fluctuation between bipartition and tripartition of soul. At 237DE, for example, we read how there are *two* ruling principles in us, the one an "innate desire for pleasure," the other an "acquired judgment that aims at what is best." These two elements, it is said, are "sometimes in accord, sometimes at variance." (237D9-E1) In an earlier dialogue, the *Republic*, Plato had used the term "judgment" (δόξα) in a highly technical manner (477D ff.), but here he seems to have reverted

19 See especially 34C4-5 for the relationship between World Soul and the world's body.
20 See below, 148ff.
21 Arist. *Ph.* 241B34-242A54 (in the alternative text 241B24 ff.). See also *Metaph.* 1071B3-22.
22 Aquinas (*Summa Theologiae*, pars Ia, quaest. 2, art. 3) talks of the "prima et manifestior via quae sumitur ex parte motus." Cf. *Summa contra Gentiles,* cap. 13, and *Commentarium in Physicorum Aristotelis,* liber VII, cap. I, lectio I. (For further references see E. Krebs, *Thomas von Aquin, Texte zum Gottesbeweis*, Bonn 1921). For the same theme in literature see the opening lines of the *Paradiso:* "La gloria di Colui che tutto move/per l'universo penetra e risplende/in una parte più e meno altrove."
23 J. B. Skemp (1) 6; R. Hackforth (7) 68.
24 *Phd.* 67C3, *Phdr.* 239A5, 239C1, 249C5.

to its more popular use: what he seems to mean is that state of care and reflection which tends to curb and check the inborn urge towards immediate pleasure. This popular bipartition of soul we saw in the *Gorgias* and early *Republic*; that it *is* popular is perhaps hinted at by the way Socrates puts the whole doctrine into the mouth of "a wily lover" (αἱμύλος τις ἐραστής).[25] This view, while accepting that soul does enjoy certain pleasures, still takes a somewhat disparaging view of them, and it is noteworthy that in the rest of the dialogue, even where Plato seems to be talking in terms of a tripartite soul, the black horse which represents the lowest part is seen as uncompromisingly evil. (253E ff.) One is reminded of the many-headed beast of *Republic* 588C ff., except that in that dialogue the desiderative element has a clear and legitimate part to play in the right functioning of soul. Though in the *Phaedrus* myth lip service is paid to tripartition, and the good horse is called a "lover of honour" and "a friend of genuine δόξα" (253D6–7), in practice it cannot be distinguished from the charioteer. Their desires and aims are invariably one and the same; there is no hint of that rebellion which so characterizes *Republic* VIII. This is true both on earth, where they act in unison to subdue lust (254A ff.), and in the "region beyond the heavens" where they are united in their struggle for a view of the eternal Ideas. (247B) Not that desires are uncontrollable; the good man can subdue them. (247B, 254E) But their tendency is invariably to mischief. This fact, coupled with the fundamental lack of distinction between good horse and charioteer, leads one to suspect that Plato's basic allegiance still lies with that popular bipartition of soul (first seen in the *Gorgias*) into a set of desires and a principle of reflection.

In conclusion, it may perhaps be significant that the "likening to God" advocated for the philosopher in other dialogues is somewhat different from that put forward in the *Phaedrus*. In earlier dialogues the model for imitation is the world of Ideas (*Phd.* 79D, *R.* 500BC); in the *Phaedrus*, where the life and movement of soul have been stressed, it is that particular *deity* who was one's companion in the region beyond the heavens. (252E7 ff.) This suggests that the model for imitation is now living and moving, as well as divine (i.e., it is something other than the Ideas), and at first sight this appears to be an attempted solution of the "two worlds" problem presented by the *Phaedo* and *Republic*. The gods themselves, however, are unequivocally said to receive their own divinity from their "nearness to" the Ideas (249C6), and so the problem in fact remains the same, though now it has been promoted

25 237B3–4. See R. Hackforth (7) *ad loc.*

to a celestial level. More significantly, if souls (and *a fortiori* gods) are themselves genuinely principles of movement and eternally moving, and individual gods, as we saw above, are now seen as objects of imitation, the efficient and exemplary causality of the Ideas (as seen, for example, in the *Republic*) begins to look a little superfluous. This had been hinted at even in the *Republic* itself, where efficient causality in the universe had been attributed to the Demiurge as well as to the Idea of Good (see above, 66–7). The *Timaeus* had clarified the matter a little by clearly differentiating between the exemplary causality of the Ideas and the efficient causality of the Demiurge and lesser gods. Now, finally, in the *Phaedrus*, the doctrine of psychic autokinesis suggests a reason *why* a god (or gods) is better seen as the efficient cause of the sum of things. For gods are souls, and souls are (by definition) efficient causes. But this does not mean that Plato is now ready to concede that the Ideas are superfluous. Their role may now only be an "exemplary" one, but this role is re-affirmed in the most striking possible way by the statement that "nearness" to the Ideas makes the gods themselves to be divine. Not even the *Timaeus* presents us with so uncompromising an affirmation.

7

Tripartition, Immortality, and the After-Life

Apart from the *Republic*, the two other dialogues in which tripartition of soul seems to be propounded in detail are the *Timaeus* and *Phaedrus*. In both cases there are one or two notable changes of emphasis, though over and above these is a note of hesitancy common to all three dialogues. The evidence for this in the *Republic* has already been discussed. In the *Phaedrus* the same doubts are expressed. To discover the nature of soul (οἷόν ἐστι) "would be a long tale to tell, and most assuredly a god alone could tell it." (246A4–5) So, as in the case of the Idea of Good, we can only approach it by way of simile (ᾧ ἔοικεν 246A5), in keeping with our human limitations. In the *Timaeus*, too, when the whole account of the human soul's tripartition is completed, we are told that it can only be affirmed with assurance if some god were found to agree with it (72D6); all that has been offered is a "likely" account, in keeping with the general contention that the dialogue is a "likely story." (72D7, 29D2)

With this by way of introduction, we can now turn to the two accounts. At *Timaeus* 41C ff. and 44D–45B we have an outline of the creation of the immortal part of the soul by the Demiurge, and its installation in the head by the lesser deities. This part is called immortal and divine, and is described as the ruling element in all who pay service to the gods and justice. It is said to be a direct creation of the Demiurge, and on this score participates in (his) life and is equal to the gods.[1] The created gods are assigned the task of adding to it a part which is called mortal (41D1), and the process is described at 69C ff. The distinction between mortal and immortal parts of the soul is

---

1 41C2–3. Such is the clear implication, if not the direct statement.

in keeping with the dualism of the whole dialogue, where Plato is at pains to distinguish the world of becoming, transience, and mortality from the world of Ideas, authentic existence, and immortality. Even if the soul is further subdivided (69E ff.), the basic stress is upon its *bi*partition into mortal and immortal parts, the foundation of its amphibian status and cause of its ability to bridge the hiatus between the two worlds of authentic existence and quasi-existence. At 69C7-8 the "other part" of the soul is introduced as "another form ... the mortal one," and later we read twice of the "mortal type" of the soul, and how "the divine" must not be defiled by the presence of "the mortal." (69D5-E4) At this stage the "mortal form" is further subdivided into a part which is "better" and a part which is "worse" (69E5), and it is easy to recognize the "spirited" and "desiderative" soul of *Republic* IV. The two are described in some detail, and then the passage concludes, as it had begun, in terms of *bi*partition into mortal and immortal. (72D4 ff.) This is not to argue, of course, that Plato no longer believes in tripartition; but in a dialogue where matters political are no longer to the fore the notion receives less prominence. In the *Republic* all three parts of soul were involved in his account of the cardinal virtues; here the two lower parts are important more for their common attribute of mortality than for any differences which divide them, and the characteristics attributed to them jointly as "the mortal form" at 69D reads like the lists of those bodily and equally mortal experiences which so trouble the immortal soul in the *Phaedo*. (65C6-9, 83B6-7) In all such passages where the mortal element in human activity is being stressed the characteristics of "spirited" and "desiderative" soul are invariably treated as forming a single group. When they *are* clearly separated, as in the *Republic*, I have suggested that this is to suit a particular political analogy.[2] There is some evidence for this even in the *Timaeus* (although the subject-matter could hardly be further removed from politics). For the entire battery of metaphors used in describing the activities of the "spirited" soul is drawn from the state and the military machine, and indicates a view of soul as a state-in-miniature much the same as that outlined in the *Republic*. One need only point to the military flavour of words like "injunction" (ἐπίταγμα), "hand down word" (παραγγέλλειν), the "guard-room" (ἡ δορυφορικὴ οἴκησις), or other such clear verbal echoes of the *Republic* as "plan" (βουλεύεσθαι), "contentious" (φιλόνικον), and "citadel" (ἀκρόπολις).[3] So that even though the context is now a biological one, the source of Plato's

2 See above, 42ff.
3 70A6, 70B4, 70B2, 70E6-7, 70A3.

inspiration is evidently to be found elsewhere. If this analysis is correct, the "spirited element" of soul in the *Timaeus* rests on the same flimsy foundations as its counterpart in the *Republic*, and this would be one good reason for the note of hesitancy in both dialogues.

It could be argued that the stark and unequivocal assignment of each of the three parts of soul to specific parts of the body shows the depth of Plato's commitment to the idea of tripartition, particularly in a context where biology, not politics, is involved. To this one could reply that any apparent commitment to the idea is the result of that political analogy which is still very much before Plato's mind, as is evidenced by the metaphors (quoted above) which are used in describing the "spirited" soul. As for the so-called tripartition itself, it is in fact more fairly described as *bi*partition with a further subdivision within it. The neck is seen as an isthmus which divides the two important parts of soul, "immortal form" and "mortal form,"[4] and any further subdivisions cannot be said to compare with this initial one. But it is nonetheless true that a number of remarkable similarities with the *Republic* in thought and language still remain. At 70E4, for example, the "desiderative" soul is called a "wild beast" (see *R.* 588C9), and the idea that it is necessary (ἀναγκαῖον 70E5) to feed it, while keeping it chained down, if the human race is to exist at all, finds its parallel in the notion of "necessary" desires at *Republic* 558D5. The evaluative language which characterizes the intellective soul as "the best" (70B8) and the other two parts as "better" and "worse" (relatively to each other) is also a noticeable feature of the *Republic*.[5] So, too, the φιλο-compounds of the *Republic*, which suggested that "parts" might be better translated as "drives,"[6] have their counterpart in a description of the "spirited" soul as "contentious" (70A3). All this suggests that Plato is still heavily influenced by ideas expressed in the *Republic*, and might perhaps be used to bolster the argument of Owen (which I have provisionally accepted) that the *Timaeus* and *Critias* are the crowning works of the *Republic* group. But this would be a study in its own right. For the

---

4 69A1. On the basic dualism of the individual psychology of the *Timaeus*, see R. Hackforth (7) 41, and S. Pétrement 59. Although at *de An.* 432A25–26 Aristotle seems to distinguish Plato's tripartite psychology from the bipartite one advocated by many, and at *E.N.* 1102A26 characterizes bipartition as an opinion current in the ἐξωτερικοὶ λόγοι, the author of the *Magna Moralia* (1, 1182A23) says that Plato divided soul into τὸ λόγον ἔχον and τὸ ἄλογον. As Hicks sees (note on *de An.* 432A26), the two points of view are not irreconcilable: any tripartition of soul is ultimately based upon a bipartition into θνητόν and ἀθάνατον εἶδος, as outlined at *Ti.* 67C ff. See also D. A. Rees (1) 113–14.

5 431A4–5, 432A7–8, 603A4–5, 604D5, 606A7.

6 See above, 56.

moment the point of interest is that the "tripartition" of soul in the *Timaeus*
is somewhat different in detail and emphasis from that found in the *Republic*,
while still apparently drawing its basic inspiration from a common political
analogue. *Plus ça change, plus c'est la même chose.*

The passage in the *Phaedrus*, in which the soul is compared to a charioteer
driving two winged horses, is usually taken as an allegorical reference to the
tripartite soul.[7] The passage follows immediately upon a proof of soul's
immortality, in which "soul" has been taken in its most general sense,
perhaps best translated, as we saw above (111) by "soul in all its forms."
The same seems to be true in the myth of the winged chariot. The souls both
of gods and "the other beings" (246B1) are described according to the
allegory as multipartite. In the case of the souls of the gods, the charioteer
and his team (whatever their number – it is not specified) are classed as
"good and of good stock,"[8] so that the question of strife does not arise.
Their souls exhibit that state of "ordered harmony" of reason and impulse
already seen at *Gorgias* 503E ff., and there is no need to assume any division
among the steeds equivalent to "spirited" and "desiderative" soul. The souls
of "the rest" are then passed over, and Plato confines himself to human souls.
These have a charioteer and two steeds, one "noble and good and of good
stock" (246B2–3), the other just the opposite, making the task of the charioteer a difficult one. The ascent to the "place beyond the heavens" is described
as easy for the chariots of the gods, for they are "well-balanced and easily
guided," but more difficult for the rest "by reason of the heaviness of the
steed of wickedness, which pulls down his driver with his weight, unless
that driver has schooled him well." (247B2–3) If this is a reference to tripartition, it is slightly different from that outlined in the *Republic*. There,
apart from a single disclaimer (440B4 ff.), it is consistently maintained that
the "spirited" soul can and does occasionally ally with the "desiderative"
soul against reason; here the "noble" horse is invariably docile, and it is the
activities of the evil horse alone which account for the charioteer's inadequate
vision of True Being. (248A) Again, in the *Timaeus* we are explicitly told
that only the intellective soul is immortal; the other parts are "built on"
to us as necessary adjuncts during our mortal lives. (69C5–8). Here in the
Phaedrus the (immortal) souls of both gods and men are seen as multipartite,
and so presumably subject, even if in the gods' case only potentially, to the
cravings of impulse. The apparent discrepancies have led some to believe

7 E.g., R. Hackforth (7) 72.
8 246A8. See R. Hackforth (7) 69 n3.

that the chariot allegory has nothing to do with tripartition; instead the two
horses are thought to represent what in the *Timaeus* is called Necessity or the
Different, while the charioteer represents Intelligence or the Same. This
minority opinion was sponsored by the neo-Platonist commentator Hermias,
and supported in the last century by Hermann and in this by Robin.[9] By the
time he came to edit the *Phaedrus*, however, Robin had changed his mind,
and was prepared to accept the view that the *Phaedrus* teaches tripartition
of all souls, divine and human.[10] This is perhaps to go to the opposite
extreme, since the compelling evidence there supports multipartition of
divine souls, but not specifically tripartition.[11] Presuming, however, that both
types of soul *are* tripartite, he is at a loss to explain the function of "spirited"
soul in them, and would be glad to see it explained away.[12] This particular
difficulty is self-made, but perhaps he is right in saying that, after the more
cautious talk in *Republic* x, Plato has at this point firmly committed himself
to tripartition when describing the human soul in its "true state," that is,
when it is unencumbered by the body.[13] But again we must remind ourselves
about Plato's hesitancy concerning the whole idea of tripartition,[14] and interpretation becomes doubly hard when we are dealing with myth.

It could be argued that, if we confine ourselves to the view of soul as
it appears in the myths, there is every reason to think that Plato intended
a place for the ordinary desires in the discarnate soul. In the eschatological
myths of the *Phaedo, Gorgias,* and *Republic,* for example, souls before and
after incarnation are anything but disembodied intellects, and this passage
of the *Phaedrus* is as much a myth as they are. When Plato the devotee of
Orphism is talking he tends to assume a basic bipartition of soul into reason
and impulse both in this world and the next. The difficulties begin when he
tries to square this religious belief with his more elaborate philosophical

9 For the references see L. Robin (2) 162–3.

10 L. Robin (4) cxx. Robin opts for tripartition, but a comment on the same page, outlining the difficulties which this involves, makes it clear that he would still prefer bipartition.

11 See R. Hackforth (7) 69 n3.

12 L. Robin (4) cxx.

13 *Ibid.* W. K. C. Guthrie (1) 9 ff., while agreeing that the chariot-image refers to the
tripartite soul, tries to explain away discrepancies by suggesting that the difference between
mortal and immortal soul is not that of being in or out of a body but that of being in or
out of the Wheel of Birth. Only the latter group (i.e., the gods and the fully purified) are
immortal. If this is true, however, one is still left to explain the presence in the celestial
world of the two εἴδη of soul which only appear to make sense when seen as part and
parcel of the human condition here and now. The *Timaeus* faces the difficulty squarely.

14 See above, 42, 119.

views on tripartition. In *Republic* x he is in doubt as to whether soul in its true, discarnate nature is single and homogeneous or manifold, though he makes it clear that he himself tends towards the view that it is single and homogeneous, if only in the minimal sense that its tripartition is subsumed into a higher unity.[15] In the *Timaeus* the true soul is still thought of as single and homogeneous, but now only because the soul which survives is nothing but intellective soul anyway. (69C5–6, 41C6–D1) Whether Plato felt later that this was perhaps oversimplifying the position we do not know, but at all events in the *Phaedrus* he opts equally firmly, it seems, for the tripartition of the discarnate soul. (246A7 ff.)

Apart from a vague and unclear sentence at *Sophist* 228B2–3, which may just perhaps be a reference (albeit a rather chaotic one) to the earlier doctrine of tripartition, there seems to be no other clear allusion to the doctrine in any dialogue later than the *Phaedrus*. This is true, I take it, even of the *Laws*, though this latter point has recently been disputed by T. J. Saunders.[16] As Saunders himself admits, however, "there is no *explicit* evidence for a tri-partite soul in the *Laws*,"[17] and many of the passages which he cites hardly corroborate his own thesis. At 935A4–6, for example, we read of a man who "brutalizes" an element in his soul, and at 731B3–4 we are told how every man should be both "spirited" and "mild." But if this has any counterpart at all, it is in the two characteristics "mild" ($\pi\rho\hat{a}ov$) and "great-hearted" ($\mu\epsilon\gamma\alpha\lambda\acute{o}\theta\upsilon\mu\omega\nu$) of *Republic* 375C, where Plato is still content with a *bi*partite division of soul. "Spirit" ($\theta\upsilon\mu\acute{o}s$) is indeed mentioned in the *Laws* on a number of occasions, but Plato seems unsure of its status, now placing it among the ordinary desires, along with "pleasure," "grief," and "envy" (863E7–8), now *distinguishing* it (along with "fear") from "pleasure" and "desires." (864B3–6) The same hesitation is found at 863B3, where he leaves open the question whether spirit is to be called an *experience* ($\pi\acute{a}\theta os$) or a *part* ($\mu\acute{e}\rho os$) of soul. The phrase "the spirit of covetousness in a soul" ($\phi\iota\lambda\acute{o}\tau\iota\mu\omega\nu$ $\psi\upsilon\chi\hat{\eta}s$ $\acute{e}\xi\iota s$ 870C5) has something in common with the description of the spirited soul as "covetous of honour" ($\phi\iota\lambda\acute{o}\tau\iota\mu\omega\nu$) at *Republic* 581B2, but more often than not the term "spirit" is used pejoratively, and included in long lists of harmful desires very reminiscent of the *Phaedo*.[18] Though spirit can perhaps on one occasion be seen as legitimate and justifiable anger

---

15 See above, 50 ff.
16 T. J. Saunders 37–55. See also V. Martin 125.
17 *Ibid.* 37 (my italics).
18 E.g., *Lg.* 649D5 ff., 943A3–6.

(865D7), it is more often than not treated as an evil influence in the soul, as Saunders admits.[19] All this sounds like the familiar bipartition into reason and impulse, and is perhaps corroborated by the talk of "self-conquest" and "self-defeat" at 645B2–3 (cf. R. 432A7–9). That this bipartition (here and in the early part of the *Republic*) is such that it can easily be expanded into tripartition is no doubt true, as Saunders suggests,[20] but there seems no clear evidence that in the *Laws* Plato is particularly interested in doing this. The strength of the case for tripartition in the *Republic* lay in stressing the noble rather than the less noble senses of spirit,[21] whereas in the *Laws* just the opposite seems to be the case. Even in the *Republic* and *Timaeus* he was prepared to express doubts about the whole notion of tripartition, though it proved a convenient enough concept in the context;[22] in the *Laws*, where the political context would have given most plausibility to the idea's resuscitation, tripartition is never mentioned at all, and doubts about its continued acceptance are thereby if anything intensified.

II IMMORTALITY
(AND DOUBTS CONCERNING IT)

Did Plato himself ever doubt the soul's immortality? Certainly in the *Apology* Socrates makes no claim to be able to prove it,[1] and it has been argued that in the *Symposium* we have evidence of a "temporary scepticism" about soul's immortality, and along with it a (temporary) dropping of the Theory of Ideas and Recollection.[2] The only immortality envisaged, apparently, is the vicarious immortality involved in the begetting of virtue (ἀρετή) in the soul of another (212A2 ff.). The *argumentum e silentio*, however, is notoriously slippery. With equal plausibility it can be used to show either tacit affirmation or tacit denial, and in most cases context and general purpose of the dialogue will prove safer guides to interpretation. In this case we have a dialogue dealing with the nature of love, and one can expect at the outset that topics such as soul's immortality will only be of peripheral interest. It does seem, however, to affirm (at least in embryo) the Theory of Ideas

19 T. J. Saunders 40 n1.
20 *Ibid.* 37.
21 See above, 44 f.
22 See above, 42, 119.
1 See R. Hackforth (3) 43.
2 *Ibid.* 45, 46.

(*pace* Hackforth),[3] and in the *Phaedo* this particular doctrine is seen to go hand in hand with that of soul's immortality. (77C1–5) In particular the final argument of the *Phaedo* depends for its cogency on the Theory of Ideas; Socrates expects a belief in this from his hearers before he can hope to make his conclusions plausible.[4] So that if, as Hackforth believed, the *Symposium* is to be dated very soon after the *Phaedo*,[5] it is odd that the one theory should be (implicitly) maintained and the other apparently abandoned, without some attempt at explanation. However, it is notoriously difficult to decide which dialogue precedes the other, and it is at least possible that the *Symposium* is the earlier,[6] and that in it Plato is feeling his way towards the doctrine of Ideas without yet seeing its valuable implications for the doctrine of immortality.[7] Certainly the dialogue does not seem to be interested in the soul as potentially separable from the body and the human condition; if anything the stress is upon those human qualities which make it mortal rather than that divine aspect which, in the *Phaedo*, makes it immortal. In other words, as Luce has argued, the soul which is envisaged is the embodied soul rather than the discarnate soul, the ἀνθρωπίνη φύσις rather than the θεία ψυχή.[8] Vicarious immortality is attributed to the ἀνθρωπίνη φύσις, or to the soul as we know it in its embodied condition only. Such a view is in keeping with the *Phaedo*, where the soul *qua* divine is immortal, and with the *Timaeus*, where this divine, immortal aspect is classified as reason. If the vocabulary of the *Republic* and *Timaeus* had been used, Plato might have said that the two lower parts of soul, while being themselves expendable and mortal, could still achieve a vicarious immortality.[9]

In the *Laws* we find both ideas combined in a single dialogue; at 713E8 on the one hand we seem to have a reference to the genuinely immortal soul or part of soul in the phrase "the immortal element within us," with another unequivocal reference at 959B3–4 to the "immortal soul" (ἀθάνατον ψυχήν), while at 721B7–8, on the other hand, the "human race" (ἀνθρώπινον

---

3 *Ibid.* 46.

4 See J. V. Luce 137.

5 R. Hackforth (3) 43.

6 For the view that it precedes the *Republic* see L. Robin (2) 81, and R. K. Gaye 18. More recently, J. S. Morrison has argued that it precedes the entire group *Meno, Gorgias, Phaedo,* and *Republic*, on the grounds that it does not betray their Pythagorean influence (44). For a reply to this see K. J. Dover 16–20.

7 See J. S. Morrison *ibid.*

8 J. V. Luce 139.

9 *Ibid.*

γένος) is said to "share in immortality," and at 773E5 ff. Plato talks of the vicarious immortality which a man achieves by leaving children behind him. The distinction, as in the *Symposium*, is again apparently between the discarnate soul and the embodied soul. It also seems to underlie two important passages in the Seventh Letter, where we read that "no *man* is *naturally* [πέφυκεν] immortal" (334E3–4); nevertheless we must accept on the authority of divine revelation that "the *soul*" (ψυχήν) is immortal.[10] Much the same idea is to be found at *Phaedrus* 276E–277A, where truth is seen as something undying (ἀθάνατον), passed on as it is from one generation to the next; as Hackforth notes, the word ἀθάνατον "might equally well have been applied to the possessor of truth (τὸν ἔχοντα), for he does attain immortality so far as an ἄνθρωπος can ..."[11]

A final compelling passage is *Timaeus* 90C1–3, where we are told that by "having immortal thoughts" a man "must altogether be immortal, insofar as human nature is capable of sharing in immortality." The soul as such (in this dialogue synonymous with intellect) is immortal; the ἀνθρωπίνη φύσις, a conglomerate of soul as such, body, and the two "mortal forms" of soul consequent upon incarnation, can at best achieve only a vicarious immortality.

This evidence shows, I think, that Plato at no time doubted the immortality of soul as such, and is sufficient to absolve the *Symposium* from the charge of temporary scepticism. But it would perhaps be unwise to assert that there is positive evidence in the *Symposium for* the doctrine of immortality.[12] The phrase "what is immortal" (ἀθάνατον) at 208B4 is much more naturally taken as referring to the gods than to the (intellective) soul,[13] particularly if the *Symposium* precedes the *Phaedo* and *Republic*. In the same way the phrase "discerning beauty itself through what makes it visible" (212A3) is inconclusive; to a reader knowing the *Phaedo* and/or *Republic* it may naturally be taken as referring to the immortal (intellective) soul, but this would not necessarily follow if the *Symposium* is the earliest of the three dialogues in question. The most one could then say is that Plato is feeling his way towards a philosophic statement of the immortality of soul, and in the process saying nothing incompatible with what is to come later.

10 335A4. See J. V. Luce 140–1.
11 R. Hackforth (7) 160 n3.
12 See J. V. Luce 140.
13 G. M. A. Grube (2) 149.

III THE AFTER-LIFE

One of the most noticeable facts about the *Phaedo* and *Republic* was the fluidity of the notion of soul, even within the compass of a single dialogue. This is less evident when we turn to the great eschatological myths of the *Gorgias*, *Phaedo*, *Republic*, and *Phaedrus*. In all cases the soul is seen as a counter-person, or "double" of the person known to us in the present life. It qualifies for the name of "person" because it is shown as a free and responsible moral agent, capable of good and evil even in its discarnate state.[1] Its joys and punishments, and the places in which they are supposed to take place, are simply glorified versions of earthly counterparts.[2] This view may seem far removed from that of soul as an incarcerated intellect, but it has much in common with another view, frequently noticed already, of man's true self as his soul. Pindar[3] and Empedocles[4] seem to have envisaged the soul in the same way, and a passage of *Odyssey* XI (568 ff.) entertains the same idea. Whether all those accounts draw upon a common body of doctrine roughly labelled "Orphism" elicits contradictory answers from scholars, and can be passed over as not germane to our purpose.[5] The important point is that Plato is prepared to accept in his myths a view of soul which stems from religious circles and is often apparently at variance with much of what he has to say about soul in the body of the dialogues. The whole burden of the *Republic*, for example, is that true justice and happiness coincide; the one state of soul entails the other. Such a conclusion is an answer to that more general problem that has troubled men from the beginning; why do the unjust prosper, and why is the just man so often rewarded with slights and oppression? It is a remarkable conclusion indeed, and one, it might have been thought, sufficient to render superfluous that other, more popular, view expounded in the myths, where a *future life* is seen as the abode of divine and inexorable justice. In the one case virtue is its own reward; in the other it seems to be the preliminary to a reward bestowed elsewhere. However, Plato does not seem to have viewed the two conclusions as incompatible. On the contrary, they seem to be actually conflated in the theory of "philosophic" virtue, which is found at its starkest in the

---

1 J. A. Stewart 85 ff.
2 *Phd.* 107C–114C, *Grg.* 523A–526D, *R.* 614B–621D.
3 P. O. II, 53 ff.
4 DK[12] B 142 (Empedocles).
5 For the two extremes see I. M. Linforth and W. K. C. Guthrie (2).

Phaedo and *Republic*.[6] The "virtue" (ἀρετή) practised by the greater part of mankind, it appears, has about as much value on the ethical plane as "true opinion" on the epistemological. In the *Phaedo* the results of this are bad enough; the man who has practised merely "popular" virtue (i.e., virtue without intelligence) in this life can expect to become an animal or insect in his next incarnation, according to his character. (82B2–7) In the *Republic* the results are much worse, for the crucial choice of a future life, and all its attendant risks, are seen to depend upon one's type of virtue in this. The man who has practised only "popular" virtue may perhaps enjoy *one* period of bliss, but Plato makes it clear that, when it comes to choosing another life, he stands even less chance than the sinner of making a wise choice, and indeed runs the severe risk of choosing a life which will involve lengthy, if not eternal, punishment after it. (619B2 ff.) The only guarantee of eventual happiness is to practise "philosophic" virtue.[7] In this way the philosophic life of the *Republic*, besides ensuring complete contentment of mind in this life, is also seen as an indispensable preliminary to eternal bliss in the next. This may seem like a reconciliation of the two views of justice mentioned above, but, as Dodds has stressed, the implication that all except the philosopher are on the verge of becoming subhuman is still hard to reconcile with the view that every human soul possesses an essentially rational part or aspect.[8]

Involved in the problem of the soul's virtue is that of its free will. One strain in religious thought had summed up this present life as an "entombment," a punishment for some sin before birth.[9] This hard saying could perhaps be construed as detracting from the justice of the gods (or god), but for Plato it is axiomatic that gods are the authors only of what is good. (R. 379C5–7) So when he combines the previously mentioned notion with his own views on virtue, and applies both to a mythical account of the soul's previous existence, one can expect incongruities to appear. This is nowhere more evident than in the famous sentence of the Myth of Er, "Responsibility lies with the chooser; God is not responsible." (617E4–5) At a stroke Plato seems to have solved the problem of free will by placing in another life the entire choice of this one. But the assertion is belied by the context. The man who has been rewarded, it seems, is less likely to choose well than one who

---

6 See R. D. Archer-Hind (2) app. A, for the major references.
7 See also *Phd.* 114BC.
8 E. R. Dodds (2) 215.
9 See *Grg.* 493A3, with Dodds' comment *ad loc.*

has just been punished, and the ludicrous system of lots diminishes even further the scope of his choice, as Plato himself implicitly admits. (*Republic* 619D8–E2) Even if such a soul is lucky enough to have first choice in the lots, he is hindered by the fact that the one aspect of the patterns of life which matters, its disposition (τάξις) to good or evil (618B3), is unknown to him till the fateful choice, soon to be inexorably implemented by Necessity, has already been made. (619C2 ff.) And yet, from the point of view of the rest of the *Republic*, problems such as these should hardly arise. For the true philosopher, if anyone, is supposed to be master of himself, and fully happy, just, and free in the most authentic sense.[10] By contrast, the degree of a man's *injustice* is the degree to which he is enslaved to the lower elements in his soul. (577D1 ff.) This seems such a satisfying answer to the central problem of good and evil, justice and injustice, that many have been led to question the very *raison d'être* of the myths as a result. An easy solution is to explain them away as "popular," pictorial representations of Plato's more abstruse philosophical beliefs, which could hardly be expected to have very much meaning for the greater number of people, in much the same way as M. Jean-Paul Sartre uses the art-form of novels and plays.[11] If this is true, however, it is hard to account for the discrepancies which exist between the two. These discrepancies do exist, and if Plato allows them to stand side by side one can only assume that he was loath to say dogmatically that the one account was any more "true" than the other. Certainly his commitment to the "religious" view of man and his destiny is evidenced at all stages of his writing career; his doctrine of the soul, for example, appears as a truth of religion in the *Gorgias* before appearing later as a truth of reason in the *Phaedo*,[12] and the divinity of the heavenly bodies is asserted in the *Republic* (508A4) and assumed in the *Timaeus* (39E ff.) before any "proofs" are offered in the *Laws*. (891E ff.) Even in the *Phaedo*, for all its rationalizing, the "safer raft" of divine revelation is envisaged (85D1–4), and, if the Seventh Letter is genuine, it is interesting how in extreme old age Plato points to "the old and sacred doctrines which reveal that the soul is immortal" rather than to any of his own philosophical "proofs."[13]

Stewart argues at great length that the myths express a truth deeper

---

10 587B8 ff., 591C1 ff., 586E4–587A1.

11 Compare, for example, *La Nausée* with *L'Etre et le Néant*. For Schleiermacher's interpretation along these lines see P. Frutiger 154 ff.

12 See E. R. Dodds (1) 24.

13 *Ep.* VII, 335A3–4; E. R. Dodds *ibid.*

than anything which philosophical speculation can penetrate.[14] If this is true, however, it is hard to see how a mythological truth in one dialogue could be philosophically "demonstrated" to be true in another. Yet this happens in the case of immortality, which is accepted as a truth of religion in the *Meno* (81A5 ff.) and "proved" a short while later in the *Phaedo*. Again, on Stewart's analysis one would be hard put to it to account for apparently important changes of viewpoint within the myths themselves, let alone the oddity of the fact that a revealed truth should be in disaccord with a "truth" known by reason alone. In the *Meno*, for example, Pindar is taken as the authority, and the cycle of births is seen as a penalty for sin committed in a previous existence. (81B3 ff.) The same doctrine seems clearly present at *Republic* 613A1-2. In the *Timaeus*, however, a much more optimistic view emerges, and the incarnation of soul, far from being any sort of "fall," is seen as the direct result of divine providence and benevolence.[15] The difference between these optimistic and pessimistic strains within the myths themselves is reflected in the body of the dialogues, where Plato himself wavers between two estimates of man, in the one case seeing him as "a plant of heavenly, not of earthly growth" (*Ti.* 90A6-7), a god and a sharer in the life of the immortals, and in the other as a shadow like those which flit through Homer's Hades.[16] In other words the myths, as well as the body of the dialogues, are liable to reflect Plato's varying moods and convictions. To look for an organized body of "religious" truth in the one is perhaps as illusory as to search for a totally coherent philosophical system in the other.

14 J. A. Stewart *passim*.
15 41B7-C2. On this see A.-J. Festugière's chapter on the *Timaeus* in (1) II.
16 *Men.* 100A2-7; cf. E. R. Dodds (2) 214-16.

8

The Politicus

The *Politicus*, like the *Timaeus*, is a dialogue difficult to date. For reasons which will transpire I take it as coming some time after the *Timaeus* and *Phaedrus* (in that order), though its most recent English editor takes it either as preceding, or as being written concomitantly with the *Timaeus*.[1] Certainly the cosmology and cosmogony of both *Politicus* and *Timaeus* are strikingly similar. The cosmos is a living creature, possessing intelligence (φρόνησις),[2] and so presumably qualifying for the title of "ensouled," in much the same way as the world is said to possess a soul in the *Timaeus*.[3] As a living creature it owes its origin to a "craftsman (Demiurge) and father" (273B1–2), and, while possessing immortality of a sort, possesses it only in a contingent manner, having received it as a gift from the Demiurge.[4] The Demiurge is not omnipotent; he is subject, like the Olympians of Homer, to Necessity and Law and Fate.[5] He is divine, but probably only in a referred manner, in much the same way as the gods in the *Phaedrus* are said to receive their divinity from their nearness to the Ideas.[6] All the world's good stems from its Demiurge and father (273B6–7); evil is to be attributed

1 J. B. Skemp (5) 237 and *passim*.
2 269D1; cf. 269D9, τοῦ γεννήσαντος.
3 J. Bidez 71 claims that there is no idea of World Soul in the *Politicus*. The sentence 269C4–D2 (especially D1–2) would seem to be enough to disprove this, however. For fuller notes on World Soul in the *Politicus* see J. B. Skemp (5) 105–6.
4 270A4–5; cf. *Ti.* 41A8–B6.
5 269D3 (ἀνάγκη), 269E7 (θέμις), 272E6 (εἱμαρμένη).
6 *Phdr.* 249C6. I take it, with Van Camp and Canart (219 n3), that the phrase τοῖς πάντων θειοτάτοις (269D6) is a veiled reference to Ideas. It can hardly mean intelligences, or souls, or divinities, since such beings are said to possess motion of one type or another (see 269E1–6, 270A5–8), while the θειότατα and they only (μόνοις 269D6) are described as enjoying τὰ κατὰ ταὐτὰ καὶ ὡσαύτως ἔχειν ἀεὶ καὶ ταὐτὸν εἶναι (*ibid.*). The phrase is identical with that of a description of the static Ideas in the *Phaedo* (80B2–3), and it is hard to see how it can apply to anything subject to motion, however minimal. Even in the *Timaeus* the Demiurge still looks to the Ideas for his model (32C ff.). For another apparent reference to the Ideas in the *Politicus* see 285D10–286A7.

to the presence of the bodily element in it (273B4), and to its forgetfulness of his instructions. (273C6) For all its self-induced ills and sicknesses he is the Great Healer.

As in the *Timaeus*, he is or represents good, intelligent, and purposive activity, though now it is explicitly stated that he has a movement of his own, described as "everlasting self-sustained rotation in a single sense" (αὐτὸ ... ἑαυτὸ στρέφειν ἀεί 269E5).[7] Whether such talk of rotation has any meaning at all will depend on one's view of the Demiurge as real or as a symbol; and if he is to be taken as real there could be further dispute as to whether his "rotation" is local or otherwise.[8] If one accepts that here and in the *Timaeus* the Demiurge is nothing but a symbol or personification of the logical abstraction "intelligent causation" in general, a symbol of the class of causes "which are endowed with mind and are the workers of things fair and good,"[9] one is still left facing the question why no movement of the Demiurge (nor self-movement of soul, for that matter) is mentioned in the *Timaeus* when it is in the *Politicus*. An extreme answer is to say that the notion of movement in soul or intelligence is not introduced in the *Timaeus* because it seems to run counter to the particular type of myth in which Plato there chooses to express his thoughts: that is, to talk of soul as eternally self-moving "would have deprived the creation myth of all literary plausibility."[10] If this is true, Plato has only himself to blame if he is misunderstood; soul as self-moving is necessarily eternal and *non*-contingent, as the *Phaedrus*[11] (and later the *Laws*)[12] make clear, whereas the burden of the *Timaeus* is that all soul (except, presumably, that of the Demiurge), even if it does enjoy a quasi-eternity, does so inasmuch as it is *dependent* upon a reality itself independent. How Plato could have written so misleading an account if his views on the autokinetic nature of soul were already developed is not immediately clear.

7 Tr. J. B. Skemp. I understand ἡγουμένῳ at 269E6 to refer to the Demiurge. (For Campbell it is "Pure Soul in general, of which the Deity, who sustains the universe, is a particular example." (L. Campbell *ad loc.*)) This is to say that it is νοῦς and ψυχή at their purest, since the Demiurge is presumably their most perfect embodiment.

8 J. B. Skemp (5) 105 takes it that the motion of the Demiurge is not ἐν τόπῳ, but "psychic" only, and interprets 269D5–6 as a reference to God. This involves taking the phrase as meaning not absolute rest but to "revolve ever in the same sense" (*ibid.*). For my own view see above, 132n6.

9 *Ti.* 46E4; cf. H. Cherniss (3) 207 n1.

10 H. Cherniss (2) 26 n4; cf. H. Cherniss (5) 428–31.

11 See above, 111 ff.

12 See below, 147.

As has been suggested earlier, a plausible solution to this problem is to suggest that the *Phaedrus* is to be dated a little after the *Timaeus*, which in turn follows close on the *Republic*.[13] The *Politicus* will then be seen to incorporate into a single Weltanschauung the cosmology of the *Timaeus* and the *Phaedrus* doctrine of soul as a "source of motion." In the *Phaedrus* a single and oversimplified principle was announced; now it is seen that it will not account for all of the facts. To posit soul as the source of all activity in the universe is in itself no guarantee that the universe is under intelligent and beneficent direction; one must still assume a supremely intelligent and provident soul, the Demiurge, who takes as his model the perfection of the Ideas and guarantees the basic victory of Intelligence over Unreason.[14] He will now, of course, have the characteristic attributed to *all* (noetic) souls in the *Phaedrus*, namely autokinesis. World Soul, too, will possess autokinesis; but its ultimate dependence upon the Demiurge, and its association with the bodily, will render such autokinesis less perfect in its operations. This does seem to be an advance upon the views of the *Timaeus*, where World Soul was in everlasting motion, but less obviously itself a principle of movement. As far as the Demiurge is concerned, however, it only makes explicit what in the *Timaeus* was implicit. For in the *Timaeus*, too, the Demiurge was by implication a soul who was a *principle* of movement (and to that degree exceptional) as well as a soul who was in everlasting motion.[15] By the time of the *Politicus*, however, the exception has become the rule, thanks to the fresh analysis of the *Phaedrus*.

If, as I believe, the Demiurge of the *Politicus*, like his counterpart in the *Timaeus*, is meant to be a person, we are presented with what looks like a hierarchy of existents. Foremost stand the static and exemplary Ideas,[16] followed by the Demiurge, whose particular quality is that eternal self-motion which is rotation in the same sense, local or otherwise. (269E5–6) Being a person, he *is* intelligence and soul, rather than represents them, and he is non-contingent. Below him comes World Soul. This receives its eternity from him and so is contingent (270A4–5), and its basic characteristic is apparently that self-motion which is rotation in the same sense, like his own. This, at any rate, is true in theory, since he has endowed it with life

13 See L. Robin (2) 116–17, and G. E. L. Owen (1) 79–95.
14 See J. B. Skemp (1) 112.
15 His eternity and his activities of creation and formation seem sufficient evidence of this.
16 269D6, 285D9–286A7; see also above, 132n6.

and intelligence like his own.[17] But in practice World Soul is inseparable from the world's body, and the bodily element, inducing forgetfulness, stops World Soul from performing its task correctly. (273B4, C6) It is reduced to a second-best activity, that of rotation in reverse (ἀνακύκλησις).[18] Perfection lies in the static Ideas; the world, being other than these, is necessarily subject to change, and so undergoes movement. So, too, does the Demiurge, since he too is other than the uniquely static Ideas. But he, being intelligence and soul at their purest, possesses the noblest form of change, that self-motion which Plato sees as self-sustained rotation in one sense; lesser souls approximate to this as best they can, and in doing so come as near as their station permits them to the perfection of the Ideas.

17 269D1. Most scholars assume that the phrase ζῷον ὂν καὶ φρόνησιν εἰληχός at 269D1 is causal, but this need not be so. If ζῷον ὄν is seen as in apposition to τὸ δέ ("the desire to run in the opposite direction is a characteristic of refractory ζῷα"), καὶ φρόνησιν could then be treated as concessive. That which possesses φρόνησις ought in theory to work in harmony with the wishes of the Demiurge; why in fact the world does not is later explained in terms of the "bodily element" in it (273B4) and the "forgetfulness" of the Father's instructions which this induces (273C6). The world in the *Timaeus* is a ζῷον ἔμψυχον ἔννουν τε and a god, and in itself (without reference to ἀνάγκη) affords no trouble to the Demiurge; in the *Politicus* this is hardly the case, since any intelligence possessed by the world eventually turns to λήθη, making it more refractory than amenable. For a similar view see J. B. Skemp (5) 106, and J. Gould 207, and n4. The former sees World Soul as a battleground between φρόνησις and σύμφυτος ἐπιθυμία, with ἐπιθυμία largely prevailing. With reservations he follows Plutarch (*de An.* 1014D) in seeing similarities between σύμφυτος ἐπιθυμία and the ἀνάγκη of the *Timaeus* (89). But the opposition, if any, is more likely to be between φρόνησις and τὸ σωματοειδές, that bodily and irrational element in the universe whose presence and influence conditions the σύμφυτος ἐπιθυμία into being the type of drive it is. See A.-J. Festugière (1) 123, A. Diès (3) xxxii, and my own comments later in this chapter.

18 269E3. The phrase τὴν ἀνακύκλησιν εἴληχεν (269E3-4) is strange, suggesting as it does that the ἀνακύκλησις has been received from the Demiurge, rather than as the result of its own σύμφυτος ἐπιθυμία. But the difficulty is perhaps only apparent. Both World Soul and its ἐπιθυμία are the Demiurge's creation and so ultimately within his control; the alien force with which he must reckon is τὸ σωματοειδές. So, in giving the world an ἀνακύκλησις he could be said to be catering for the element of σωματοειδές in the universe and its inevitable influence upon the ἐπιθυμητικόν of World Soul. When this is said, however, one must face the further difficulty that it is not θέμις (269E7), apparently, for the Demiurge to initiate two contrary motions. Light may be thrown on the problem if we examine the implications of the phrase δι' ἑαυτοῦ at 270A5. This phrase is particularly ambiguous, capable as it is of a mechanistic or non-mechanistic interpretation. I take it as non-mechanistic (accepting at its face value Plato's view of the cosmos as a ζῷόν τι), and indicating proximate causality, by contrast with the remote and more fundamental causality exercised by the Demiurge on the one hand (εἰληχός 269D1) and by τὸ σωματοειδές on the other. If the distinction is a legitimate one it could be argued that the troublesome reference at 269E7 is to direct and proximate causality only.

By writing in this way Plato seems to be clarifying a point left unclear in earlier dialogues. In the *Republic* he had suggested that the Idea of Good and the Demiurge were both of them efficient causes, the one of the sun (508B12–C2), the other of "the universe" (530A6), but he had said nothing to suggest what rapport (if any) there was between the two agents, or whether they were not indeed merely different descriptions, one personal, one impersonal, of one and the same efficient cause. This obscurity was clarified to some degree in the *Timaeus*, as we saw, in that efficient causality was now attributed pre-eminently to the highest soul, the Demiurge, while the Ideas were left with exemplary causality only. However, there was nothing to suggest that the Ideas were in any way "higher" than the Demiurge; they were merely over and against him. This being the case, it seemed natural for a reader to assume that the Ideas and the Demiurge, enjoying as they both did eternal and non-contingent existence, were on an ontological par. Whether Plato really thought this was so at the time he wrote the *Timaeus* is not capable of demonstration, but his comments on the matter in the *Phaedrus* suggest that at that period of his life at any rate he thought that the Ideas in some way *transcended* the gods, since the latter are said to be divine only because of their "nearness" to them. Finally, in the *Politicus*, he is in a position to state succinctly (and defend precisely) exactly what he thinks the relationship to be, thanks to his new description of soul, in the *Phaedrus*, as autokinetic and a principle of change in other things. The Ideas *do* indeed transcend the gods – and even the highest god, the Demiurge – precisely because they are *static*; the Demiurge, by contrast, being a soul, *moves*, and is to that degree less perfect than they.

Has there been any change in his views on the physical world and Necessity? In the *Timaeus* Necessity or the Wandering Cause stood over and against the Demiurge; it was a *datum* with which he had to grapple; he did not create it. In the *Politicus* we read of an "inborn urge" (σύμφυτος ἐπιθυμία) of the world, which causes it to rotate in a direction counter to that imparted by the Demiurge. (272E6) More remotely, it is said to be "the bodily" which accounts for the evil in the world, and this, if anything, has some affinities with the Necessity of the *Timaeus*.[19] This is not to say that the body or the bodily as such is positively evil; it can mean simply that, in any complex involving body or the bodily, results tend to be less perfect than in a complex which does not.[20] In the same way a virus could be said to be neutral as such;

19 273B4; cf. *Ti.* 47E4–5.
20 See S. Pétrement 47 and G. Vlastos (1) 78 f.

it becomes harmful when allowed to contact a particular living organism. Again, the motion of the "inborn urge" is rotatory, whereas the movements of Necessity in the *Timaeus* are rectilinear.[21] The movements of the bodily (τὸ σωματοειδές) in the *Politicus* are no doubt equally rectilinear, and this will be another reason for seeing *it*, rather than the "inborn urge," as the equivalent of Necessity. If this is the case, however, the status of the world's "inborn urge" becomes very ambiguous, and the evidence of the text seems to point to Plato's discomfort about the whole matter. A view of the world as a living creature leads him to talk of its activities as one would those of a person, and the picture which emerges is that of a refractory infant. (272E6, 273C6–7) Laying stress on this, Skemp sees the "inborn urge" as the equivalent of that (psychic) Necessity which he finds in the *Timaeus*, a Necessity in opposition to the Demiurge, but amenable to his persuasion.[22] But even if this were true, one would still be in doubt about its genuine status. Is it supposed to be an irrational urge within World Soul, or an irrational force over and against World Soul? Hardly the latter, for Plato explicitly rejects the notion of two deities in opposition in the universe. (270A1–2) But if it is supposed to be within World Soul it will also be within the Demiurge's general control, since it is he who formed the world and its soul. Its refractory nature will then be accounted for by the presence of the bodily. In this case the more genuine opposition force to the Demiurge will be the same "bodily" element, and hence *it* will be a more exact equivalent of Necessity.

On the other hand, the imagery of the spindle which Plato employs to illustrate the world's periodic inverse rotation could lead one to imagine that any such rotation is of a purely mechanical, rather than psychic nature, and the simple result of relaxed tension, as in the case of any spring or spindle tightly wound and then allowed to uncoil under the impetus of its own stored momentum. If one lays stress on this image, as does M. P.-M. Schuhl, the "inborn urge" can be explained away as a colourful expression for what is a purely mechanical, non-psychic phenomenon.[23] This would be extremely

---

21 For references and comment see J. B. Skemp (1) 26–7.

22 See above, 135n17.

23 Holding, like Bidez (see above, 132n3), that there is no case for World Soul in the *Politicus*, he takes it that σύμφυτος ἐπιθυμία is a colourful expression for a physical impetus of a purely mechanical nature, rather than some sort of personal desire (47). In his edition of the dialogue J. B. Skemp concedes (103) that Plato's explanation in terms of "unwinding" does seem mechanical, but feels that "the real motive power of the world is its own Soul and that the Framer and Maker works upon it essentially by persuasion" (102). For a similar criticism of Schuhl see A. Diès (3) xxxi and H. Herter (2) 109n13.

convenient, but it does little justice to the earlier imagery in which the world is a living creature, and liable to act like a refractory child. If we take this at its face value, Plato seems to be carrying to their logical conclusion on a *cosmic* scale views expressed about the *human* soul in earlier dialogues. When discussing the newly incarnate infant soul in the *Timaeus*, for example, he showed how the purely rational circles of its soul could be bent awry by the incursions of the bodily and its demands (43A ff.); however rational soul may be in theory, contact with the bodily is liable to influence it for harm. This is seen to be true as early as the *Phaedo*, where even the noetic soul can end by "thinking to be true whatever the *body* says is true." (83D6) In similar strain is a quotation at *Phaedo* 83D7–8: "The result of agreeing with the body and finding pleasure in the same things is, I imagine, that it *cannot help* [ἀναγκάζεται] becoming like it in character and training." If this analysis is correct, Plato is implicitly criticizing his earlier concept of World Soul (as seen in the *Timaeus*) by reference to truths outlined in his individual psychology. But he expresses himself so obscurely on the point that confident assertion is hazardous. As so often, he seems content to let two views stand side by side, an abiding monument to his caution or confusion, according to one's prejudices.

Another point of interest is that in the *Politicus* the activity of soul is the originating force, not simply of movement, but of a very particular type of movement – rotation. In its perfect state soul can initiate rotation in one sense only, it seems; rotation in the opposite sense is of a less perfect nature, and is the result of the soul's association with the bodily. (273B4, C6) *Why* the Demiurge cannot initiate rotation now in one sense now in another is left obscure; Plato himself is satisfied to say that this would be "impious" (οὐ θέμις).[24] It is more than likely, however, that the idea stems from a conflation of ideas already expressed in the *Timaeus* and *Phaedrus*. For in the *Timaeus* the movement initiated by the Demiurge is of a circular kind only (rectilinear motion being caused by Necessity),[25] while in the *Phaedrus* no limitation seems to be set upon the kinds of motion which soul can originate. (245C8–9) By the time of the *Politicus*, however, the inadequacies of the *Phaedrus* statement appear to have been noticed, and while soul is still seen as a "self-moving" entity, the motions initiated by it are once again said to

---

24 269E7. This sounds very like the ἀνάγκη and εἱμαρμένη which govern the actions of the Olympian gods, even Zeus himself, in the Homeric poems. In the activities of Xenophanes' god the controlling factor is "seemliness," or "what is fitting for a god." See DK¹² B 26 (Xenophanes).

25 *Ti.* 34A4–5, 43B1–5. See J. B. Skemp (1) 82.

be of a *circular* kind only (269E5–6); deviations from this norm can be attributed to "the bodily." (273B6) But if soul is self-moving, and if what it moves is moved in a circle, the logical corollary is that its own motion is rotatory. For this reason the Demiurge, the most perfect soul, is given rotatory movement (269E5–6), and so is World Soul. (269E3–4) These types of rotation are different, as we have seen, and Plato's οὐ θέμις, offered in explanation, is hardly enlightening. One might perhaps hazard a guess that rotation in a single sense – that exercised by the Demiurge – epitomizes the eternal, underived and *undisturbed* nature of his autokinesis (cf. the *Phaedrus* [245C8], where a self-moving entity never "breaks contact" with itself), while the backward-and-forward rotation of World Soul epitomizes its "eternity" as ultimately derivative from the Demiurge and subject to the disturbing exigencies of the bodily. Another possible reason would be that offered in the *Timaeus*: the heavenly gods have uniform motion in the same place "because their thoughts never vary" (40AB); their manner of cognition is an indication of their perfection.

9

The Philebus

A notable difference between the *Phaedo* and the *Republic* lay in their doctrines of pleasure and desire. In the *Phaedo* both are taken to be of bodily provenance, and thereby suspect; in the *Republic* they achieve a more reputable status, and are looked upon as a characteristic of soul. The body is now no longer a source, but a channel, of pleasures and desires. In the *Philebus* this doctrine is amplified, and subjected to much more scientific analysis with the new logical tool of Division. By and large the conclusions of the *Republic* are reaffirmed. Pleasures are psychic rather than bodily, though in some cases the body will have a more significant part to play in their production than in others. Pleasures of anticipation, for example (32B9 ff.), are purely psychic, as are the pleasures of knowledge (66c6), while others are psychic in a rather different way, since they have their origin in the physical process of depletion and replenishment.[1] It is true that on no occasion does Plato say explicitly that all desires and pleasures are activities of soul, but the doctrine is implied throughout. (See for example 55B3 and 35D1-3 where, by contrast with the *Gorgias* [499D4 ff.] and the *Phaedo* [66c7], he denies that hunger and thirst are bodily activities.) In view of the whole tenor of the dialogue it seems not unfair to claim that on the rare occasions when he does talk of "bodily" pleasures and desires he is talking carelessly, and can be taken to mean (psychic) pleasures and desires of bodily provenance.[2]

But even here the earlier, more negative, psychology of the *Phaedo* is not dead, and is allowed to stand side by side with a much more advanced psychology, as in *Republic* IX. At 63DE, for example, pleasures other than the "purest," that is, other than knowledge or appreciation of such things as pure shapes and colours, are spoken of in very much the same disparaging terms as the "bodily" pleasures and desires of *Phaedo* 65A-67A. In the fresh

1 See R. Hackforth (8) 140 n2.
2 E.g., 45A5-6, 46B8-C4. See R. Hackforth (8) 61.

terminology of the *Philebus*, the greater number of pleasures are "without limitation" (ἄπειρα), and to that degree not true or pure pleasures at all; worthwhile pleasures are those with a suitable admixture of "limitation" (πέρας) in them. (52CD) To the modern mind it is odd to find truth and falsity affirmed of anything other than propositions, but Plato takes it that the ontological status of the objects of pleasures and desires characterizes the pleasures and desires themselves.[3] While even the least "true" of pleasures are considered now to be at any rate psychic processes, in practice they seem to be viewed with the same depreciation as when they were once called "bodily." Here, as elsewhere, the old and the new psychologies jostle awkwardly for supremacy.

As for the notion of soul itself, Plato shows himself as fluid as ever in his views. It is taken to be a substance, complete in itself, distinct from body and enjoying a parallel ontological status with it.[4] In the *Phaedo* the life-soul and the noetic soul were taken to be one and the same; in the *Philebus*, as in the *Timaeus* and *Sophist*, their position appears to be such that, if they are logically separable, the one cannot exist without the other: "Wisdom and intelligence would never come into being without soul."[5] Again, the soul is frequently treated as if it is a sort of inner person. This is particularly evident when he is discussing the nature of sensation. The body is said to undergo certain sensations which are likened to an earth tremor which may or may not be communicated to the inner soul, as the case may be. (33D2–E1)[6] Hackforth may be right in assuming that "whereas the body (i.e., the sense organ) suffers a literal "shaking," the soul or consciousness, not being an extended magnitude, can only be shaken figuratively."[7] But this is not the first time that Plato has spoken of soul in a highly materialistic and spatial fashion, and I have argued elsewhere that it takes its place as one of a number

3 See A. E. Taylor (4) 64.

4 On the extreme dichotomy between ψυχή and σῶμα in the *Philebus* see M. Vanhoutte 237.

5 30C9–10; cf. *Sph.* 249A4–8, *Ti.* 30B3.

6 For a similar view of soul as the inner recipient of sense-impressions see *Tht.* 184–6. The epistemology involved in the passage is a complex one, but for present purposes it is enough to notice that sense-organs are seen, not as perceivers, but as *receivers*; only the inner soul can be said to "perceive." This view bears a close affinity to a view seen earlier, in *Alcibiades* I, the *Phaedo,* and the *Republic*, that "soul" and "self" are synonymous; the body is a medium, with no claim to a share in the title "man," or even (strictly speaking) to a share in the activity called perception. It is the soul which, having received the παθήματα (passive impressions) which have been transmitted to it *via* the sense-organs, in the more precise sense of the word "perceives" anything.

7 R. Hackforth (8) 63 n3.

of conflicting views of soul which he takes over from his contemporaries and predecessors and seems content to leave unresolved.

A notable feature of the *Philebus* is Plato's continued belief in a cosmic intelligence and a cosmic soul, though now they are seen as the *source* from which our own intelligence and soul are derived, as our body is said to owe its origin to that of the physical world.[8] The idea of the world as a living creature, and operating in a way which manifests intelligence, has its roots deep in pre-Socratic thought; the Socrates of the *Phaedo* longed for explanations in terms of intelligent purpose (97C ff.), and as early as the *Republic* the world was seen as a living creature (546B3), and the divinity of the heavenly bodies was taken for granted. (508A4) In later dialogues, as we have seen, Plato takes the further step of applying his individual psychology on a cosmic scale. The dualism of soul and body is seen as a characteristic of the cosmos itself;[9] man is to the world as microcosm to macrocosm. This raises a number of problems of its own, tackled already at length in the *Timaeus* and *Politicus*, and a summary outline of Plato's position, with one or two interesting changes of emphasis, is found in the *Philebus*. Of the four "types" making up the sum total of reality the last mentioned is the αἰτία μείξεως, or Efficient Cause, as Aristotle would no doubt have called it.[10] This cause is called wisdom and intelligence (30C6), and in the context can only mean cosmic intelligence, rather than individual. But, once this is said, Plato's further comments on the subject are singularly obscure. The wisdom and intelligence in question are said to be "unable to come into existence without soul." (30C9–10) In itself this is nothing new. That soul and intelligence go hand in hand is simply the weaker statement of the extreme position of the *Phaedo*, where soul and intelligence are taken as identical,[11] and finds parallel expression at *Timaeus* 30B3 and *Sophist* 249A6–7. But the point is obscured by a statement at 30D1–3 that "in the nature of Zeus a royal soul and a royal reason come to dwell by virtue of the power of the Cause." Is this the same cause as the αἰτία μείξεως or a different one? The language leads one to think

---

8 29B6 ff. This view of individual souls as ἀποσπάσματα of a cosmic soul caught the imagination of many later thinkers, particularly those of Stoic sympathies. See Epict. *Ench.* I, 14, 6; II, 8, 11; M. Ant. v, 27; D.L. VII, 156; Ph. *De Opificio Mundi* 146; *De Somniis* I, 34; *De Mutatione Nominum*, 223; Seneca, *Epistles*, 66, 12; 92, 30, etc. (The Philo references are to the Cohn-Wendland-Reiter edition (Berlin 1896–1930). For these I am grateful to Prof. A.-J. Festugière, o.p.)

9 See the account of the operations of the Demiurge, *Ti.* 29D7 ff.

10 30A10. That it is to be equated with Aristotle's Efficient Cause is agreed upon by R. G. Bury (xliv–xlv), A. E. Taylor ((4) 47), and R. Hackforth ((8) 36).

11 E.g., *Phd.* 67C3, where διάνοια is apparently substituted for ψυχή.

it is different. For it is said to be responsible (the basic meaning of αἰτία) for the *coming into being* (ἐγγίγνεσθαι) of what are called the "royal soul" and the "royal intelligence." (30D1–3) This need not necessarily involve a relationship of temporal anteriority and posteriority, but it does appear to indicate that the one cause is derivative in a way that the other is not. If one takes "the nature of Zeus" as a mythical expression for the cosmos,[12] the two causes may be seen perhaps as transcendent and immanent intelligence respectively, or as non-contingent and contingent.[13] If this is true, it will only be in the case of the derivative cause that intelligence and soul will come into being together; it will be this derivative soul and intelligence which "orders and regulates the years, the seasons and the months." (30C5–6) Such an interpretation leaves us with the awkward picture of a transcendent, non-psychic Intelligence, remarkably similar to the God of Aristotle. Proclus faces the problem squarely, and in true neo-platonic fashion concludes that the one cause is a self-projection of the other: Intelligence has no particular need of soul for its *own* existence, but if it wishes to manifest itself in the objects of the physical world it needs the intermediate receptacle which is soul.[14] Thus existence in soul will only be a characteristic of derivative intelligence. This solution which Proclus profers may be right, but Plato's confusing account makes confident analysis difficult. The nature of an intelligence divorced from life and personality is hard to envisage, and in the *Timaeus* its equivalent is seen as a personal Demiurge. (29D ff.) In this case the transcendent Efficient Cause is endowed with life and personality as well as intelligence, and it is at least possible that Plato's description of it as such springs from an awareness of the awkwardness of an Efficient Cause which is supposed to be intelligent yet in some way not alive. In the more summary *Philebus* the question is not raised specifically, but a possible pointer to Plato's sympathies lies in the qualification of the Efficient Cause as "fashioning" (δημιουργοῦν) and "making" (ποιοῦν) things (27B1, 26E6). Such, however, were not the sympathies of neo-Platonism, and it is easy to see how an

---

12 I take it that the *body* of the world is the "nature of Zeus," and that the world's βασιλικὸς νοῦς and βασιλικὴ ψυχή are equivalent to the World Soul and Intelligence of the *Timaeus*. In this I follow P. Shorey (2) 608. For Wilamowitz, "Da ist Zeus die Weltseele" (1 640).

13 See R. Hackforth (8) 56–7 n1.

14 Procl. *in Ti.* 122E (Diehl 1 402/15 ff.); cf. R. Hackforth (8) 57n. For his own view of Plato's God as transcendent νοῦς see R. Hackforth (1) 4–9. For notable criticisms of this see J. B. Skemp (1) 114, J. H. M. M. Loenen 252, F. Solmsen (4) 138, and H. Cherniss (5) app. 11. In agreement, however, are A. Diès (1) II 541 f. and H. Görgemanns 205 n3.

interpretation of this passage and its *Timaeus* counterpart could lead to an assertion that there is a transcendent Intelligence enjoying a higher degree of existence than soul. Such a view would seem to be corroborated by a statement at 30B that the Cause (which is intelligence) "furnishes the elements that belong to our bodies with soul," or by the statement that the power of "the Cause" is responsible (αἰτία) for the *coming into existence* of that soul and intelligence which pervade the universe. (30D1–3) Be this as it may, it seems clear enough that both *Timaeus* and *Philebus* are in agreement that the soul and intelligence of the visible cosmos are *dependent for their being* (whether temporally or otherwise) on some transcendent Cause (αἰτία). That is, World Soul is in either case *contingent*.

Whether this World Soul is one or many, or one when viewed collectively and many when viewed distributively, seems to be of little importance to Plato. More often than not he sees it as one, but occasionally (as at 30B4–5) he sees it as plural, and one finds the same apparent indifference at *Laws* 898C7–8, where he talks of "one soul or many." More important for present purposes is the fact that in both *Timaeus* and *Philebus* World Soul (or Souls) is thought of as a matrix for intelligence. There is no hint of any irrationality in it, still less of ethical neutrality. But one apparently significant difference, which we have already noticed *en passant*, is the account given of the relationship between World Soul (or Souls) and individual human souls. At *Timaeus* 41D4–7 the account of the individual creation of human souls by the Demiurge suggests the antithesis of pantheism; we are hardly meant to be parts of, or derivations from, or emanations of World Soul. Now, however, at *Philebus* 29B6 ff., it is stated that we *do* owe our intelligence and soul to cosmic intelligence and soul. At first sight the contradiction looks complete, but this may turn out to be not quite the case. For even in the *Timaeus* account the ingredients of cosmic soul and individual souls are basically the same; difference is in degrees of purity, not of substance. (41D4–7) If one lays stress on *this* aspect of Plato's account one is extremely close to the position adopted in the *Philebus*, and the comments of the latter can be plausibly seen as a development rather than a contradiction. Certainly the soul as a "fragment" (ἀπόσπασμα) of World Soul fired the imagination of many ancient thinkers,[15] and this is the sort of passage which provides them with their scriptural text.

15 See above, 142n8.

10

The Laws and the Epinomis

To one examining Plato's psychology in the *Laws*, the *locus classicus* can only be book ten, with its defence of the divine in human and cosmic affairs, and its championing of the primacy of soul as the source of all activity. This has much in common with the *Phaedrus* in particular, and has led some scholars to think that the two dialogues must have been composed fairly closely together in time.[1] Against this, however, the greater number of references to soul which abound throughout the rest of the dialogue reminds us much more of the Plato of the *Gorgias, Meno, Phaedo,* and *Republic*. In particular, the strain of religious enthusiasm which burns bright in the *Phaedo* is still very much aglow, and that "safer raft" of Divine Revelation mentioned there (85D3) seems at times to count for much more than does philosophical argument. Life is a process of purification and assimilation to the divine (716CE); the soul is the true self and enjoys personal immortality. (959B3–4) The just man is rewarded in a future life, and there are sanctions reserved for the wicked.[2] A basic substantial distinction of soul and body is taken for granted, and "pleasures" are once again treated with distrust.[3] The finer distinctions of the *Republic* are passed by, and "soul" is called divine, and man's most precious possession. (728B1, 726A2–727A2) Presumably Plato means by this "reason" or the "noetic soul," since the familiar bipartition of soul into reason and impulse is taken for granted throughout. (E.g., 689AB, 714A3) These two parts or aspects of soul are again spoken of as though they possessed size and occupied space (689A9), and the Hippocratean view of disease as imbalance of parts underlies a description of the incontinent soul as "in the grip of disease" (νοσήματι συνεχομένην).[4] The

---

1 See J. Stenzel (1) and O. Regenbogen.
2 904DE, 881A ff., 727D, 870DE, 927AB, 959B.
3 672D8–9, 727CI ff., 714A2 ff., 689AB.
4 714A5–6. England *ad loc.*, following Hermann, doubts the word νοσήματι. It is defended by Ast and Stallbaum, and included in Burnet's Oxford Text.

truly good state of soul or body is seen as one of "measured balance,"[5] and this *fil conducteur* of the *Republic* is now perhaps corroborated by the further suggestion that man, in manifesting such measured balance, is imitating God, the measure (μέτρον) of all things. (716C4–5 ff.) Even the notion of metempsychosis seems to be covertly introduced, though now in a much more philosophically respectable guise.[6] Free will ultimately accounts for the good or evil estate of any soul, but this is seen now within the broader context of a divine Chess Player, who moves the chess pieces in a way which suits their individual merits and qualifications and which always coincides (or is made to coincide) with the good of the whole. (904AE) Whatever may have happened in the meanwhile, we seem to be back to the standpoint of the *Republic*, where "responsibility lies with the chooser – not with God" (617E4–5), except that what was there enunciated as a particular proposition to suit a particular case – the choosing of a new life – is now asserted as true of man in any and every condition: "... for the cause of change lies within themselves."[7] Finally, the evaluative language used in describing "good" and "bad" elements of soul in the early *Republic* is now reintroduced without qualification,[8] and shows that the psychology of the *Gorgias, Phaedo* and early *Republic* is still a powerful driving force, and has as strong a hold on Plato as the more balanced and penetrating views of *Republic* IX and the *Philebus*. In spite of the more sophisticated metaphysics of middle age, Plato the old man seems equally content to return to the sources which inspired him in earlier times.[9]

The view of soul just outlined can, for all its inadequacies and internal inconsistencies, be roughly described as that single general view running through the *Gorgias, Meno, Phaedo, Republic*, and (in part) *Phaedrus*: the (noetic) soul is in some way divine, precious, worthy of respect, superior to and natural master of the body. Book ten, however, introduces us to a very different view of soul, first seen in embryo in the *Phaedrus* (245C5 ff.), as a "source of motion," and discussed above in chapter 6. If the earlier account deals with the *human* (or at any rate *noetic*) soul and its status, this one purports to be an account of soul as such, without further qualification. The

---

5 728DE. See also England's commentary on 716D1.

6 904A ff. See F. Solmsen (4) 158.

7 904C7. E. Magotteaux 349–51 stresses the similarity of R. 617E and Lg. 904C, but for an important account of their differences see England *ad loc.*

8 904B2–3; cf. R. 431A, 432A.

9 G. Müller 190 finds the whole thing a parody of Plato's philosophy, and, but for Aristotle's testimony, would excise the *Laws* from the Platonic corpus. P. Shorey, by contrast, finds the *Laws* "almost a complete compendium of Platonic philosophy" ((1) 347).

distinction is vital, for in the context (an apologia for theism, 887C ff.) Plato must have a definition of soul wide enough to cover the souls of gods as well as men and other living things, if he is to have an adequate reply to the pure mechanists who, he asserts, deny the existence of the divine. Soul as such, it transpires, is "in the first rank" in the order of coming into being, coming to birth before any body and "exercising unequivocal control over any change or rearrangement a body might undergo." (892A4–7) It is then stated as a "necessary" conclusion that what is "cognate" to soul is in the same way older than body (892A7 ff.), and such cognate activities are later described as wishes, calculations, true judgments, purposes, and memories. (896C9–D1) This is already an argument against mechanism; it shows, in the words of England, that "ψυχή is more φύσει than body – for the sceptics mean by φύσις to denote *primary production*, and that, as we say, is the work of ψυχή."[10]

After an elaborate account of the different types of motion, soul is eventually defined as "the movement which is able to move itself" or "the activity which can activate itself" (896A1–2), and this is expanded into "the first coming-into-being and movement of those things which are, have been, and will be, together with the sum total of their contraries," on the grounds that "in every instance it is soul which is responsible for any change and motion they undergo."[11] What is more, the priority of soul is not simply ontological; it is temporal. Such seems to be the only possible meaning of a sentence like: "Soul comes into being prior [προτέραν γεγονέναι] to body, while body is secondary and derivative [δεύτερόν τε καὶ ὕστερον], with soul governing in the real order of things, and body being subject to governance." (896C1–3) This soul is finally described as "responsible for those things which are good and bad, beautiful and ugly, just and unjust, and in general for the opposites." (896D5–7)

It is fairly clear that so far the only soul under discussion has been soul-in-general, perhaps better translated as soul-stuff or psychic force.[12] There has been no indication that it is particular or personal. To this extent

10 E. B. England II 26, summarizing *Lg*. 892.

11 896A6–8, 896A8–B1. What the "contraries" are meant to be is not clear. C. Ritter's suggestion (quoted by England) that it means τὰ μὴ ὄντα καὶ διαφθαρημένα καὶ διαφθαρησόμενα may be correct, but it seems possible to infer from 896D6 ff. that Plato had in mind the different *moral* opposites, despite England's disclaimer. For ψυχή as πρώτη γένεσις see also 899C7.

12 For the translation see England on 896E8 and W. J. W. Koster 60. Cf. also J. Moreau (2) 68, and E. Bréhier (quoted with approval by S. Pétrement 69). For the notion of ψυχή as "stuff" of some sort see *Ti*. 35B ff.

the argument first seen in the *Phaedrus*[13] has been broadened already. Again, in the *Phaedrus* the (intellective) soul whose immortality Plato was attempting to prove was purely and simply a self-moving entity, and in eternal motion, and it was natural in the context to assume that such a soul was non-contingent. Now the position has been clarified, and soul as such is seen to belong to the order of Becoming, though it is still said to be "older" than the body and deathless.[14] And even more searching questions are being posed. "Are we to say," asks the Athenian, "that soul rules over and dwells in all things which undergo every type of movement and that it controls the universe?" (896D10 ff.) Clinias replies in the affirmative; but to what has he agreed? To the view that there is a World Soul, whose (intelligent) activities are best seen in the movements of the heavens (οὐρανός), as in the *Timaeus*? Or to the view that the entire universe (οὐρανός) is charged with a psychic force or soul-stuff which is somehow superior to or controls what is material and physical? From what has gone before, the second answer must be said to have *prima facie* plausibility: it is *soul* (ψυχή), not a *particular* soul (ψυχή τις), which is under discussion.[15] But the sentence which follows creates immediate difficulties. Soul, it appears, is multiple, not single. This would be understandable if Plato could be taken to mean that there are several types or brands of soul-*stuff*; but the Greek, as it stands, can hardly be translated except as "more than one (individual) *soul*" (πλείους, 896E4). These "souls" are said to be "at least two" in number (896E5–6), thus accounting for that minimal division of things into moral opposites seen above at 896D. The word "two" need hardly be stressed; it is simply the minimum number required to make the souls "many" rather than "one."[16]

---

13 See above, 111 ff.

14 892A4–5, 892C4, 896C1–3, 967D5. See *Ti.* 41D4–7, 34B3, *Plt.* 273B1–2.

15 For a view that οὐρανός means the heavens, see England's note on 896E1. This draws its cogency from a reference to τὰ κατ' οὐρανὸν καὶ γῆν at 896E8–9, where οὐρανός is clearly meant to be the heavens. But the most natural translation of οὐρανός in its context at 896E1, as W. Spoerri sees (212), is "l'Univers tout entier." See also 899B8. However, the ambiguity inherent in the word οὐρανός makes certainty of interpretation a rare occasion, and has led Reich to conclude that we find *two* notions of cosmic soul in the *Laws*: (a) ψυχή as World Soul (as in the *Timaeus*), which "rules" the οὐρανός, (b) ψυχή "as such" (i.e., ψυχή as soul-stuff, or life-force), which "goes through all things" (πάντα περιάγει). (K. Reich 66–7)

16 In the context δύο seems to be chosen as befitting one particular division of reality – i.e., into moral opposites. But this is not to say that a different approach would not have resulted in a different number of "divisions." For Pétrement Plato's ultimate aim is to show that the heavens are governed by a number of good souls; this can only be achieved by an initial division of souls into good and bad, to point the contrast. (S. Pétrement 67 n136)

It is a particular division of soul which is meaningful and useful in a context of polemical apologetics, rather than an exhaustive analysis. But the whole sentence is couched in very misleading Greek; so much so that many have seen here a reference to the "two gods" theory of Mazdaism.[17] All difficulty would perhaps have been avoided if Plato had talked about different "types" of soul instead of about particular souls, and many have referred to the phrase "types of soul" (γένος ψυχῆς 897B7) as expressing his true opinion on the matter.[18] Certainly, as soon as the Athenian returns to the subject he seems to be talking once again about soul in general or psychic force, which is said to lead or guide all things, in heaven, on earth, and under the sea, by means of "its own [i.e., soul's] movements." (896E9) As such, this soul-stuff would appear to be ethically and intellectually neutral. Its activities take on ethical and intellectual colour when it operates "with wisdom as its helper" (νοῦν προσλαβοῦσα) or "when it companies with folly" (ἀνοίᾳ συγγενομένη).[19] This distinction is now applied in an attempt to answer the question, Which type (γένος) of soul can be said to control "heaven and earth and their whole circuit"? (897B7-8) Is it "that which is intelligent and replete with goodness" (i.e., soul when seen as νοῦν προσλαβοῦσα) or the opposite (i.e., soul when seen as ἀνοίᾳ συγγενομένη)? (897B8-C1) The interlocutors agree that the movements of the heavens manifest nothing if not intelligence, and so conclude to the prior alternative. (897C4 ff.) But again, before this conclusion is reached, much of the language is misleading. Hardly has the useful concept of a "type of soul" been introduced than the two "types" are described as "the best *soul*" (τὴν ἀρίστην ψυχήν) and "the bad *soul*" (τὴν κακήν).[20] For many this is simply evidence of careless writing; the doctrine of different *types* of the *same soul* remains Plato's basic position.[21] For others Plato is envisaging the possibility of two World Souls, one good and one evil, but only as a "provisional hypothesis."[22] For others, whom we might call Mazdaists, Plato is definitely stating the existence of two World Souls; if the heavens manifest the good one, one can take it that the sublunary world

17 See especially W. Jaeger (1) 132, R. Reitzenstein and H. H. Schaeder 6, 32-7, and J. Geffcken 517 ff. For more recent upholders of the theory see H. Cherniss (1) 53-7.

18 England ad loc.; S. Pétrement 68; H. Cherniss (2) 26 n29; R. Hackforth (1) 6; V. Martin 121; W. C. Greene 311; H. Görgemanns 201; R. Schaerer 69 n1.

19 897B1, 3. See V. Martin 120.

20 897C7, D1. Cf. 896E5-6, τῆς εὐεργετίδος, etc.

21 See above, n18.

22 L. Robin (1) 227; A.-J. Festugière (1) II 126. Earlier, however, Robin had talked of a good and bad element within the one soul ((2) 114).

will be the province of the other.[23] It is then only a short step to identify this latter with the Necessity of the *Timaeus*.[24]

The Mazdaist case seems to rest upon a literal interpretation of statements taken out of context. It is true that Plato's writing is very unguarded, but strong evidence against a "two souls" theory can be found at the end of the argument, where he concludes that "it would be blasphemy to ascribe the work to anything but a soul or souls – one or more than one – of absolute goodness." (898C7–8) Whether it is one or many good souls that govern the heavens seems a matter of indifference to him.[25] The important point is that the psychic force manifest in the operation of the heavens is of a type recognizably "good," whether one chooses to look upon it collectively or distributively.[26] The "hypothesis" theory is attractive, but it does not follow that the hypothesis would involve two and only two World Souls; however careless Plato's language, the "one" or "many" of 898c makes it clear that he wants to talk about *at least* two types of soul, one or both of which might be viewed as *further* subdivided. If, in spite of this, one continues to posit the (hypothetical) existence of an Evil World Soul, its nature must still remain in doubt. For Plato himself seems to vary in his appraisal of it, now dubbing it categorically as "the bad soul" ($\tau\grave{\eta}\nu$ $\kappa\alpha\kappa\acute{\eta}\nu$), now less roundly as "that which is *capable of* the contrary effect" (i.e., of evil) ($\tau\hat{\eta}s$ $\tau\acute{\alpha}\nu\alpha\nu\tau\acute{\iota}\alpha$ $\delta\upsilon\nu\alpha\mu\acute{\epsilon}\nu\eta s$ $\grave{\epsilon}\rho\gamma\acute{\alpha}\zeta\epsilon\sigma\theta\alpha\iota$).[27] His imprecision of language throughout the whole passage makes any interpretation hazardous, but the least unsatisfactory is perhaps that of England, Moreau, Cherniss, and others, who feel that he is trying to distinguish two basic types of single psychic energy.[28] If one interprets such dubious phrases as "the best soul" and "the bad soul" in the light of this the passage makes some sense, but a number of questions remain unanswered. If the heavens manifest the presence of a "best type of soul" ($\check{\alpha}\rho\iota\sigma\tau o\nu$ $\psi\upsilon\chi\hat{\eta}s$ $\gamma\acute{\epsilon}\nu os$), are we to conclude that the "bad type of soul," having served its purpose as an hypothesis, does not really exist at all? If not,

23 See S. Pétrement 70–2 for references. To these add A. Rivaud (1) 351–2, G. M. A. Grube (2) 147 n1, and G. Müller 87.

24 U. von Wilamowitz-Moellendorff II 321; Th.-H. Martin 356–7 (following Plutarch); E. R. Dodds (1) 21.

25 See 898B5–6, and *Phlb.* 30B4–5.

26 See England on 896E4, and *Phlb.* 30B4–5.

27 897D1, 896E6. It is the less strong of the two assertions which lends strength to the claim that the $\psi\upsilon\chi\acute{\eta}$ in question is the equivalent of $\grave{\alpha}\nu\acute{\alpha}\gamma\kappa\eta$ in the *Timaeus*. See T. Gould 134.

28 For references to Burnet, England, Taylor, and Moreau, see S. Pétrement 68. To this add W. C. Greene 311, W. Spoerri 211, R. Hackforth (1) 6, H. Cherniss (2) 26 n29, T. Gould 134.

where is it? Totally in the sublunary world, or partly in the heavens as well?[29]
Is it perhaps a collective term for the evil in men's souls,[30] or a popular term
for that element of cussedness in the world of physical things more strikingly
described elsewhere as Necessity?[31] The answers to such queries have been
legion, and the imprecise nature of Plato's language leaves each one open
to question. Perhaps the safest policy is to look for his "philosophy of evil,"
if he has one, amidst less dubious texts.

The broadening of the definition of soul has already taken us some way
from the schematized reasoning of the *Phaedrus*; we now go even further,
when an account of the *nature* of soul's motions is offered. These psychic
movements, by which soul is said to lead or control all things in heaven,
earth, or sea are given in full: "Wish, reflection, foresight, counsel, judgment,
true or false, pleasure, pain, hope, fear, hate, love, and whatever other
kindred or primary [πρωτουργοί] motions there may be."[32] This very
"personal" or "spiritual" description is in marked contrast with the
"physical" description of the movements of soul, personal and cosmic, in
the *Timaeus*. (36c ff.) It is tempting, of course, to explain away the "crudities"
of the *Timaeus* by reference to this passage and *Sophist* 249A, where the
movements of soul are again fairly clearly not spatial, but totally spiritual.[33]
But, quite apart from the general hazardousness of "explaining" any earlier
dialogue by a posterior one, in this case we do not seem to be considering
identical types of movement. Here in the *Laws* it is the self-induced and
self-sustained movement of the non-contingent and autonomous soul that
is under discussion; in the *Timaeus*, I have suggested, the soul (apart from
the presumptive – and exceptional – soul of the Demiurge) is merely *in*
everlasting motion only, not a *principle* of motion, and is basically contingent. In view of this I take it that Plato is here expressing a rather different
view of soul, and one that implies a possibly more profound view of the
nature of its activities. These (psychic) activities, the primacy of whose
motion is stressed (πρωτουργοί), are remarkably "personal" in appearance,

29 Scholars who are convinced that Plato *is* talking about an Evil World Soul tend to
place it in the sublunary world. E.g., H. Cherniss (3) 208 n2, G. Müller 87, and R. W. Hall
77. Hall stresses that Evil World Soul is inferior to Good World Soul.
30 G. M. A. Grube feels that the evil soul(s) must be the souls of ignorant men ((2) 146).
See also P. Stöcklein 45.
31 E. R. Dodds (1) 21, following Plutarch.
32 897A1–4. W. Theiler (2) 70 goes too far, I feel, in saying that the movement of soul in
the *Phaedrus* is *Ortsbewegung* only. The argument at 245c ff. seems to me generic and
non-committal. For non-material psychic motions see R. 583D ff. and *Tht.* 153B9–10.
33 See J. B. Skemp (1) 21, 86.

and include a large element of providence (cf. especially the verbs "examine" σκοπεῖσθαι, "care for" ἐπιμελεῖσθαι, and "plan" βουλεύεσθαι).[34] This is a useful elucidation of what was implicit in the *Phaedrus* account, where soul's providence was equally evident. (246B6–7) But it is worth noticing that the providence of soul in the *Laws* is not necessarily beneficent; it can be directed to ends other than good.[35] Nor need it be particularly intelligent; the most that Plato says is that it "plans" and can (but need not) "opine correctly," (897A1–2) and that it can be motivated by hatred as much as by love. (897A3)

Soul's movements are said to "take over" "the secondary movements of bodies," thus inducing "growth and decrease," "separation and combination," and other like characteristics of the physical world. (897A4 ff.) Such secondary movements are the material with which soul must work; the perfection or imperfection of the results will depend upon whether it acts with intelligence or unintelligence. (897B1–3) All of this has much in common with what is said in other dialogues about individual (intellective) souls, or about the Demiurge. But the differences are even more noticeable. The Demiurge can do nothing but good and is himself totally good (*Ti.* 29E1–3, *Plt.* 273B6–7); soul as such can do good or evil, depending on whether it "has wisdom as its helper" or "companies with folly." (897B1–3) The Demiurge can be meaningfully (if misleadingly) seen as a doublet of World Soul or the intelligence of World Soul; soul as such need *not* use intelligence, and any providence it exercises can be directed to ends other than good. This final point serves also to distinguish it from that totally intelligent, beneficently provident and divine World Soul which we saw in the *Timaeus*. It is much more correctly described as cosmic soul-stuff or psychic force, ethically and intellectually neutral, which takes on ethical and intellectual colour when and as it operates in accordance with wisdom (νοῦς) or folly (ἄνοια).[36] (The distinction is no doubt a logical one only; it would be hard to imagine a soul in a state where it *neither* "has wisdom as its helper" *nor* "companies with folly.") Its essential neutrality makes it very like the "life-soul" to which we were first introduced in the *Phaedo*,[37] and

---

34 897A4, 897A1. With 897A4 compare 897A5 (παραλαμβάνουσαι) and 897B2 (παιδαγωγεῖ).

35 See especially 897A3, 897B1–4.

36 W. Theiler (2) 69 n1, apart from a misleading introduction of the phrase World Soul, gives an admirable definition of ψυχή in the *Laws*. "Weltseele," he writes, "ist ja nur der zusammenfassende Ausdruck für den geistigen Ursprung aller im Weltall erschienenen Bewegungen."

37 I.e., in the argument from Opposition.

Martin, thinking along similar lines, points out how biological existence is the *sine qua non* of any action, good or bad, intelligent or insane.[38] But here again, as in the *Phaedo*, life-soul and cognitive soul are presumed to be one and the same, and the problems which might have been raised there (and were not) are once more bypassed.

The discussion of causes and *sine quibus non* in the *Phaedo* also seems to find its counterpart in the *Laws*. The true cause of Socrates' sitting down, according to the *Phaedo*, is to be found in the psychic "movement" of volition (cf. *Laws* 897C1, βούλεσθαι); any flexing of muscles or bending of joints is seen as an indispensable physical condition (συναίτιον) rather than as a genuine cause. (98C ff.) In spite of the difference of language, this reads very like the "primary" and "secondary" motions of *Laws* x. If this analysis is correct, the soul of *Laws* x seems to be a cosmic version of the individual soul seen as a *life*-soul, just as the individual soul seen in its *noetic* or cognitive aspect had its cosmic equivalent in the rational World Soul of the *Timaeus* and *Politicus*. We first met these two types of soul in the *Phaedo*, in the Opposition and Recollection arguments respectively, and noticed how their assumed oneness created problems rather than solved them. Later, when tackling the same questions on a cosmic scale, Plato stresses the operation now of one type of soul, now of the other, though apparently never doubting that the two are really one and the same principle. Therein, it seems, lies the source of so many confusions. Not the least of these is the way in which soul is claimed to be a source of motion and *per se* autokinetic yet still subject to Becoming.[39] Soul may be either contingent or non-contingent, but hardly both. The puzzle deepens when *all* motion is implicitly declared to be eternal – for Anaxagoras is criticized for his audacity in imagining that movement could originate from a state of primeval immobility.[40] One quasi-solution would be to bring in the Demiurge once again; his soul will be the exceptional, all-important one that is *not* subject to Becoming, as in the *Timaeus* and *Politicus*. As it happens, the Demiurge as such is not to be found, but his clear counterpart appears in the divine Chess Player, who arranges the pieces in a way which will fit the whole. This is the god who is called "not inferior to human workmen" (902E4–5) and in his care

---

38 V. Martin 120.

39 967D4–5, 892A4–5, 892C4. A. Diès (1) II 567 thinks that Plato is here accommodating himself to his readers (who are presumably not overinterested in the niceties of metaphysical speculation). M. Guéroult 38 feels that we are left to understand that soul is created by a Demiurge, as in the *Timaeus*.

40 895A6 ff., and M. Guéroult 43. His exposition of the problems seems to me admirable, his solution (in terms of the Hegelian triad) preposterous.

for the whole is compared to "a doctor or skilled craftsman" (δημιουργός).[41]
But how the soul dependent on him for its existence can still be autokinetic
remains as puzzling as ever; either it or the god himself must prove superfluous, it seems. Certainly the problem is now much more acute than in the
Timaeus, for there World Soul was simply an entity *in* everlasting motion
but apparently not itself *self*-moving; now soul *as such* is seen to be *both*.
(896A1–B1) Aristotle sees the implications of this, if Plato does not, and
fuses Demiurge and soul-as-source-of-motion into the ultimate Unmoved
Mover. But Plato tries to the end to preserve his two principles, at the risk
of incoherence.

In context, the psychology of *Laws* x is an uncompromising apologetic.
Plato's views of soul as such, seen in abstraction, are simply the prelude to
his major thesis that the heavens and their operations manifest the activity
of one special type of soul or souls exercising intelligence and providence,
and hence clearly qualifying for the title of divine. Their intelligence can be
inferred from their circular motion;[42] their providence and care can be denied
only by the impious. (898C3–8) At 898D it is finally agreed that *all* the
heavenly bodies can be said to have an individual soul, and the interesting
problem is raised of how such a soul is related to the body in question. From
the very beginning the body-soul relationship in Plato's works has been
something never clearly formulated, and even at the end he seems as unsure
as ever. Taking the sun as his example, he mentions three possible ways in
which soul might control body; from within, as does "our own soul"; from
without; or by "guiding" it in some other mysterious way "stripped of
body and in possession of other wonderful powers."[43] It is worth noticing
that the "inner person" view of the *individual* human soul still holds sway,
but for the rest his conclusions could hardly be more unsatisfactory. The
reason is not far to seek. However much soul and body are supposed to differ
in ontological status, in practice, whether we are dealing with the soul of the
Phaedo or of *Laws* x, the two are treated as being equally substantial. Though
soul is supposed in both dialogues to be indiscernible to the senses,[44] and

41 903C5–6. Like the Demiurge, he is also called βασιλεύς (904A6). See *Phlb.* 28C7, and
H. Görgemanns 202.

42 See *Ti.* 36E3–5 and *Plt.* 269E5.

43 898E8–10, 898E10–899A2, 899A2–4. This perhaps indicates that, while Plato may still
feel that it is meaningful to talk about the heavenly bodies as ζῷα, he is beginning to
think that the genus ζῷον may have to be widened when we are dealing with objects in a
superlunary world beyond the reach of exhaustive sense perception. See V. Martin 119.

44 898E1, *Phd.* 79B12 ff. At 898D11–E2, however, it is noteworthy that Plato is not dogmatic

though its movements are anything but bodily, in two out of his three guesses its actions are simply those of any three-dimensional body. The third guess, however, while telling us nothing very illuminating, is perhaps a hint that Plato sensed the implausibility of the first two.

His final conclusions are then drawn.

> *Athenian*: Of all the planets, of the moon, of years and months and all seasons, what other story shall we have to tell than just this same, that since soul or souls, and those souls good with perfect goodness, have proved to be causes of all, these souls we hold to be gods, whether they direct the universe by inhabiting bodies, like animated beings, or whatever the manner of their action. Will any man who shares this belief bear to hear that all things are not "full of gods"?
> *Clinias*: No man, sir, can be so much beside himself.[45]

With this the case against the atheists is complete.

The *Epinomis*, which may be the last of Plato's works or one written by another shortly after Plato's death,[46] has little new to say about soul, though changes of emphasis abound. In particular, the dichotomy of soul and body is trenchantly reaffirmed (980D6 ff.), and we are treated to a number of familiar epithets. The soul is the ruling element in the living being (980E2), older than body (980E5), more godlike, and "better" (980D8); whatever the type of body-soul complex, cosmic or otherwise, this will invariably be the case. (980D7) New, however, is the more extravagant statement at 983D2–E3, where the sum total of reality (τὰ ὄντα) is divided into two, soul and body; everything that is will be a species of one or other of these genera. The author goes on: "The first we shall, of course, take to be intelligent, the second unintelligent; the first sovereign, the second subject; the first the universal cause, the second a cause of no effect whatsoever." (983D3–7) Intelligence and causal responsibility (αἴτιον), it seems, are confined to soul only. This marks a considerable change from the *Timaeus*, where room is

about the imperceptibility of soul in all cases (τὸ παράπαν). For his own purposes it no doubt is, but he is not sufficiently confident to write with complete assurance. Even in the *Phaedo* the soul is said to be only *like* the invisible Ideas.

45 899B3–C1. In this account I have stressed the fact that if ψυχή is an ἀρχὴ κινήσεως it is non-contingent. A writer more interested in *Lebensphilosophie* will emphasize that, when applied to the human soul, it is an assertion of its autonomy and free will. See H. Barth 288, following Hegel.

46 For a full discussion see the preface to the Budé edition.

left for the Ideas, the only true ὄντα, and where Necessity is seen as a powerful force in the world process, though not, apparently, a psychic one. In the *Laws*, however, soul was seen as the cause of the activity of all things, and no stress was laid upon the Ideas. The *Epinomis* seems to be pushing the latter position to its extreme conclusion.

The old problem of soul's contingency or non-contingency is still with us. Soul is asserted to be self-moving (988D2), and one is tempted at once to think that its reality is non-contingent; against this, it is said that only a god (θεός) can bring about the ensoulment of any body (983B2-3), and one must therefore conclude that soul must be to some degree dependent for its existence, temporal or otherwise, upon a reality other than itself. The θεός in question is called "father," like the Demiurge of the *Timaeus* (978C4; *Ti.* 37C7), but the author seems equally willing to identify him with what appears to be World Soul, called now Uranus, or Cosmos, or Olympus. (977A4, B2) This does make it appear that, in the *Epinomis* at any rate, the θεός or Demiurge is simply a doublet for World Soul;[47] but if soul is supposed to be self-moving, why is a θεός mentioned at all? Perhaps the author saw a difference in kind between the non-contingent World Soul and/or Demiurge and other contingent souls who owe their existence to it. But, if this is true, the difficulties have only been shelved, not solved, since even the contingent souls of the heavenly bodies are said to be themselves self-moving (988D2); unless their autokinesis is of a different kind, why must *their* embodiment have an αἴτιον other than themselves, while World Soul apparently needs none? The author gives no hint, however, that their autokinesis *is* different in kind, and we are left with a confusing picture: Soul is either (a) of two kinds, the one (explicably) non-contingent, and the other (inexplicably) contingent, or (b) of one kind, but somehow contingent or non-contingent according to the plane of its activity. Either way, we have not yet progressed from the stage of assertion to that of argument.

The problem of a good and a bad soul is raised briefly once again, but remains as obscure as ever. "The good soul" is the origin of all that ends in good, and the bad (soul) of the opposite. (988E2-3) Is this simply loose writing for two different *types* of soul, as is perhaps the case in the *Laws*, or is the author really thinking of two opposed deities? A third view, that bad soul is

---

47 The "demiurgic" activities of soul on a cosmic scale are clearly outlined at 984B6-7 (πλάττειν) and 984C2-5 (πλάττειν ... δημιουργήσασαν). To this degree Demiurge and cosmic ψυχή might well be called a doublet (see above, 100n18, for references to Theiler and Festugière). But, in view of the doubtful authenticity of the *Epinomis*, it would be hazardous to apply this view directly to the *Laws*.

introduced only as a provisional hypothesis,[48] can be excluded, since stress is laid upon both the good and the bad in the cosmos, rather than just the good, and the author clearly intends to posit a psychic origin for both. (988D4 ff.) But here, as in the *Laws*, the evidence from the text is still unclear, and one can only outline the balance of probabilities. It does seem highly unlikely that Plato, even in old age, should have gone over to such an extreme position as that of Mazdaism, without explaining himself more fully to his startled readers. A less unsatisfactory solution is to take the two "souls" as meaning two types of soul, and to seek for their origin in the Love and Strife of Empedocles rather than in the two gods of Mazdaism. Such a conclusion would more than adequately account for the author's final assertion that "good [τὰ ἀγαθά] must be, and ever has been, triumphant over its contrary." (988E3–4) This conviction is in keeping with his views that the heavenly bodies and their movements manifest the operation of divine intelligence in the universe (982A7 ff.), and that the product of intelligence of such a perfect order will inevitably be that which is itself perfect. (982C1–2) The ordered progress of the heavens is seen as the result of an antecedent Master Plan (982C4–5), and reads like a primitive cosmic version of the theory of pre-established harmony. Convictions such as these seem hard to square with the notion that there is an evil god in the universe competing on equal terms with the good. If anything, they are nearer to the position adopted in the *Timaeus*, where the Necessity associated with the body is largely open to the persuasion of intelligence, and allows itself to be directed towards what is good. (48A2–3) To say that "things that are good" prevail over their opposite is to voice one's ultimate conviction that, in spite of its evident recalcitrance, the universe is subject to the guiding hand of an intelligent providence, with whom the forces of evil can never hope to compete on exactly equal terms.

48 See above, 149n22.

I I

Coda

The complexity and subtlety of thought which Plato manifests on almost every topic makes it hazardous for a commentator to attempt to reduce it to a small, unified, easily-digested summary and conclusion. Bearing this in mind, I shall here simply review the strains and tensions that have become apparent during the discussion of Plato's concept of soul and leave the reader to judge for himself what unifying factors (if any) underlie them and/or what progress (or regress, depending on one's viewpoint) in Plato's writings on the subject can be discerned.

Several distinguishable senses of soul emerged from the Socratic dialogues. It is a cognitive principle (e.g., in the *Charmides* and *Protagoras*) and a principle of moral activity (e.g., in the *Gorgias* and *Meno*). It is also meant to be seen as the "true self" in the *Charmides*, *Alcibiades* I, and *Protagoras*, and as what I call a "counter-person" in the myth of the *Gorgias* (and other, later, myths). As far as the body-soul relationship is concerned the *Charmides*, *Alcibiades* I, and *Protagoras* are united in asserting that self and soul are one and the same, but differ in their accounts of its relationship to the body. In the *Protagoras* the body is simply a possession of the soul; in *Alcibiades* I it is likewise a possession and an "instrument" of the soul, but enjoys a "special relationship" with soul that other possessions do not; in the *Charmides* it is seen to be itself an integral and inalienable part of soul, and the two enjoy the sophisticated relationship of biological part to biological whole. In two dialogues, the *Gorgias* and *Meno*, there are hints of partition within the soul, and its continued existence after separation from the body is asserted.

In the *Phaedo* soul as cognitive principle, moral principle, true self, and counter-person is once more evident, though now there are added the notions of soul as life-principle (or "life-carrier") and soul as some sort of spatialistic fluid in the body, rather like ectoplasm. More confusing is a description of the similarities between soul and the Ideas, in which soul seems to be something static, homogeneous, and atomic. In all these descriptions soul is clearly meant to be a substance on a par with body, so that their numerical addition would make two. As for the body-soul relationship, this is one of extreme dualism. Body is at best a nuisance and at worst an evil, and in no way part of the true self, which is exhausted in content by the soul. Equally suspect are the pleasures and desires of the body and the bodily, which are to be distinguished in kind from the more reputable desires of the soul. The body, in a word, is an influence for harm, and the life of the good man will be a process of "purification" from it, in the hope of achieving a reward elsewhere. As for the proofs of soul's immortality which take up a large part of the dialogue, these, I suggested, are largely vitiated by the continual exploitation (witting or unwitting) of the ambiguities within the notion of soul itself.

In the *Republic* most of the senses of soul seen in the *Phaedo* re-emerge, and confusion between two of them, soul as life-principle and soul as moral principle, casts serious doubts on the validity of the argumentation about soul's well-being in the crucial closing pages of book one. By and large soul and self are accepted as synonymous, though in a few curious passages the self seems to be seen as a biological combination of soul and body (as in the *Charmides*) or as a super-Ego transcending the body-soul complex. How seriously such passages are to be taken, however, is very much open to question.

Apparently to suit a political analogue, the soul is declared to be tripartite, and this is a notable advance over the *Phaedo*, in that desires and pleasures, which were there written off as of "bodily" provenance and hence suspect, are now seen to have a part to play in the balanced personality, if they are sensibly canalized. Conversely, conflict in a person is conflict within his soul, not conflict (as in the *Phaedo*) between soul and body. Virtue is health of soul, and health of soul is balance between its different constituent elements or parts or "drives."

In book ten a new argument for immortality is introduced, and I defended a minority opinion in arguing that the "soul" whose immortality is under discussion is the whole (tripartite) soul, not simply that element in it which is called reason or the reasoning part in book four. This is not to argue that it survives in its tripartite state; it is simply to maintain that the soul which survives, perhaps as a unity, has the same gamut or extension as that soul which is claimed to be in some way tripartite *ici bas*.

In the *Timaeus* we saw the full-blown elaboration of what had been hinted at even in the *Republic* – that is, that the world, analogously with the human being and other living things, is itself alive and has a "soul." This soul, I argued (against Cornford), is purely noetic, and is in most respects the analogue of the "reasoning" part of human soul as described in *Republic* IV. It is also, like the human reason, everlasting, though not eternal; that is, the everlastingness of its duration is a "temporal" one (as distinct from the non-temporal "eternity" of the Ideas and of what Plato calls the Demiurge)., It is dependent for its being on the Demiurge, and so is contingent, by contrast with the Demiurge and the Ideas, which are non-contingent. It possesses everlasting circular motions, called the Same and the Different, which, I argued (again against Cornford), both demonstrate its inherent rationality; even though the Different has as its province the subrational world of transient existence, its approach is the most rational one compatible with the exiguous amount of being and intelligibility that such a world enjoys.

In much of my interpretation I criticized the views of Proclus and Plutarch (and their modern followers) and defended the more "literalist" interpretation of Aristotle. This included a defence of the very "physical" language used of World Soul; it seems to me to find its analogue in the physical language sometimes used of individual soul in the *Phaedo*.

Equally "physical" language is used in the *Timaeus* of the individual human soul, which is again said to be tripartite, and each "part" is spoken of as though it is located within a particular part of the body. The "tri-partition," however, seems somewhat different from that outlined in the *Republic*, and is probably more fairly described as *bi*-partition with a further subdivision within it; the essential division of human soul is into its mortal and immortal aspects. For it is now *unequivocally* asserted (by contrast with *Republic* X) that the only part of human soul which is immortal is reason. The two "lower" parts are mortal, being merely aspects of soul in its incarnate state.

I followed Taylor in taking the Demiurge, father and organizer (but not creator) of the Universe, to be a person, rather than simply a symbol of intelligence. He is soul and intelligence at their most untrammelled. Against Festugière (who sees the Demiurge as simply a doublet of World Soul) and against Cornford (who sees him as a doublet of the "rational element" in World Soul) I suggested that the Demiurge is a being quite different in kind from World Soul. He is uncreated, eternal, and *non*-contingent; World Soul is created, *temporally* everlasting, and contingent.

"Necessity" I took to be an eternal, non-psychic datum, over and against the Demiurge, epitomizing the nuisance-value of "the bodily" (as it is later called in the *Politicus*) to any planning intelligence which is compelled to have dealings with it. Being eternal, it is to be found in both the pre-cosmic chaos and the formed cosmos. In either case its causality is non-teleological, though by the time the cosmos is formed it has been so "persuaded" and tamed by the Demiurge that its causality is now the predictable, mechanistic one enjoyed by formed physical objects – that mechanistic causality on whose general reliability and predictability we base our everyday lives.

Distinguishing as I do between World Soul and the soul of the Demiurge, I argued that the later doctrine of soul as a source of motion and self-moving can hardly refer to World Soul, since the latter is dependent for its origin on the Demiurge. At most one will be able to say that it could by implication apply to the eternal, non-contingent soul of the Demiurge. World Soul may be in everlasting motion, but it is not that eternal, self-originating, and self-sustained motion which the *Phaedrus* and *Laws* are at pains to affirm as the essence of soul in any form. One might concede that statements about soul's power of self-motion are to be found in embryo in the notion that soul is a life-principle (e.g., in the *Phaedo*), but, in view of the very "static" image of soul which emerges in dialogues like the *Phaedo*, one can legitimately doubt whether at such a stage Plato is aware of some of the implications of his assertions. As for the doctrine of the "motions" of World Soul (and, by analogy, of individual soul) in the *Timaeus*, these seemed to be readily explicable in terms of the observable motions of the heavenly bodies, without reference to the more sophisticated and all-embracing doctrine of soul propounded in the *Phaedrus*.

In the *Phaedrus* a view of soul is put forward which, I argued, is a considerable advance over the one which prevails in the *Timaeus*. It concerns soul as such, rather than cosmic or individual soul, and maintains that it is a source of motion and is eternally self-moving, as well as exercising a providential care over what is not ensouled. I took this to mean that all soul is non-contingent and eternal; what was true only of the Demiurge in the *Timaeus* is now seen to be universally true of any soul. "Soul," however, in this argument I took to mean noetic soul only, following Hermias.

Concomitant with this advanced view is the sort of image of soul already seen in the earlier dialogues. In the mythological section, for example, it is seen as a counter-person (as in all the myths), though it is still apparently the same tripartite soul as in *Republic* IV. This seems to be a definite *volte-face* from the position adopted in the *Timaeus*, where only the reasoning part of soul is said to be immortal, but can probably be squared with the discussion in *Republic* x.

The myth of the *Politicus* seemed to me an interesting conflation of views expressed in both the *Timaeus* and the *Phaedrus*. As in the *Timaeus*, World Soul is contingent and the Demiurge non-contingent. The findings of the *Phaedrus*, however, have led Plato to depict the Demiurge as himself enjoying eternal rotation, this being the logical corollary of his combined non-contingency and autokinesis. In the light of the discussion of soul in the *Phaedrus*, autokinesis is attributed to World Soul, but its basic contingency upon the Demiurge suggests that such "autokinesis" is of a qualified nature only; the global claims of the *Phaedrus* have been seen to be less absolute than Plato at first imagined. World Soul also seems now to have a partly irrational element in it (cf. the *Phaedrus*, where even the immortal souls of the gods seem to have a "desiderative" element), by contrast with the *Timaeus*, while the non-rational datum called Necessity, with which the Demiurge had to grapple in the *Timaeus*, has its clear counterpart in what the *Politicus* calls "the bodily."

In the *Philebus* the parallelism between World Soul and individual soul is again stressed, but is given a different emphasis by the assertion that World Soul is the *source* of human soul and World Mind the *source* of human mind. World Soul is seen as essentially a matrix for intelligence (cf. the *Timaeus* and *Sophist*): there is no hint of any irrationality or ethical neutrality about it. It is also, it appears, contingent upon a "transcendent" Intelligence, and this would seem to be the fairly clear counterpart of the Demiurge of the *Timaeus* and *Politicus*. As far as human soul is concerned, there is the usual fluidity in the descriptions given of it, though a notable point, in line with *Republic* IX, is the assertion that all pleasures and desires are of psychic origin. The break with the viewpoint of the *Phaedo* seems just about complete.

In the *Laws* soul is again said to be a source of motion and eternally self-moving, but the argument of the *Phaedrus* has been broadened considerably. For now the stress is upon soul as life-force, or cosmic-stuff, rather than on soul as a cognitive principle (cf. the *Timaeus* and *Politicus*). We are no longer dealing with a (beneficently provident and rational) World Soul whose activities are supremely manifest in the operations of the heavenly bodies, but with an ethically and intellectually neutral cosmic-stuff or life-force, the *sine qua non* of all ethical or intellectual activity. It can (but need not) act intelligently, and its providence can (but need not) be directed to laudable ends. This soul-stuff, like World Soul in the *Timaeus*, is older than the world's body (just as individual soul is older than individual body in the *Phaedo*), and comes into being. That is, it is contingent upon some other being. This latter is the divine Chess Player, the fairly clear counterpart of the Demiurge in the *Timaeus* and *Politicus*, and of the transcendent Intelligence in the *Philebus*. The softening of the *Phaedrus* argument implied in the *Politicus* is of relevance to the *Laws*: soul-stuff may be a source of motion and self-moving, but its self-motion will be of a special order, contingent as it is upon a soul higher than itself.

The claim that there are "two souls," one good, one bad, struggling for the supremacy of the cosmos, is one that I rejected, while admitting that Plato expresses himself most unfortunately.

The *Epinomis*, whether written by Plato or another, largely reiterates the viewpoint of the *Laws* concerning soul-stuff, but talk about its "demiurgic" activities suggested that the author was trying to equate it with the (rational) World Soul of the *Timaeus* and also, perhaps, with the Demiurge himself. A similar attempt to equate life-soul and intellective soul at the individual level was seen in the *Phaedo*.

As for individual soul, it was suggested that the *Laws* and *Epinomis* present us with an almost complete compendium of Plato's views. Remarkable for its omission is tripartition, particularly in so obviously political a context. Whatever the development in sophistication of his views on World Soul, in the matter of individual soul Plato the old man, it was suggested, seems content to abide by the popular, bipartite view originally propounded in the Socratic dialogues.

Abbreviations

AC   *Acta Classica*
AJP   *American Journal of Philology*
AntCl   *L'Antiquité classique*
ArchGPh   *Archiv für Geschichte der Philosophie*
ArchPh   *Archiv für Philosophie*
ArchPhilos   *Archives de philosophie*
BonnJbb   *Bonner Jahrbücher*
CP   *Classical Philology*
CQ   *Classical Quarterly*
CR   *Classical Review*
DK¹²   *Die Fragmente der Vorsokratiker,*¹²
   eds. H. Diels, W. Kranz (Dublin/Zürich 1966)
HSCP   *Harvard Studies in Classical Philology*
JClS   *Journal of Classical Studies*
JHI   *Journal of the History of Ideas*
JHPh   *Journal of the History of Philosophy*
JHS   *Journal of Hellenic Studies*
JP   *Journal of Philology*
PhQ   *Philosophical Quarterly*
PhR   *Philosophical Review*
PP   *La Parola del Passato*
ProcArSoc   *Proceedings of the Aristotelian Society*
ProcBritAc   *Proceedings of the British Academy*
ProcPhilSoc   *Proceedings of the American Philosophical Society*
RBPh   *Revue Belge de philosophie et d'histoire*
REA   *Revue des études anciennes*
REG   *Revue des études grecques*
REL   *Revue des études latines*
RhM   *Rheinisches Museum für Philologie*

RMM   *Revue de métaphysique et de morale*
RPh   *Revue de philologie, de littérature et d'histoire anciennes*
RThPh   *Revue de théologie et de philosophie*
SBBay   *Sitzungsberichte der Bayerischen Akademie der Wissenschaften, Phil.-hist. Klasse*
SBWien   *Sitzungsberichte der Oesterreichischen Akademie der Wissenschaften, Phil.-hist. Klasse*
StPh   *Studia Philosophica*
TAPA   *Transactions of the American Philological Association*

Bibliography

Ackrill, J. L. Review of R. Hackforth (7) *Mind* LXII (1953) 277–9
Adam, J. (ed.) (1) *Plato's Crito* Cambridge 1888
  (2) *The Republic of Plato*² Cambridge 1963
Allan, D. J. (ed.) *Plato: Republic, Book I*² London 1944
Allen, R. E. (ed.) *Studies in Plato's Metaphysics* London 1965
Archer-Hind, R. D. (1) "On some Difficulties in the Platonic Psychology"
  JP X (1882) 120–31
  (2) *The Phaedo of Plato* London 1894

Baldry, H. C. "Embryological Analogies in pre-Socratic Cosmogony" *CQ*
  XXVI (1932) 27–34
Ballard, E. "Plato's Movement from an Ethics of Individuals to a Science of
  Particulars" *Tulane Studies in Philosophy* VI (1957) 5–41
Bambrough, R. (ed.) *New Essays in Plato and Aristotle* New York 1965
Barth, H. *Die Seele in der Philosophie Platons* Tübingen 1921
Bäumker, C. *Das Problem der Materie in der griechischen Philosophie* Münster
  1890
Bidez, J. *Eos, ou Platon et l'Orient* Bruxelles 1945
Bluck, R. S. (1) "The Phaedrus and Re-incarnation" *AJP* LXXIX (1958)
  156–64
  (2) "Plato, Pindar and Metempsychosis" *AJP* LXXIX (1958) 404–14
Boeckh, A. *Untersuchungen über das kosmische System des Platon* Berlin 1852
Boll, F. (1) *Sphaera* Leipzig 1903
  (2) *Sternglaube und Sterndeutung* Leipzig-Berlin 1926
Boyancé, P. *Le Culte des Muses chez les philosophes grecs* Paris 1937
Brémond, A. "De l'âme et de Dieu dans la philosophie de Platon" *ArchPhilos*
  II (1924) 372–404

Buford, Th. O. *The Idea of Creation in Plato, Augustine and Emil Brunner* Boston 1963

Burnet, J. (1) "The Socratic Doctrine of the Soul" *ProcBritAc* VII (1916) 235 ff.

(2) *Early Greek Philosophy*[2] London 1908

(3) *Plato's Euthyphro, Apology of Socrates and Crito* Oxford 1924

(4) *Plato's Phaedo* Oxford 1911

(5) *Greek Philosophy* I: *Thales to Plato* London 1914

Bury, R. G. *Plato's Philebus* Cambridge 1897

Callahan, J. F. *Four Views on Time in Ancient Philosophy* Cambridge, Mass. 1948

Campbell, L. *The Sophistes and Politicus of Plato* Oxford 1867

Chaignet, A.-Ed. *De la Psychologie de Platon* Paris 1862

Cherniss, H. (1) "Plato (1950–7)" *Lustrum* IV–V (1959–60)

(2) "The Sources of Evil According to Plato" *ProcPhilSoc* XCVIII (1954) 23–30

(3) Review of A.-J. Festugière (1) II *Gnomon* XXII (1950) 204–16

(4) "The Philosophical Economy of the Theory of Ideas" *AJP* LVII (1936) 445–56

(5) *Aristotle's Criticism of Plato and the Academy* I Baltimore 1944

(6) "The Relationship of the Timaeus to Plato's later Dialogues" *AJP* LXXVIII (1957) 225–66

Claghorn, George S. *Aristotle's Criticism of Plato's "Timaeus"* The Hague 1954

Comau, J. "L'immortalité de l'âme dans le Phédon et la resurrection des morts dans la littérature chrétienne des deux premières siècles" *Helikon* III (1953) 17–40

Cornford, F. M. (1) "The 'Polytheism' of Plato: An Apology" *Mind* XLVII (1938) 321–30

(2) "The Division of the Soul" *Hibbert Journal* XXVIII (1929–30) 206–19

(3) "Psychology and Social Structure in the Republic of Plato" *CQ* VI (1912) 246 ff.

(4) *The Republic of Plato* Oxford 1941

(5) *Plato's Cosmology* London 1937

Courcelle, P. (1) "Le corps-tombeau" *REA* LXVIII (1966) 101–22

(2) "Tradition platonicienne et traditions chrétiennes du corps-prison" *REL* XLII (1966) 406–43

Couvreur, P. (ed.) *Hermiae Alexandrini in Platonis Phaedrum Scholia* Paris 1901

Croiset, A. (ed.) *Platon: Oeuvres complètes* II: *Hippias Majeur, Charmide, Lachès, Lysis* Paris 1921

Crombie, I. M. *An Examination of Plato's Doctrines* 2 vols. London 1962, 1963

de Mahieu, W. "La doctrine des athées au Xe livre des Lois de Platon" *RBPhil* XLI (1963) 5–24

des Places, E. (1) "Platon et l'astronomie chaldéenne" in *Mélanges Franz Cumont* Bruxelles 1936, 120–42

    (2) *Syngeneia: La parenté de l'homme avec Dieu, d'Homère à la patristique* Paris 1966

de Vogel, C. J. (1) "Het godsbegrip bij Plato, II" *AC* VIII (1965) 38–52

    (2) "On the Neoplatonic Character of Platonism and the Platonic Character of Neoplatonism" *Mind* LXII (1953) 43–64

Diano, C. "Quod semper movetur aeternum est" *PP* II (1947) 189–92

Diès, A. (1) *Autour de Platon* 2 vols. Paris 1927

    (2) "Le dieu de Platon" in *Autour d'Aristote* (Festschrift for A. Mansion) Leuven 1955, 61–7

    (3) (ed.) *Platon: Oeuvres complètes* IX: *Le Politique* Paris 1935

Dodds, E. R. (1) "Plato and the Irrational" *JHS* XLV (1945) 18–25

    (2) *The Greeks and the Irrational* Berkeley 1951

    (3) *Plato: Gorgias* Oxford 1959

Disertori, P. *Il Messaggio del Timeo* Padova 1965

Dover, K. J. "The Date of Plato's Symposium" *Phronesis* X (1965) 2–20

Edelstein, L. Review of M. Pohlenz *Hippokrates und die Begründung der wissenschaftlichen Medizin* (Berlin 1938) *AJP* LXI (1940) 221–9

Einarson, B. "A new edition of the Epinomis" *CP* LIII (1958) 91–7

England, E. B. *The Laws of Plato* 2 vols. Manchester 1921

Festugière, A.-J. (1) *La Révélation d'Hermès Trismégiste* II and III Paris 1949, 1953

    (2) "Platon et l'Orient" *RevPhil* III, 21 (1947) 5–45

    (3) *Contemplation et vie contemplative chez Platon*[2] Paris 1950

    (4) "Les trois vies" *Acta Congressus Madvigiani* II (Hafniae 1954) 131–74

    (5) "Les 'Mémoires Pythagoriques' cités par Alexandre Polyhistor" *REG* LXVIII (1945) 1–59

Ferguson, J. *Plato: Republic, Book* X London 1957

Flasch, K. von (ed.) *Parusia: Studien zur Philosophie Platons und zur Problem-geschichte des Platonismus* Frankfurt 1965

Freire, A. "Aspectos da ideia de Deus em Platão" *Revista Portuguesa de Filosofia* XXIII (1967) 135–60

Friedländer, P. *Plato* I: *An Introduction* New York 1958

Frutiger, P. *Les Mythes de Platon* Paris 1930

Gaye, R. K. *The Platonic Conception of Immortality, and its Connexion with the Theory of Ideas* Cambridge 1904

Geffcken, J. "Platon und der Orient" *Neue Jahrbücher für Wissenschaft und Jugendbildung* V (1929) 517–28

Görgemanns, H. "Beiträge zur Interpretation von Platons Nomoi" *Zetemata* xxv (München 1960)

Gould, J. *The Development of Plato's Ethics* Cambridge 1955

Gould, T. *Platonic Love* London 1963

Greene, W. C. *Moira: Fate, Good and Evil in Greek Thought* Harvard 1944

Grube, G. M. A. (1) "The Composition of the World-soul in Timaeus 35A–B" *CP* XXVII (1932) 80–2

(2) *Plato's Thought* London 1935

Guéroult, M. "Le Xe livre des Lois et la dernière forme de la physique platonicienne" *REG* XXXVII (1924) 26–78

Guthrie, W. K. C. (1) "Plato's views on the nature of the soul" in *Recherches sur la tradition platonicienne* (Fondation Hardt, Entretiens III) Van-deuvres-Genève 1957, 3–19

(2) *Orpheus and Greek Religion*[2] London 1952

Hackforth, R. (1) "Plato's Theism" *CQ* xxx (1936) 4–9

(2) "Plato's Cosmogony (Timaeus 27D ff.)" *CQ* n.s. IX (1959) 17–22

(3) "Immortality in Plato's Symposium" *CR* LXIV (1950) 43–5

(4) "Moral Evil and Ignorance in Plato's Ethics" *CQ* XL (1946) 118–20

(5) "The Modification of Plan in Plato's Republic" *CQ* VII (1913) 265–72

(6) *Plato: Phaedo* Cambridge 1955

(7) *Plato's Phaedrus* Cambridge 1952

(8) *Plato's Examination of Pleasure* Cambridge 1945

Hager, F.-P. *Die Vernunft und das Problem des Bösen im Rahmen der platonischen Ethik und Metaphysik* Bern 1963

Hall, R. W. "ψυχή as Differentiated Unity in the Philosophy of Plato" *Phronesis* VIII (1963) 63–82. This article now appears, revised, as a chapter in his book *Plato and the Individual* The Hague 1964

Hamlyn, D. W. "The Communion of Forms and the Development of Plato's Logic" *PhQ* V (1955) 289–302

Handley, E. W. "Words for 'soul,' 'heart' and 'mind' in Aristophanes" *RhM* N.F. XCIX (1956) 205–25

Hardie, W. F. R. *A Study in Plato* Oxford 1936

Herter, H. (1) "Bewegung der Materie bei Platon" *RhM* N.F. C (1957) 327–47

(2) "Gott und die Welt bei Platon (Eine Studie zum Mythos des Politikos)" *BonnJbb* CLVIII (1958) 106–17

Hicken, W. F. "Phaedo 93A11–94B3" *CQ* n.s. IV (1954) 16–22

Hicks, R. D. (ed.) *Aristotle: De Anima* Cambridge 1907

Hirzel, R. "Die Person" *SBBay* X (1914)

Hoffmann, E. (1) *Die griechische Philosophie bis Platon* Heidelberg 1951

(2) *Drei Schriften zur griechischen Philosophie (Platons Lehre von der Weltseele)* Heidelberg 1964

Jaeger, W. (1) *Aristotle*[3] (tr. R. Robinson) Oxford 1948

(2) "A new Greek word in Plato's Republic" *Eranos* XLIV (1946) 123–30

(3) *Paideia: The Ideals of Greek Culture* (tr. G. Highet) Oxford 1939

Jäger, G. "Nus" in Platons Dialogen Göttingen 1967

Joseph, H. W. B. *Essays in Ancient and Modern Philosophy* Oxford 1935

Jowett, B. *The Dialogues of Plato*[2] Oxford 1953

Kerschensteiner, J. *Platon und der Orient* Stuttgart 1945

Keyt, D. "The Fallacies in Phaedo 102A–107B" *Phronesis* VIII (1963) 167–72

Koster, W. J. W. "Le Mythe de Platon, de Zarathoustra et des Chaldéens" *Mnemosyne* suppl. III (1951)

Kranz, W. "Platon über Hippokrates" *Philologus* XCVI (1944) 193–200

Kucharski, P. (1) "Eschatologie et connaissance dans le 'Timée'" *ArchPhil* XXIX (1966) 5–36

(2) "L'Affinité entre les idées et l'âme d'après le Phédon" *ArchPhil* XXVI (1963) 483–515

Kusayama, K. "On the Disorderly Motion in the Timaeus" (Eng. résumé) *JClS* XII (1964) 56–73

Laemmli, F. *Vom Chaos zum Kosmos* Basel 1962

Lee, E. N. "On Plato's Timaeus, 49D4–E7" *AJP* LXXXVIII (1967) 1–28

Legido, L. M. *El problema de Dios en Platón: La teología del demiurgo* Salamanca 1963

Leyden, W. von "Time, Number and Eternity in Plato and Aristotle" *PhQ* XIV (1964) 35–52

Linforth, I. M. *The Arts of Orpheus* Berkeley–Los Angeles 1941

Litsenburg, P. J. G. M. van *God en het goddelijke in de dialogen van Plato* Nijmegen–Utrecht 1954

Loenen, J. H. M. M. *De Nous in het systeem van Plato's philosophie* Amsterdam 1951

Lopez-Doriga, E. "Inmortalidad y personalidad en Platón" *Pensamiento* XXIII (1967) 167–76

Luce, J. V. "Immortality in Plato's Symposium: A Reply" *CR* n.s. II (1952) 137–41

Magotteaux, E. "Manes virgiliens et Démon platonicien" *AntCl* XXIV (1955) 341–51

Maier, H. *Sokrates, sein Werk und seine geschichtliche Stellung* Tübingen 1913

Martin, Th.-H. *Etudes sur le Timée de Platon* 2 vols. Paris 1841

Martin, V. "Sur la condamnation des athées par Platon au Xe livre des Lois" *StPh* XI (1951) 103–54

McGibbon, D. D. "The Fall of the Soul in Plato's Phaedrus" *CQ* n.s. XIV (1964) 56–63

McMinn, J. B. "Plato as a Philosophical Theologian" *Phronesis* V (1960) 23–31

Meldrum, M. "Plato and the 'ἀρχὴ κακῶν'" *JHS* LXX (1950) 65–74

Merlan, P. "Religion and Philosophy from Plato's Phaedo to the Chaldean Oracles" *JHPh* I (1963) 163–76, II (1964) 15–21

Michel, A. *La Lecture de Platon* Paris 1967

Moreau, J. (1) "Platon et la connaissance de l'âme" *REA* LV (1953) 249–57
(2) *L'Ame du monde de Platon aux Stoiciens* Paris 1939

Morrison, J. S. "Four Notes on Plato's *Symposium*" *CQ* n.s. XIV (1964) 42–55

Morrow, Glenn R. (1) "Necessity and Persuasion in Plato's Timaeus" *PhR* LIX (1950) 147–63
(2) "Plato's Gods" *Rice University Studies* LI (1965) 121–34

Mugler, C. "Démocrite et les postulats cosmologiques du Démiurge" *REA* LXIX (1967) 50–8

Müller, G. *Studien zu den platonischen Nomoi* München 1951

Murphy, N. R. *The Interpretation of Plato's Republic* Oxford 1951

Naddei, M. C. "L'immortalità dell'anima nel pensiero dei Greci" *Sophia* XXXIII (1965) 272–300

Nilsson, M. P. "The Immortality of Soul in Greek Religion" *Eranos* XXXIX (1941) 1–16

North, H. "Pindar, Isthmian 8, 24–28" *AJP* LXIX (1948) 304–8

O'Brien, D. "The Last Argument of Plato's Phaedo" *CQ* n.s. XVII (1967) 198–231; n.s. XVIII (1968) 95–106

Olerud, A. *L'Idée de macrocosmos et de microcosmos dans le Timée de Platon* Uppsala 1951

Onians, R. B. *The Origins of European Thought about the Body, the Mind, the Soul, the World, Time and Fate*[2] Cambridge 1954

Owen, G. E. L. (1) "The Place of the Timaeus in Plato's Dialogues" *CQ* n.s. III (1953) 79–95

    (2) "Plato and Parmenides on the Timeless Present" *The Monist* L (1966) 317–40

Patterson, R. L. *Plato on Immortality* University Park, Pa. 1965

Pépin, J. *Théologie cosmique et théologie chrétienne* Paris 1964

Pétrement, S. *Le Dualisme chez Platon, les Gnostiques et les Manichéens* Paris 1947

Pfeiderer, E. (1) *Zur Lösung der Platonischen Frage* Freiburg 1888

    (2) *Sokrates und Plato* Tübingen 1896

Pieper, J. *Ueber die Platonischen Mythen* München 1965

Pohlenz, M. *Aus Platos Werdezeit* Berlin 1913

Popper, K. R. *The Open Society and its Enemies*[3] 2 vols. London 1957

Raeder, H. *Platons Philosophische Entwickelung* Leipzig 1905

Rankin, H. D. *Plato and the Individual* London 1964

Rees, D. A. (1) "Bipartition of the Soul in the early Academy" *JHS* LXXVII (1957) 112–18

    (2) "Theories of Soul in the early Aristotle" in *Aristotle and Plato in the Mid-fourth Century* (ed. I. Düring and G. E. L. Owen) Göteborg 1960, 191–200

Regenbogen, O. "Bemerkungen zur Deutung des platonischen Phaidros" *Miscellanea Academica Berolinensia* I (1950) 198–219

Reich, K. Review of J. Kerschensteiner *Platon und der Orient* (Stuttgart 1945) *Gnomon* XXII (1950) 65–70

Reinhardt, K. *Platons Mythen* Bonn 1927

Reitzenstein, R. and Schaeder, H. H. *Studien zum antiken Synkretismus aus Iran und Griechenland* Leipzig 1926

Reverdin, O. *La Religion de la cité platonicienne* Paris 1945

Rich, A. N. M. "The Platonic Ideas as the Thoughts of God" *Mnemosyne* IV 7 (1954) 123–33

Rist, J. M. (1) *Eros and Psyche: Studies in Plato, Plotinus, and Origen* Toronto 1964

(2) "The Order of the Later Dialogues of Plato" *Phoenix* XIV (1960) 107–21

Ritter, C. *Platon, sein Leben, seine Schriften, seine Lehre* 2 vols. München 1910, 1923

Rivaud, A. (1) *Le Problème du devenir et la notion de la matière dans la philosophie grecque depuis les origines jusqu'à Théophraste* Paris 1906

(2) (ed.) *Platon: Oeuvres complètes* X: *Timée, Critias* Paris 1925

Robin, L. (1) *Platon* Paris 1935

(2) *La Théorie platonicienne de l'amour* Paris 1908

(3) "La Signification et la place de la physique dans la philosophie de Platon" in *La Pensée Hellénique, de ses origines à Epicure* Paris 1942, 231–337

(4) (ed.) *Platon: Oeuvres complètes* IV: *Phèdre* Paris 1933

Robinson, T. M. "Demiurge and World Soul in Plato's Politicus" *AJP* LXXXVIII (1967) 57–66

Rohde, E. *Psyche*[8] (tr. W. B. Hillis) London 1925

Runciman, W. G. *Plato's Later Epistemology* Cambridge 1962

Ryle, G. *The Concept of Mind* London 1949

Saunders, T. J. "The Structure of Soul and State in Plato's Laws" *Eranos* LX (1962) 37–55

Schaerer, R. "Sur l'origine de l'âme et le problème du mal dans le platonisme" *RThPh* XXVII (1939) 62–72

Scarrow, D. S. "*Phaedo* 106A–106E" *PhR* LXX (1961) 245–52

Schiller, J. " 'Phaedo' 104–105: Is the Soul a Form?" *Phronesis* XII (1967) 50–8

Schipper, E. W. "Souls, Forms and False Statements in the Sophist" *PhQ* xv (1965) 240-2

Schottländer, R. "Platon und das Prinzip des Bösen" *Helikon* v (1965) 173-6

Schuhl, P.-M. "Sur le mythe du Politique" *RMM* xxxix (1932) 47-58

Shorey, P. (1) "Plato's Laws and the Unity of Plato's Thought" *CP* ix (1914) 345-69

(2) *What Plato Said* Chicago 1933

Skemp, J. B. (1) *The Theory of Motion in Plato's Later Dialogues* Cambridge 1942

(2) "Plants in Plato's Timaeus" *CQ* xli (1947) 53-60

(3) "Comment on Communal and Individual Justice in the Republic" *Phronesis* v (1960) 35-8

(4) "ὕλη and ὑποδοχή" in *Aristotle and Plato in the Mid-fourth Century* (ed. I. Düring and G. E. L. Owen) Göteborg 1960, 201-12

(5) *Plato's Statesman* London 1952

Simson, J. *Der Begriff der Seele bei Platon* Leipzig 1889

Solmsen, F. (1) "Antecedents of Aristotle's Psychology and Scale of Beings" *AJP* lxxvi (1955) 148-64

(2) "Aristotle and Presocratic Cosmogony" *HSCP* lxiii (1958) 268-82

(3) "Tissues and the Soul" *PhR* (1950) 435-68

(4) *Plato's Theology* Ithaca, N.Y. 1942

(5) *Aristotle's System of the Physical World* Ithaca, N.Y. 1960

(6) "Nature as Craftsman in Greek Thought" *JHI* xxiv (1963) 473-96

Spoerri, W. "Encore Platon et l'Orient" *RevPhil* xxxi (1957) 209-33

Steckerl, F. "Plato, Hippocrates and the 'Menon Papyrus'" *CP* xl (1945) 166-80

Stenzel, J. (1) *Ueber zwei Begriffe der Platonischen Mystik: ζῷον und κίνησις* Breslau 1914, reprinted in *Kleine Schriften* Darmstadt 1957, 1-31

(2) "Ueber Platons Lehre von der Seele: Zur Erklärung von Phaidros 245c ff." in *Festschrift des Schlesischen Philologenvereins der Universität* Breslau 1911, 87-91

Stewart, J. A. *The Myths of Plato*² London 1960

Stöcklein, P. "Ueber die philosophische Bedeutung von Platons Mythen" *Philologus* suppl. xxx 3 (1937)

Stocks, J. L. "Plato and the Tripartite Soul" *Mind* xxiv (1915) 207-21

Strang, C. "Plato and the Third Man" *ProcArSoc* suppl. xxxvii (1963) 147-64

Tait, Marcus D. C. "Spirit, Gentleness and the Philosophic Nature in the
    Republic" *TAPA* LXXX (1949) 203–11
Tarán, L. "Phaedo 62A" *AJP* LXXXVII (1966) 326–36
Taylor, A. E. (1) "The 'Polytheism' of Plato: An Apologia" *Mind* XLVII
    (1938) 180–99
    (2) *Plato, the Man and his Work* London 1929
    (3) *A Commentary on Plato's Timaeus* Oxford 1928
    (4) *Plato: Philebus & Epinomis* (ed. R. Klibansky) London 1956
Tejera, A. D. "Die Chronologie der Dialoge Platons" *Das Altertum* XI
    (1965) 79–86
Tenkku, J. *The Evaluation of Pleasure in Plato's Ethics* Helsinki 1956
Theiler, W. (1) "Demiurgos" in *Reallexicon für Antike und Christentum* III
    Stuttgart 1955
    (2) *Zur Geschichte der teleologischen Naturbetrachtung bis auf Aristoteles²*
    Berlin 1965
    (3) Review of F. Müller *Stilistische Untersuchung der Epinomis des
    Philippos von Opus* (Berlin 1927) and A. E. Taylor *Plato and the
    Authorship of the Epinomis* (London 1930) *Gnomon* VII (1931) 337–55
Thévenaz, P. *L'Ame du monde, le devenir et la matière chez Plutarque* Paris 1938
Topitsch, E. (1) "Die platonisch-aristotelischen Seelenlehren in weltanschau-
    ungskritischer Beleuchtung" *SBWien* CCXXXIII 4 (1959)
    (2) "Seelenglaube und Selbstinterpretation" *ArchPhil* (1959) 1–36
    (3) *Vom Ursprung und Ende der Metaphysik* Wien 1958
Tsirpanlis, E. C. "The Immortality of the Soul in Phaedo and Symposium"
    Platon XVII (1965) 224–34
Turnbull, R. G. "The Argument of the Sophist" *PhQ* XIV (1964) 23–34

Van Camp, J. and Canart, P. *Le Sens du mot Θεῖος chez Platon* Leuven 1956
Vanhoutte, M. "La Genèse du plaisir dans le Philèbe" in *Mélanges Diès*
    Paris 1956
Verdenius, W. J. (1) "Platons Gottesbegriff" in *La notion du divin depuis
    Homère à Platon* (Fondation Hardt, Entretiens 1) Vandeuvres-Genève
    1952, 241–82
    (2) "Notes on Plato's Phaedo" *Mnemosyne* IV 11 (1958) 193–243
    (3) "Notes on Plato's Phaedrus" *Mnemosyne* IV 8 (1955) 265–89
Vlastos, G. (1) "The Disorderly Motion in the Timaios" *CQ* XXXIII (1939)
    71–83, reprinted in R. E. Allen 379–99

(2) "Creation in the Timaeus: Is it a Fiction?" in R. E. Allen 401–19
(3) "Postscript to the Third Man: A Reply to Mr. Geach" *PhR* LXV
(1956) 83–94

Waszink, J. H. *Studien zum Timaioskommentar des Calcidius* I Leiden 1964
Webster, T. W. "Psychological Terms in Greek Tragedy" *JHS* LXXVII
(1957) 149–54
Wilamowitz-Moellendorff, U. von *Platon*² 2 vols. Berlin 1920
Wilford, F. A. "The Status of Reason in Plato's Psychology" *Phronesis* IV
(1959) 54–8
Winspear, A. D. *The Genesis of Plato's Thought*² New York 1956
Wippern, J. "Eros und Unsterblichkeit in der Diotima-Rede des Sym-
posions" in *Synusia: Festgabe für W. Schadewaldt* (ed. H. von Flashar
and K. Gaiser) Pfullingen Neske 1965, 123–9
Witte, B. "Der εἰκὼς λόγος in Platos Timaios" *ArchGPh* XLVI (1964) 1–16
Wolfe, J. "A Note on Plato's 'Cyclical Argument' in the Phaedo" *Dialogue*
V (1966) 237–8
Wrobel, J. (ed.) *Platonis Timaeus interprete Chalcidio cum eiusdem commentario*
Lipsiae 1876

Zeller, E. *Die Philosophie der Griechen* II, 1⁴ Leipzig 1876

Indexes

The Index of Passages Cited (179–84) offers a complete listing of passages in the ancient sources that are explicitly quoted or referred to. For those citations of ancient sources that do not involve explicit quotation of, or reference to, specific passages, the Subject Index should be consulted.

The Author Index (185–7) covers references to all authors other than classical.

The Subject Index (188–99) attempts to give a comprehensive conspectus of subjects touched on or discussed in the book, but the following points should be noted:

1 The names Socrates and Plato, being ubiquitous, are not indexed.
2 The word "soul" has been indexed, but without claims to comprehensiveness. What one has attempted is simply to give some idea of the wide range and flexibility of the concept as Plato uses it.
3 References to particular Platonic dialogues do not cover those found in the chapter specifically devoted to the dialogue in question.

INDEX OF PASSAGES CITED

AUTHOR INDEX

INDEX OF GREEK WORDS